Human Resource Management for MBA Students

IAIN HENDERSON

The Chartered Institute of Personnel and Development is the leading publisher
of books and reports for personnel and training professionals, students,
and all those concerned with the effective management and development
of people at work. For details of all our titles, please contact the publishing
department:
tel: 020-8612 6204
e-mail publish@cipd.co.uk
The catalogue of all CIPD titles can be viewed on the CIPD website:
www.cipd.co.uk/bookstore

Human Resource Management for MBA Students

Iain Henderson

Chartered Institute of Personnel and Development

Published by the Chartered Institute of Personnel and Development,
151 The Broadway, London, SW19 1JQ

This edition first published 2008
© Chartered Institute of Personnel and Development, 2008

Typeset by Fakenham Photosetting Ltd, Norfolk

Printed in Great Britain by The Cromwell Press, Trowbridge, Wiltshire

British Library Cataloguing in Publication Data

A catalogue of this publication is available from the British Library

ISBN 978 1 84398 147 3

Chartered Institute of Personnel and Development, CIPD House,
151 The Broadway, London, SW19 1JQ

Tel: 020 8612 6200
E-mail: cipd@cipd.co.uk
Website: www.cipd.co.uk
Incorporated by Royal Charter.
Registered Charity No. 1079797

Contents

List of figures and tables

Acknowledgements

I could not have written this book without the unstinting support of my wife Morag.

Ruth Lake of CIPD Publishing first encouraged me to write a text on HRM for MBA students, and she and her colleagues Jenna Steventon and Kirsty Smy continued to give patient and uncomplaining support and guidance throughout.

I must also acknowledge the kind support and encouragement I received from Professor Keith Lumsden and Professor Alex Scott at Edinburgh Business School. The influence of the 'EBS way' is evident on every page of the text.

The comments of several anonymous referees unquestionably improved the final text although of course any remaining deficiencies are wholly my responsibility.

I should like to thank Mike Beer and Bert Spector for their kind permission to use their 'Harvard Model of HRM' in Fig 1; Blackwell Publishing for their permission to base Fig 2 on material first published in the *Journal of Management Studies*; Cengage Learning for permission to reproduce Fig 14.1 from the text *Understanding Industrial Relations* (1995) by David Farnham and John Pimlott as Fig 3 in the present text; and the Work Foundation for allowing me to base the Caledonian Healthcare case in chapter 1 on material from their report *Achieving Strategic Alignment of Business and Human Resources*.

Iain Henderson
Edinburgh
December 2007

Preface

I have taught the fundamentals of Human Resource Management (HRM) to Masters in Business Administration (MBA) students over the past 15 years at several Scottish universities and this text is the fruit of my labours.

There is a plethora of excellent textbooks and collections of case studies on HRM, written by experts, which is available to teachers and lecturers. But these books are almost always aimed either at highly academic niche markets, such as final-year honours undergraduates or postgraduate students who already possess an extensive and sophisticated background in the social sciences; or, conversely, they attempt to cover the whole range of HRM teaching, which nowadays encompasses basic management training, professional courses for practitioners, all levels of undergraduate teaching and specialist Masters degrees. So there is no shortage of material for teaching the subject, but I have felt for many years that there was a need for a single text which was comprehensive enough to cover the subject at a serious and intelligent level but which did not require students to possess an extensive prior knowledge of management theory or the social sciences.

The MBA market has particular needs. A text for such students, some of whom will already occupy senior executive positions, and more of whom will be aiming to, needs to provide a guide to the landscape of this difficult area of management, help equip them to put the basic principles and techniques into action, and enable them to discuss the issues meaningfully with specialists in the field. But managers have to travel light. They need the essence with minimal baggage.

I have attempted to make the text as accessible as possible without losing the nuances and subtleties of a complex and important subject. I will have succeeded if this text is helpful to MBA students and their lecturers and yet can also be read by a busy general manager who wishes to learn about the subject but has not the time to embark on a formal academic course.

I have drawn on the latest HRM research where I thought this was necessary or useful to MBA students, but this unavoidably had limits given the purpose and scope of the text. No doubt I have made some errors and omissions but I trust I will have the understanding of any academic colleague who feels that their own area of expertise has been somewhat ignored.

The text is designed to cover the needs of a stand-alone, one term/semester MBA course in HRM with no need for prerequisite studies. It should be read and worked through sequentially. In chapter 1 the development of HRM in the modern organisation is traced and an account of its essential nature is given.

Key themes in HRM in the twenty-first century are identified from recent empirical research, in particular the 2004 UK Workplace Employee Relations Survey. Subsequent chapters deal with specific areas in HRM. The chapters have a common structure. Learning outcomes are stated at the beginning of the chapter; the topic is then developed, with empirical information and activities being introduced where appropriate. Finally the key issues which the student should have mastered before proceeding with the text. Most chapters conclude with an illustration of 'HRM in action'. Additional material for both lecturers and students will be available on the publisher's accompanying websites.

To the memory of my parents, Andrew and Elizabeth Henderson.

CHAPTER 1

People management: personnel management and human resource management

INTRODUCTION

Good managers are not only effective in their use of economic and technical resources, but when they manage people they remember that these particular resources are special, and are ultimately the most important assets. People are the only real source of 'core competence' (Prahalad and Hamel, 1990) and thus of continuing competitive advantage. Good managers also remember that these particular assets are human beings.

LEARNING OUTCOMES

On completion of this chapter you should:

- have a good appreciation of what the 'people management' function in contemporary organisations comprises

- know what we mean by the term 'human resource management' (HRM) and how this differs from the earlier 'personnel management' (PM) concept of the function

- have some appreciation of the theoretical development of HRM

- understand the relationship between HRM and business strategy

- have an appreciation of the practical application of HRM

- recognise some of the key themes of HRM in the early twenty-first century.

The definition of terms such as 'personnel management' and 'human resource management' is one area of particular confusion and irritation to general managers, and we will discuss later the differences between what typically is meant by these terms. We will use the phrase 'people management' as a generic term to cover both 'personnel management' (PM) and 'human resource management' (HRM) in the absence of a specific definition of either.

But broadly, we can say that the 'people management' function – whether we wish to define it as 'personnel management' or as 'human resource management' – may be described as:

> All the management decisions and actions that directly affect or influence people *as members of the organisation rather than as job-holders.*

In other words, people management is not executive management of individuals and their jobs. Management of specific tasks and responsibilities is the concern of the employee's immediate supervisor or manager – that is, the person to whom his or her performance is accountable (sometimes this might be the person's team). So people managers – whether 'personnel managers' or 'human resource managers' – do not have line authority over employees.

The term 'human resource management' was being used by Peter Ducker and others in North America as early as the 1950s without any special meaning, and usually simply as another label for 'personnel management' or 'personnel administration'. By the 1980s, however, HRM had come to mean a 'radically different philosophy and approach to the management of people at work' (Storey, 1989; pp4–5) with an emphasis on performance, workers' commitment and rewards based on individual or team contribution, differing significantly in all of these from the corresponding aspects of traditional personnel management

One of the main characteristics of HRM is the devolution of many aspects of 'people management' from specialists directly to line managers. HRM itself has been called 'the discovery of personnel management by chief executives'. So line managers over the past ten years or so have frequently been confronted with HRM decisions and activities in their day-to-day business in a way that was not the case previously.

This process has been accelerated by a more recent development which adds to the burden of the line manager while increasing the effectiveness of the organisation as a whole. Outsourcing of large areas of the traditional personnel management department's routine functions is happening on a massive scale (*The Economist,* Dec 2001). This is unlikely to be a passing fad. Outsourcing of non-core functions, allowing the organisation to concentrate on its core competencies, has been one of the single most important organisational factors in both business and the public sector in recent years. It is extremely unlikely that this will be set in reverse in the foreseeable future.

This outsourcing does not remove the day-to-day burden of HR from line managers: it increases it. Nor does it remove the need for HR specialists, but these people are just that – highly specialised, technical experts who act as consultants, either internally in the case of larger organisations, or externally (eg as a specialised bureau service used by line mangers as required). This means that it will be more important than ever for line managers to communicate effectively with HR specialists and be able to weigh up their advice in an intelligent and knowledgeable manner – and to do that they have to speak the language and understand the concepts of the expert.

REFLECTIVE ACTIVITY

Write down what you think personnel or human resource managers are actually supposed to do.

WHAT DO PEOPLE MANAGERS DO?

Torrington *et al* (2002), an authoritative text widely used in teaching managers who are studying for the professional exams of the Chartered Institute of Personnel and Development (CIPD), describe the general role of people management as comprising specific objectives under four headings: staffing, performance, change management, and administration.

- *Staffing objectives* are firstly concerned with 'getting the right people in the right jobs at the right times' – ie the recruitment and selection of staff, but increasingly these days also advising on subcontracting and outsourcing of staff. Staffing also concerns managing the release of employees from the organisation by, for example, resignation, retiral, dismissal or redundancy.

- *Performance objectives*: people managers have a part to play in assisting the organisation to motivate its employees and ensure that they perform well. Training and development, reward and performance management systems are all important here. Grievance and disciplinary procedures are also necessary, as are welfare support and employee involvement initiatives.

- *Change management objectives* include employee relations/involvement, the recruitment and development of people with the necessary leadership and change management skills, and the construction of rewards systems to underpin the change.

- *Administration objectives* include the maintenance of accurate employee data on, for example, recruitment, contracts and conditions of service; performance; attendance and training; ensuring organisational compliance with legal requirements, for example in employment law and employee relations; and health and safety.

General managers are increasingly involved directly in all of the first three types of objectives. Other than in managerial oversight for legal compliance issues, administrative objectives tend to remain the preserve of dedicated PM/HR support staff.

The above closely reflects the arguments in David Ulrich's highly influential *Harvard Business Review* article of 1998, 'A new mandate for human resources', which has helped to shape human resources (HR) in the new century. After acknowledging that some commentators had been calling for the 'abolition of HR' on the grounds of serious doubts about its contribution to organisational performance, Ulrich agreed (Ulrich, 1998; p.124) that:

> there is good reason for HR's beleaguered reputation. It is often ineffective, incompetent and costly.

His solution was for HR to be 'reconfigured' to focus on outcomes rather than on traditional processes such as staffing or compensation:

> HR should not be defined by what it does but by what it delivers – results that enrich the organisation's value to customers, investors and employees.

His recommendations were that:

- First, HR should become a 'partner' with senior and line managers in strategy execution.

- Second, it should become an 'expert' in the way work is organised and executed, delivering administrative efficiency to ensure that costs are reduced while quality is maintained.

- Third, it should become a 'champion for employees', vigorously representing their concerns to senior managers and at the same time working to increase employees' contribution – 'that is, employees' commitment to the organisation and their ability to deliver results'.

- Finally, HR should become an 'agent of continuous transformation', shaping processes and a culture that together improve an organisation's capacity for change.

Ulrich's model of the HR role has set the agenda for people management in the twenty-first century as being essentially about its contribution to organisational performance.

Linda Holbeche, the Director of Research and Policy for the CIPD, recently wrote (Holbech, 2007; pp10–11) that building organisational capability is HR's heartland,

and she added that HR managers

can help make capitalism human.

These two statements more or less sum it all up.

SO WHAT IS HRM?

What exactly does this rather self-important-sounding phrase 'human resource management' actually mean? To many people it is seen as just a fancy or pretentious re-labelling of what used to be called 'personnel management'. But to many managers and management theorists it is vital to the survival and success of organisations in the twenty-first century. Why they think so really derives from one single, simple idea: that people – their skills, knowledge and creativity – are *the* key resource for economic and organisational success in what Peter Drucker (1993) called 'the knowledge-based economy'.

By the 1970s a settled idea of people management in large organisations had evolved in developed free-market economies, and this was typically termed 'personnel management' (PM) or sometimes 'personnel administration' (PA). It reflected the predominantly Taylorist[1] organisation of work, which in turn had developed to exploit the technology available for the mass production of industrial goods. It acknowledged and incorporated the institutions of collective industrial relations recognising the role and power of trade unions.

The extraordinary economic success of Taylorist industrial practices ensured that this became the standard model for all large organisations, even those in service industries and in the public sector, and PM techniques used in industry – eg in recruitment and selection – were usually assumed to be best management practice.

Something of a revolution in people management occurred in the 1980s which seemingly overturned the established paradigm[2] of personnel management in favour of 'human resource management' (HRM). If today, some quarter of a century later, one surveys the academic and professional management literature on people management, whether aimed at specialists or at general managers, one would think the revolution had been total. Normative models[3] of HRM and examples of HRM 'best practice' abound, with little or no trace of traditional personnel management.

However, if in fact we look at the empirical evidence, we are forced to conclude that indeed there has been a revolution, but that it is not complete in terms of either organisational culture or management practice.

Few, if any, new techniques of people management have been developed within HRM. It is often the scope and manner of their use, and the intent behind their employment, that differs in the two approaches. For example, psychometric testing and personality profiling have been available for decades but in PM these were used only for executive and other highly paid appointments. Many firms adopting HRM now routinely apply such techniques to all appointments, the intention being not to predict whether one high-cost appointment will be successful in a particular role but rather to ensure that all employees can accept a strong common culture.

As we will discuss in some detail in the following section, it makes sense to talk of two paradigms in people management: 'personnel management' ('PM') and 'HRM', the latter being predominant, and increasingly so, but with most organisations still showing some mixture of the two.

We will first discuss the evolution of each of these paradigms.

THE EVOLUTION OF PEOPLE MANAGEMENT AND THE EMERGENCE OF 'PERSONNEL MANAGEMENT'

People management originated in the UK in the nineteenth century amidst the factory conditions of the first Industrial Revolution. The unrestrained capitalism of the initial industrialisation of the UK was restricted by the Factory Acts of the 1840s, which compelled factory owners to consider the well-being of their workforces, at least to some degree. Enlightened capitalists such as Rowntree and Cadbury, who were often motivated by religious convictions, appointed 'welfare officers' to monitor and improve the conditions and lives of workers. Their actions would often seem intrusive and paternalistic today – for example, they discouraged drinking out of work hours as well as during. Caring for the welfare of employees was thus the first true 'people management' role in the sense of organisational responsibility beyond that of specific job performance.

With the rise of industrial trade unionism in the twentieth century another role evolved in people management – that of negotiating and communicating with the collective representatives of the workforce (the workplace 'shop stewards' and the full-time paid trade union officials) on behalf of the organisation.

The rise of scientific management and the organisation of industrial work along Taylorist lines also led to increased interest in more rigorous selection of personnel administered by management, instead of the haphazard traditional methods which often relied on the foremen or 'gangmasters' to pick men and women for work. It also led to management taking an interest in organising and providing skills training.

Following World War II, social science – particularly as employed in the Human Relations School – started to exert a direct influence on work in the areas of job design, attempting to ameliorate the worst side-effects of scientific management while still achieving its productive and economic benefits. Although such developments might not affect people management directly, they shaped the culture in which it was operating and evolving. The conscious application of social science also encouraged the use of more sophisticated techniques in recruitment and selection which did have an impact on people management policies and practice.

By the 1970s a fairly consistent set of activities and roles had developed for people management, which in most large organisations was perceived as a specialist management function, usually termed Personnel Management and comprising the areas of recruitment and selection, pay and conditions of service, employee welfare, industrial relations, training and development, and employee exit (retrenchment, redundancy or retiral). Most day-to-day people management, especially in the area of employee relations, was handled by personnel specialists and not by line managers. In the UK the professional status of personnel managers was supported by the formation of the Institute of Personnel Management (IPM) which was later to evolve and become the present-day Chartered Institute of Personnel and Development (CIPD).

Of course personnel management was not without its critics. Peter Drucker (1955) thought that 'personnel administration', as he called it, was just a set of unrelated, albeit individually important, activities. The Drucker critique can be read now as an early plea for people management to be returned to line managers as later advocated by HRM models. The ambiguity of traditional personnel management was noted with the welfare role expected by employees but efficiency and cost-control increasingly demanded of it by management (Legge, 1995). Radical critics disliked it on principle (see below).

THE DEVELOPMENT OF HUMAN RESOURCE MANAGEMENT

The people management policies and practices which are usually termed 'HRM' originated in manufacturing industry in the USA during the late 1970s and early 1980s. These represented a significant break with the personnel management paradigm. A number of factors led to this new management thinking, principally loss of faith in the traditional approach to mass production, the example of Japanese work organisation and manufacturing processes, and the realisation of the impact of new technology on work practices (Gallie et al, 1998).

The remarkable success of Japanese manufacturers in the 1970s and 1980s in capturing Western markets for sophisticated products, such as electronics and cars, brought to a head long-standing concerns about traditional Taylorist/ Fordist models of work organisation. These models were characterised by low- or semi-skilled work, close supervision, pay being linked to quantity of output, and – at least in mass-production industries – assembly-line technologies in which the pace of work was controlled by machine. Academic studies had shown concern about some of the human effects of Taylorism and Fordism for decades, and this led to the rise of the Human Relations School, but by the 1980s it was recognised by business and managers as well that the costs of such systems were becoming unacceptable in terms of low levels of job involvement and weak commitment to the employing organisation. There was an increasing willingness on the part of employees to disrupt production to achieve higher financial or other rewards despite the damage such action could have on the long-term health of the organisation. Crucially, it had also become recognised that these traditional systems of work organisation were intrinsically unable to produce the quality output now required to compete in a global marketplace (Beer *et al*, 1984; p.viii).

The perceived superiority of the Japanese model was confirmed for many Western managers and academics by an influential MIT study in the 1980s which concluded that Fordist methods would inevitably be replaced in the car industry by the 'lean production' model of work organisation typified by Toyota's work methods. This approach to work organisation was seen to combine the best features of both craft-production and mass production (Kenney and Florida, 1993) and to achieve very high levels of employee commitment with resulting benefits in quality and flexibility.

Technology also played a part in shifting managerial concern towards human resources. Managers had become aware that the rapid development of new technologies in competitive markets meant that organisations faced continual technological change, which in turn implied the need for continuous learning by employees. Employers would have to be able to assess individual employees' training needs and provide the necessary investment in changing and upgrading skills.

All this implied the development of a much closer relationship between managers and employees, and therefore also changes in the work of managers as well as that of workers. In particular, it meant that the traditional approach of managing people – 'personnel management' or 'personnel administration', which had evolved to help manage Taylorist/Fordist organisations more effectively – was no longer viable. In an increasingly competitive global economy, with advancing technology and better-educated workforces, it was not enough to manage people reactively or passively. In the industries that mattered, competitive advantage now ultimately came not from capital investment but from human resources, and these had to be managed proactively and strategically if an organisation was to be successful.

The collectivised employment relationship, in which trade unions represented the workforce and bargained with employers on its behalf for wages and conditions of employment (often on an industry-wide basis), had come to be seen by management as a hindrance to the adoption of the new technologies and work practices which were necessary to compete with the Japanese. In fact most Japanese workers in the major exporting industries were unionised but the Japanese trade unions did not share the pluralist culture of their counterparts in the West (see below).

Initially, the new human resource policies were linked to non-unionised and greenfield sites (Foulkes, 1980; Kochan *et al*, 1994). Typically, these were in large-scale manufacturing, where the Taylorist/Fordist pattern of work organisation had been most dominant, but the new approach soon exerted influence in all sorts of organisations and in every part of the economy, including services and the public sector.

Theoretical and academic models of HRM signalled from the outset the importance of strategy in normative models of HRM. HRM was regarded as superior to personnel management or personnel administration partly because it was supposed to be 'strategic' in two senses: (i) the function itself was conceived of in strategic rather than reactive ways; and (ii) the HRM strategy would be intimately linked to, and consciously supportive of, overall business and corporate strategies.

PERSPECTIVES IN THE MANAGEMENT OF PEOPLE

As we will see below, managerial perceptions of how people view relationships within their organisations are important in our analysis of human resource management. Our 'frame of reference' will influence how we expect people to behave, how we think they *ought* to behave, and how we react to the behaviour of others. We are concerned here with three major perspectives: the 'pluralist', the 'unitarist' and the 'radical' or 'critical' (Fox, 1966).

THE PLURALIST PERSPECTIVE

Until relatively recently, this reflected the typical Western industrial workplace post-World War II. It rests on the assumption that society consists of various groups which will each have its own interests and beliefs. It is naive to pretend that the interests of workers and managers/owners can be fully reconciled, and so institutions such as trade unions and arrangements such as collective bargaining are needed to achieve workable compromises between these differing interests. In the pluralist view, conflict at work is seen as inevitable, because management and workers will not have identical interests, but conflict is not in itself 'wrong'. The issue is not to try to eliminate it, which would be impossible, but rather how it should be handled. In cases where conflicts seem to be insoluble at the workplace or industry level, third-party intervention – often through state agencies (eg ACAS: the Advisory, Conciliation and Arbitration Service, in the UK) – can provide solutions.

THE UNITARIST PERSPECTIVE

From this perspective a work organisation has a purpose (or set of purposes) common to all members of it – owners, managers and workers. So there should be no real conflict of interest between these groups. Everyone has the same ultimate interest in high levels of efficiency which will generate high profits and add to shareholder value – and allow the payment of high wages.

It is a win/win situation for all concerned. Managers and those they manage are really all members of the same 'team'. Management has special leadership responsibilities and should pursue policies which allow the organisation to achieve its goals and satisfy shareholders (and other stakeholders), but which are also fair to employees. On this view, conflict within the organisation between management and the workforce is perceived as being the result of some sort of failure; it is not regarded as necessary or inevitable – in principle, at least, it could be eliminated. From this perspective trade unions are often seen as competing for the loyalty of the employees, and collective bargaining may be regarded as unnecessary.

The unitarist perspective in its purest form was traditionally found in private, typically family-owned employers, but HRM is usually associated with unitarism (sometimes termed 'neo-unitarism' to distinguish it from the earlier, more paternalistic, family-firm version).

THE RADICAL/CRITICAL PERSPECTIVE

Quite different from both the other perspectives, this derived originally from the Marxist view of society and industrial capitalism. In essence this saw all work as inevitably being exploitative of workers. Conflict between management and labour was unavoidable as part of wider class conflict in society. Management always, and inevitably, represented the interests of capital. There may be few unreconstructed Marxists in the twenty-first century, but shades of post-Marxist thought persist, and there are cultural and social radicals of various types who reject the mainstream, free-market culture in which most organisations now operate. To such radicals, as to nineteenth- and twentieth-century Marxists, work organisations reflect the inherently unfair or oppressive structures of society (for example, to radical feminists they reflect the patriarchal nature of society) and help to buttress these same structures.

Postmodern intellectuals often share this view (see McKinlay and Starkey, 1998), and many writers on HRM and management within the Critical Management School hold a radical perspective in this sense (see, for example, Legge, 1995, and Thompson and McHugh, 2002).

From this perspective even 'enlightened' management practices and philosophies such as the Human Relations School, or employee 'empowerment', or profit-sharing are really either hopelessly naive and doomed attempts to overcome the inevitable exploitative nature of capitalism/existing society, or are conscious and cynical strategies to fool the employees. Even pluralistic industrial relations structures can be seen in this light.

REFLECTIVE ACTIVITY

In terms of the perspectives examined above, how would you describe:

a) your personal perspective?

b) the managerial culture of your own organisation?

HUMAN RESOURCE MANAGEMENT IN THEORY

We noted above the practical considerations such as quality, competition and technology which led to questioning of the traditional forms of people management. Management theorists were as concerned as practising managers and governments were about the evident failure of the Taylorist/Fordist approach and produced a number of academic models of HRM.

The theoretical heritage of HRM includes the managerial writings of Peter Drucker, the Human Relations School, human capital theory, and Organisational Development. Interest in HRM proceeded alongside other developments in economics, business strategy and organisational change. Many of these ideas revolved around the notion of the resource-based theory of the firm (Barney, 1991) and core competencies (Prahalad and Hamel, 1990), which argued that sustained competitive advantage ultimately derives from a firm's internal resources provided that these (i) can add value, (ii) are unique or rare, (iii) are difficult for competitors to imitate, and (iv) are non-substitutable. Of course, human resources fit such a list of criteria well (Storey, 1995).

One of the first, and most important, intellectual proponents of HRM was the Harvard Business School (HBS). The faculty and alumni of the School agreed in the early 1980s that a new course in HRM was required to equip general managers to deal with the changes that were occurring both in society and in the competitive environment in which business had to operate. Accordingly, in 1981, HBS introduced a course in HRM in its core MBA curriculum, the first new required course since Managerial Economics twenty years before (Beer *et al*, 1984; p.ix). The primary intention of Beer *et al* was to develop a framework for general managers to understand and apply HRM in their organisations. Figure 1 shows the Harvard model of HRM.

Figure 1 The Harvard model of HRM

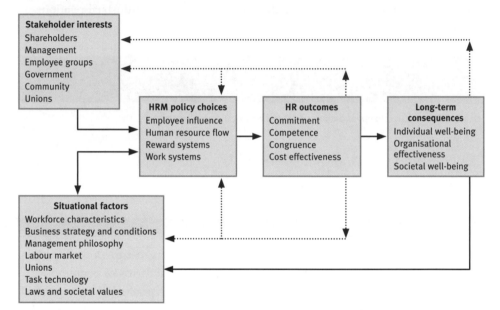

Source: Beer *et al* (1984; p.16 'Map of the HRM territory')

The central issue here is performance – managing human resources to achieve positive HR outcomes in terms of a committed workforce, working in harmony with the objectives of the organisation and achieving competence and cost-effectiveness. These outcomes in turn lead to positive long-term consequences: firstly organisational effectiveness, but also individual and society's well-being.

We should note the emphasis on policy choice. This implies that managers have at least some degree of discretion in their HR policies. The situational factors and stakeholder interests identified in the model may impact on managerial decisions on HRM, but none of these will *determine* which HRM polices are followed. The choice made will have outcomes and long-term consequences both of which, as the model shows, may feed back into policy choices, and, in the longer term, also into the stakeholder interests and situational factors.

The Harvard model has been influential worldwide. Hollinshead and Leat (1995) used the model as a framework to examine HRM in Germany, France, Italy, the Netherlands, Sweden, the UK, Japan, Australia and the USA. However, as these authors acknowledge (1995; p.27), although the fundamental principles and relationships identified by the model are pretty much universal, it is always necessary when applying it in a specific country, or in making comparisons between countries, to give due weight to specific cultural factors.

For instance, in the UK from the end of World War II to the 1980s trade unions were unusually powerful, and while their power is now much diminished, that era has left a legacy of a pluralistic industrial relations framework, especially in the public sector. In Germany and Scandinavia trade unions remain relatively powerful, whereas in the USA their influence has been waning for a generation and is practically non-existent in many industries, especially high-technology and other 'knowledge-based' ones. The wide degree of applicability of the Harvard model is one of its most useful aspects.

Of course, there have been significant developments in management practice and theory since the 1980s when the Harvard model was first conceived – for example, in areas such as knowledge management, ethics and corporate governance, the details of which often transcend the limits of the Harvard model. Technological advances also have had an obvious major impact on work including HRM (eg online recruitment, teleworking, the use of virtual teams). Nonetheless, the model has proved to be remarkably durable because, as its authors intended, it still serves as a wide-ranging 'map of the HRM territory'. It is still probably the best single model to give general managers an initial picture of what HRM entails and what it tries to achieve. The biggest single omission from the Harvard model is the neglect of learning and development.

UNIVERSALIST VERSUS CONTINGENCY

One of the faultlines in the theoretical debates on HRM has been an argument that in one form or another has run through all of management literature from the time of Taylor's 'scientific management' to the present day. This is whether there is one best way to manage – ie is there a set of principles which if applied correctly will always bring better performance, or does it depend on the particular circumstances and factors such as the nature of the work and technology that is employed? This is sometimes referred to as the 'universalist versus contingency' debate.

Somewhere between the two extremes lies the 'best fit' view: there may or may not be eternal, universally applicable management techniques but experience (sometimes supported by theory) shows that, given similar structures and contexts, successful organisations tend to employ the same methods or policies.

At the time of writing we see this debate in the arguments over whether there are specific 'bundles' of HRM which enhance performance. In reality, the debate in HRM is usually about the range and choice of techniques rather than one of absolute principle. There probably are some generic HR processes and general principles of people management common to all successful organisations (Boxall and Purcell, 2006; p.69). No one really doubts that it is best to be as systematic and accurate as possible in selecting people for work, for example, but there is much less certainty as to whether it is effective or even ethical to screen employees' personality profiles to select only those whom the organisation believes will conform to the company culture.

On the other hand, Huselid (1995) argues that there is sound evidence, gathered from over 1,000 firms in various (US) industries, for a universalist case for specific high-performance work practices impacting on firms' financial performance.

The framework presented by the Harvard model is clearly in the contingency camp, but can accommodate a variety of 'best fit' practices in various specific environments (eg industries, technology groups or cultures) as determined by the situational factors and stakeholder interests.

Critical and postmodernist interest has always been high in academic treatments of HRM, especially in the UK – for example, Legge (1995), Blyton and Turnbull (1992,), du Gay and Salaman (1992), and Kennoy (1999). As might be expected, such commentators tended to be hostile to the HRM model and were often opposed to its adoption, fearing that it represented continuing or even enhanced exploitation of ordinary employees.

On the other hand, even non-radical critics have pointed out that the specific practices associated with HRM are actually rather varied in nature, even in the theoretical models, and some have questioned whether they really can be regarded as making up a coherent approach to the management of people. For example, performance-related payment systems on the one hand seem to represent an individualisation of the employment relationship, whereas the promotion of team involvement – eg quality circles and total quality management (TQM) – represent the opposite (Gallie *et al*, 1998; pp6–7).

HARD AND SOFT MODELS OF HRM

Two main variants of HRM were identified early in academic discussions of HRM: 'hard' HRM with an emphasis on the strategic, quantitative aspects of managing human resources as an economic factor in production, and 'soft' HRM rooted in the Human Relations School and emphasising communication, motivation and leadership (Storey, 1989). All models of HRM are concerned with strategic issues, but 'hard' models typically have a stronger focus on ensuring that the

HRM strategy 'fits' and is driven by the overall corporate strategy (Keenan, 2005). This is a matter of degree, however, since all HRM models stress the importance of taking a strategic view of the human resource, but in the Harvard model, for example, the link to business strategy is implied rather than explicit. Table 1 shows a simple typology of HRM models with classification according to (i) the degree of emphasis on strategic fit, and (ii) a 'hard' or 'soft' model of HRM.

Table 1 A typology of HRM models: hard/soft, and strategic fit

	'Hard' HRM model	'Soft' HRM model
High emphasis on strategic fit	Fombrun *et al* (1984)	Mabey and Salaman's 'open approach' (1995)
Low emphasis on strategic fit	Schuler and Jackson (1987) Huselid (1995)	Beer *et al* (1984) [the Harvard model] Guest (1987)

SUMMING UP THEORETICAL HRM: KEY DIFFERENCES BETWEEN PERSONNEL MANAGEMENT AND HUMAN RESOURCE MANAGEMENT

At this stage the reader might plausibly ask, 'Why bother with personnel management? Haven't you just shown us how it has been replaced by HRM?' Well, not quite. As we shall see below, the empirical evidence is that the adoption of HRM in practice has been incomplete when compared to theoretical models. At the time of writing it can make sense to talk of two 'traditions' in people management: one largely following the 'personnel management' (PM) paradigm and the other the HRM paradigm – most organisations showing some aspects of each in their management of people, and few following either completely. Table 2 on page 17 contrasts theoretical PM with theoretical HRM along a number of key characteristics.

ARE MODELS USEFUL?

Before we look at this comparison we should deal with another question the sceptical reader might have. We acknowledge that both the HRM and PM descriptions above may never be found in their entirety in real life. So the sceptic may reasonably ask: why bother with them? The work of the great social scientist Max Weber provides an answer with his concept of 'ideal types' (Weber, 1949; p.90).

An ideal type is formed by simplifying the description of complex reality to accentuate its most important features and ignore less relevant ones, so that what is really vital about the subject under study can be identified and understood. Weber did not mean that the ideal type is some completely hypothetical entity, but rather that it possesses all of the relevant features of the type exhibited in extreme clarity. Ideal types exist, but you cannot expect to find them empirically in their purest states.

For example, no actual coin in circulation meets perfectly all the requirements of its design because of imperfections in manufacture and wear in use, yet we have complete knowledge of what the coin ideally should be like – an 'ideal type'. By comparing any actual coin to this 'ideal type' an expert can grade or classify the condition of a rare coin in terms of, for example, wear and damage, and so estimate its worth to a collector (Bailey, 1994).

The concept of ideal types is very useful in social science. For instance, an economist will not expect to find examples of 'pure competition' in any actual market in real life but by having an explicit model of pure competition he or she can make comparisons between the actual and the ideal and come to a reasoned judgement as to whether improvements in the degree of competition in the market should be pursued.

So, bearing in mind the dictum of the anonymous statistician that 'all models are wrong, but some are useful', we can regard the descriptions of PM and HRM in Table 2 as representing 'ideal types' of PM and HRM respectively. We could then study the characteristics of the people management function in a real firm or organisation, and use the descriptions in Table 2 to help us to assess whether this was closer overall to the HRM model or the PM one.

In some contexts ideal types might seem to be similar to 'normative models', as discussed in endnote 3. They are not identical, however. The author of a normative model may expect it to be fully realisable in practice, whereas for the reasons given above, ideal types are not.

We can consider the differences in the characteristics of the two models.

Strategic nature: traditional PM was usually expected to work on a short time-scale – 'fire-fighting' (ie dealing with immediate problems such as local industrial relations issues, or urgent staff shortages) rather than taking a long-term, strategic view of people management issues. Note the implications for this longer-term perspective for all HR issues, and the necessity for an articulated strategy for HRM, which should not only be coherent in itself but should be informed by, and support, the business strategy of the organisation.

The psychological contract is not to be confused with the legal contract of employment, or any written statement of terms and conditions of employment. As the term implies, it exists purely in the minds of the employee and his or her

Table 2 'Ideal types' of personnel management and human resource management

Characteristics	Personnel management (PM)	Human resource management (HRM)
Strategic nature	• Predominantly dealing with day-to-day issues • Ad hoc and reactive in nature: a short-term perspective rather than strategic	• Dealing with day-to-day issues; but proactive in nature and integrated with other management functions • A deliberately long-term, strategic view of human resources
Psychological contract	• Based on compliance on the part of the employee	• Based on seeking willing commitment of the employee
Job design	• Typically Taylorist/Fordist	• Typically team-based
Organisational structure	• Hierarchical • Tendency to vertical integration	• Flexible with core of key employees surrounded by peripheral shells • High degree of outsourcing
Remuneration	• Collective base rates • 'Pay by position' • Any additional bonuses linked to Taylorist work systems	• Market-based • Individual and/or team performance • 'Pay for contribution'
Recruitment	• Sophisticated recruitment practices for senior staff only • Strong reliance on external local labour market for most recruitment	• Sophisticated recruitment for all employees • Strong internal labour market for core employees. Greater reliance on external labour market for non-core
Training/ development	• Limited and usually restricted to training non-managerial employees. Narrowly job-related. Management development limited to top executives and fast-track candidates	• Transformed into a learning and development philosophy transcending job-related training. An ongoing developmental role for all core employees including non-management. Strong emphasis on management and leadership development • A learning organisation culture
Employee relations perspective	• Pluralist: collectivist; low trust	• Unitarist: individualistic; high trust
Organisation of the function	• Specialist/professional • Separated from line management • Bureaucratic and centralised	• Largely integrated into line management for day-to-day HR issues • Specialist HR group to advise and create HR policy
Welfare role	• Residual expectations	• No explicit welfare role
Criteria for success of the function	• Minimising cost of human resources	• Control of HR costs, but also maximum utilisation of human resources over the long term

Source: adapted and developed from Guest (1987)

managers, and so is unwritten and never clearly articulated. It has been described by Armstrong (2003; p.297) as follows:

> The psychological contract expresses the combination of beliefs held by an individual and his or her employer about what they expect from one another.

There will always be some sort of psychological contract between the employee and the organisation, but David Guest concluded (Guest, 1996) that:

> a positive psychological contract is worth taking seriously because it is strongly linked to higher commitment to the organisation, higher employee satisfaction and better employee relations.

The PM model assumed that the basis of the psychological contract was compliance – the employee would do as he or she was told and the employer in turn expected this. Management should be able to determine exactly what is required of the employee and enforce at least minimal compliance. The HRM model, on the other hand, assumes that the employee shows positive, willing commitment. Because more is expected from employees, management cannot always specify exactly what is required, and so employees must use their own judgement and initiative to a much greater extent than in the past. They must also extend and upgrade their skills and knowledge-bases.

Job design: the compliance sought in Taylorist organisational culture is reflected in the low degree of autonomy workers typically have in such a context. We would expect the PM model to be followed where jobs tend to be designed under scientific management principles (see endnote 1). The search for greater commitment in the HRM approach implies that employees should be allowed and encouraged to use self-control in matters of work and organisational discipline, rather than be driven by a system of compliance and direction imposed upon them by management. Teamworking and similar initiatives would be much more common under HRM than PM.

Organisational structure: reflecting the higher-commitment working associated with HRM, we would expect to find less hierarchical and more flexible organisational structures, with the team as the 'organisational building-block' and with fewer management levels. Organisations featuring PM will tend to be hierarchical, pyramid-shaped and bureaucratic. Those following HRM will typically be flexible with a core of key employees surrounded by peripheral shells of other workers. Note that the core employees are not all senior executives – the core is defined as comprising those members of the organisation who possess the skills, knowledge and competence necessary for the organisation's success. Core workers will possess considerable market attractiveness and will consequently enjoy better remuneration and terms of employment than others. In return, they will be expected to provide high levels of performance and flexibility in working, and accept the need for continuous learning and re-skilling to support incessant technological and process improvement. The peripheral shells of employees act as buffers against short-term market fluctuations and can be relatively easily shed or reinforced. Thus employees in those parts of the organisation will tend to be employed on short-term or temporary contracts. HRM organisations also tend to feature considerable outsourcing of non-core work.

Remuneration: PM is usually associated with traditional approaches to remuneration, long pay scales reflecting the hierarchical organisational structure mentioned above, rewarding length of service rather than current contribution. Pay structures are usually agreed via collective bargaining, at least for non-managerial employees. The HRM approach to remuneration is more focused on rewarding contribution and is likely to be individually or team-based. This implies both the use of performance management and appraisal and the setting of base rates from the market rather than by means of collective agreements.

Recruitment: sophisticated techniques such as the use of psychometric testing, psychological profiling and assessment centres have often been used with PM for recruitment and selection into senior executive posts, while much simpler and less costly methods usually suffice for non-managerial employment. With HRM these sophisticated tools are much more likely to be used for all employees, or at least core ones.

Training and development: when employees are viewed mainly as a cost (which should be minimised), commitment to training is usually negligible, employers fearing that employees will be 'poached' by free-loading competitors who do no training themselves, and this would be the typical position in the PM paradigm. An exception was often made, however, in industries with collective agreements on apprentice training. Except for large PM organisations, management training and development would be virtually non-existent. When two UK academics, Iain Mangham and Mick Silver, surveyed management development in the mid-1980s, they reported a surprisingly high proportion of firms which seemed to do no management training at all, on the grounds that, as one respondent put it, 'We only employ managers who can do the job' (Mangham and Silver, 1986).

In HRM there is a culture of continuous development of all core employees who are seen as the originators and possessors of the organisation's strategic competencies necessary for sustainable competitive advantage. Senior managers are not exempt, the directors and CEO receiving 'executive development'. This commitment would not be expected in the peripheral shells surrounding the core.

Employee relations perspective – ie the dominant managerial perspective within the organisation: personnel management typically operates in a unionised, pluralistic environment. This can be contrasted with the HRM model in which the employment relationship is much more individualised than when dealing with the workforce collectively. This is reflected in, for example, the absence of trade unions and the introduction of performance-related rewards systems.

The unitarist nature of HRM would seem to discourage the formation of a pluralist organisational culture, but in practice there have been examples where HRM has been successfully adopted within a previously pluralist culture while maintaining the pluralist style of collective bargaining in employee relations. See for example Tayeb's account of the Scottish division of the American firm NCR (Tayeb, 1998). But see also the empirical evidence from the Workplace Industrial/Employee Relations Surveys in the UK (referred to below in this chapter) on the long-term decline of trade unionism in the UK.

The organisation of the function differs in the two models. In the PM model the function tends to be seen as a specialist function which, in many important respects such as dealing with employee relations issues, is separate from line management. This often leads to the creation and maintenance of large, rather bureaucratic, personnel departments. The HRM model instead stresses that most people management, even employee relations, is actually just part of normal management, at least in its day-to-day aspects. Accordingly in the HRM model, where there are specialist HR departments they will be small and highly specialised and their function is (i) to formulate HR policies and (ii) act as internal consultants to line managers. The line managers will implement most HR policy, only seeking the involvement of HR in particularly difficult issues.

Welfare role: there are at least residual expectations under PM of a welfare role, the personnel manager being the member of the management team who could be approached with personal problems (at least if these impacted on work). This always led to ambiguous perceptions of PM. By the time the PM paradigm had become fully established, there was no doubt that it was a management function with the primary objective of reducing and controlling labour costs (see 'Criteria for success' below) but many employees expected a fuller welfare aspect than was often given, and this was a principal reason for the ambiguity with which PM was often viewed. Unreconstucted finance managers sometimes viewed PM in similar terms albeit negatively as an unnecessary cost on the organisation. So personnel managers often felt themselves to be 'the meat in the sandwich' caught between dissatisfied employees and unsympathetic management colleagues, neither of whom really understood what they were supposed to be doing. Marxist critics always saw PM as in any case reflecting the perceived contradictions of capitalism (Legge, 1989), but even dyed-in-the-wool free-marketers could see the possibility of perceived inconsistencies in the role of PM and unreconciled expectations here.

There is no explicit welfare role in HRM although proponents might argue that with its unitarist culture it is no longer necessary. Critics would not agree.

The two models also show very different *criteria for success of the function* – ie how the organisation judges the performance of the people management function. In the personnel management model, the organisation will judge the effectiveness of the function by how well it minimises unit labour costs; in the HRM model by how well it maximises the use of the organisation's human resources (while still maintaining proper control of costs).

REFLECTIVE ACTIVITY

Taking each of the people management characteristics listed in Table 2 to be represented by a seven-point scale in which 1 corresponds to 'pure PM' and 7 to 'pure HRM', profile your own organisation. Is it predominantly PM or HRM? Why is that, do you think?

It can be a useful exercise to discuss your results first with a senior line manager and then with a senior HR manager.

HRM IN PRACTICE

In addition to the theoretical literature, empirical studies have shown that significant changes in the practice of managing people in modern organisations have occurred in recent years. Interpretations may sometimes be controversial, but that there have been changes is not in doubt.

The late 1980s and early 1990s saw a transformation in the vocabulary of management in the UK, as in the USA, concepts such as 'empowerment', 'teamworking' and 'commitment' becoming widespread, along with 'human resource management' itself. Substantial survey evidence shows the adoption of a range of new practices which reflected HRM ideas: McKersie (1987); Storey (1992); Fernie *et al* (1994); Osterman (1994); Wood and Albanese (1995) – even if these studies found less evidence of integrated adoption of the whole HRM programme, or of Walton's (1985) assumed transformation of the employment relationship 'from control to commitment' (Gallie *et al*, 1998; pp9, 57).

Evidence of the adoption of a number of key HRM practices in the UK has been authoritatively established by the series of Workplace Industrial Relations/ Workplace Employee Relations Surveys. These surveys provide a nationally representative account of the state of employment relations, working life and the management of people inside British workplaces, and of how these have all been changing over a quarter of a century. The surveys were jointly sponsored by the Department of Trade and Industry (DTI), the Advisory, Conciliation and Arbitration Service (ACAS), the Economic and Social Research Council (ESRC) and the Policy Studies Institute (PSI), and were conducted in 1980, 1984, 1990,

1998 and 2004. These were all large-scale, representative surveys. The fieldwork for the 2004 survey, for example, was conducted between February 2004 and April 2005: face-to-face interviews were conducted with around 3,200 managers and almost 1,000 worker representatives. Over 20,000 employees completed and returned a self-completion questionnaire.

The 1990 survey found evidence of a shift from collectivism to individualism, with a marked decline in trade unionism, and a significant increase in the sort of approaches to participation and communication that are embraced by HRM, such as team briefings, quality circles and newsletters. There was also evidence of organisational changes such as the increasing involvement of line managers in personnel activities (Millward et *al*, 1992).

The 1998 survey found that human resource matters were often incorporated in wider business plans. They concluded that there was evidence that a number of practices consistent with a human resource management approach were 'well entrenched in many British workplaces' (Cully *et al*, 1999).

The preliminary findings of the 2004 survey showed that most of the HR practices which the earlier surveys had identified had become consolidated or were increasing in use (Kersley *et al*, 2005).

These findings reinforced the view that many organisations operated a 'flexible organisation' with a 'core' of key employees and a 'peripheral' workforce of other workers who typically enjoyed less secure and less attractive terms and conditions of employment. A large majority (83%) of workplaces had part-time employees (up from 79% in 1998). In 30% of all workplaces more than half of the workforce were part-time employees. Just under one third (30%) of workplaces had employees on temporary contracts. The use of temporary agency staff, although less prevalent than fixed-term contracts, was still quite widespread, 17% of all workplaces employing 'temps'. About one fifth (22%) gave preference to internal applicants when recruitiung, and the proportion was higher for the private sector (25%).

The selection process usually involved the use of interviews, application forms and references. Personality or competency tests, although used less frequently, had gained in importance in the search for greater objectivity in selection, even although their validity and reliability continued to be subjects of debate. Among workplaces using personality tests, three-fifths (61%) of managers said that they used these tests when recruiting core employees. Performance or competency tests were routinely used in 46% of workplaces. Performance tests were also more likely to be used when recruiting core employees, irrespective of their occupation, even more so than personality tests. Overall, one third (34%) of all workplaces used such tests for these recruits.

The use of performance appraisals had increased, 78% of managers in workplaces reporting in 2004 that performance appraisals were undertaken, compared with 73% in 1998. Two thirds (65%) of all workplaces conducted regular appraisals for most (60% or more) non-managerial employees (48% in 1998).

Most workplace managers (84%) reported that off-the-job training had been provided for some of their experienced, core employees over the previous year – an increase since 1998, when 73% of workplaces provided training for some of their experienced core employees.

The authors of the 2004 survey noted that in recent years much of the discussion about methods of work organisation had concerned 'high-performance', 'high-commitment' or 'high-involvement' work practices. These were practices that were intended to enhance employee commitment and involvement, often by increasing employees' participation in the design of work processes and the sharing of task-specific knowledge. The most commonly cited practices included teamworking, cross-training (or 'multi-skilling') and the use of problem-solving groups.

Teamworking was the most common, almost three quarters (72%) of workplaces having at least some core employees in formally designated teams. The incidence and operation of teamworking had changed little since 1998. Where teamworking was in place, it was 'usually embedded among staff': four fifths (80%) of workplaces with teamworking extended it to at least three fifths of core employees. In 83% of workplaces with teamworking, teams were given responsibility for specific products and services, and in 61% they could jointly decide how work was done. However, in just 6% they were allowed to appoint their own team leaders.

Cross-training involves training staff to be able to undertake jobs other than their own. Two thirds (66%) of workplaces had trained at least some staff to be 'functionally flexible'; again, this proportion had changed little since 1998 (69%). Around one fifth (21%) of workplaces had groups of non-managerial employees that met to solve specific problems or discuss aspects of performance or quality. The equivalent figure in 1998 had been 16%. Almost half (48%) of all workplaces had trained at least some core employees in teamworking, communication or problem-solving skills in the previous year.

Additionally the 2004 survey found that the UK trend for work culture to become more unitarist and less pluralistic was unremitting. Trade unionism continued to decline, particularly in the private sector; almost two thirds of workplaces (64%) had no union members (compared to 57% in 1998), and union members made up a majority of the workforce in only one sixth (18%) of all workplaces (22% in 1998).

SUMMING UP HRM PRACTICE

So the empirical evidence seems clear. In most UK workplaces the management of people has been progressively moving closer to the HRM model and away from the PM model over the last 20 years (see Table 2), and the most recent evidence suggests strongly that this is continuing. We can assume that the UK is not unique in this, and that giving due weight to local cultural and contextual factors, similar changes in the management of people have been happening worldwide in the developed and developing economies.

KEY THEMES IN HUMAN RESOURCE MANAGEMENT IN THE TWENTY-FIRST CENTURY

The authors of the 2004 Workplace Industrial Relations/Workplace Employee Relations Survey (2004 WERS) referred to above (Kersley *et al*, 2005) identified many of the key themes current in HRM.

The survey noted the interest in the UK in 'high-performance', 'high-commitment' or 'high-involvement' work organisation and practices. This was confirmed by a recent study funded by the UK government Department of Trade and Industry (DTI) and conducted in association with the CIPD. *High-Performance Work Strategies: Linking strategy and skills to performance outcomes* (DTI/CIPD, 2005) comprised detailed case studies of a sample of 10 firms drawn from the *Sunday Times* 100 Best Companies to Work For 2004, and a survey of nearly 300 firms.

In addition to reinforcing the findings of the 2004 WERS survey this report provided further empirical evidence on present managerial interests in the management of people in the UK.

The case studies established good practice in a range of 'high-performance work practices' (HPWPs), these being defined as

a set of complementary work practices covering three broad areas or 'bundles' of practices covering:

- high employee involvement practices – eg self-directed teams, quality circles and sharing/access to company information

- human resource practices – eg sophisticated recruitment processes, performance appraisals, work redesign and mentoring

- reward and commitment practices – eg various financial rewards, family-friendly policies, job rotation and flexi-hours.

It was found from the case studies that leadership was regarded as crucial in creating, shaping and driving these high-performing organisations. Skills development was focused on achieving specific business outcomes and levels of performance. In most of the case studies, high levels of training and continuous development were regarded as fundamental to success, and tacit skills and institutional knowledge were perceived as relatively more important than technical skills. Employees could learn all the time as part of their normal work and were encouraged to innovate and improve performance (individual, team and organisational).

High-performing organisations tended to be leaders in their industries and they set the standards for best practice. In most of the case studies HPWPs had been used to create business success from the founding of these companies, but to ensure their continued success, these practices were subject to constant modification in line with the requirements of business objectives.

The wider survey of CIPD members established how far the high-performance work practices identified in the case studies were adopted by other UK organisations, and examined the relationship between the level of adoption of high-performance work practices and a range of organisational outcomes. It was found that many of the HPWPs had been adopted by UK organisations, and there was evidence that the level of HPWP adoption, as measured by the number of practices adopted, was positively correlated with better organisational outcomes. For example, those adopting more HPWPs identified had greater employee involvement, and were more effective in delivering adequate training provision, in motivating staff, in managing change and in providing career opportunities. These organisations also had more people earning over £35,000 and fewer people earning less than £12,000.

THE INTERNATIONAL CONTEXT

The importance of high-performance working for organisational performance was confirmed in the international context by an earlier joint study from the International Federation of Training and Development Organizations (IFTDO) – of which the CIPD in the UK is a member – and the International Labour Organisation (ILO). This examined high-performance working in nine organisations around the world (ILO/IFTDO, 2000): the *Laiki Bank* (Cyprus), the *Mandarin Oriental Hotel* (Hong Kong), *SATS Security Services* and Comfort Driving Centre (Singapore), *W. H. Smith & Sons* and Thorn Lighting (UK), South African Breweries, and Motorola and the *Social Security Administration* (United States).

High-performance working was understood (ILO/IFTDO, 2000; Appendix B) to be associated with:

> the achievement of high levels of performance, profitability and customer satisfaction by enhancing skills and engaging the enthusiasm of employees.

The report also cited an Organization for Economic Cooperation and Development (OECD) definition of the characteristics of HPW organisations as:

flatter non-hierarchical structures, moving away from reliance on management control, teamworking, autonomous working based on trust, communication and involvement. Workers are seen as being more highly skilled and having the intellectual resources to engage in lifelong learning and master new skills and behaviours.

The report concluded:

Increasing evidence is becoming available about the connections between people management and development and 'the bottom line'. Researchers have identified three ways in which this occurs: through the use of best HR practice; getting the right 'fit' between business strategy and HR practices; and using specific 'bundles' of practices, varied according to organisational context. The case studies used in the ILO/IFTDO research show significant evidence of the use of all these approaches. They bear witness to the search by organisations for an alignment between practices and outcomes and active searching for examples of good practice.

The report thus also illustrates how HRM now has a global relevance beyond the US/UK industrial cultures in which it first developed.

Of course the concept of high-performance working has not been without its critics in terms of both its theoretical base and its practical effects – eg Guest (1997); Guest *et al* (2003); MacDuffie (1995); Applebaum *et al* (2000); Legge (2001); Purcell (1999) – but the International Labour Organisation (ILO) could acknowledge the validity of many of the criticisms and, while calling for more research to clarify contested areas, conclude (ILO/IFTDO, 2000) that:

Increasing evidence is becoming available about the connections between people management and development and 'the bottom line' . . . The seamless application of people management and development and line management leadership, expertise and vision provides the strategy and powerhouse for high-performance working. Finding out how to manage and develop people so as to generate freedom to learn and contribute will be a major challenge in the early part of the twenty-first century.

So the empirical evidence is mounting up to support the commonsense view that the idea that 'better' management of people should lead to 'better' performance at individual, team and organisational level – everything else being equal – is probably true. Common sense would also suggest it is wise to take what management theorists call a 'contingency' approach to this question. That is, instead of looking for a universally applicable set of HR practices that will inevitably lead to better performance in all cases, the specific circumstances of the situation should be taken into consideration. For example, individual performance-related pay might boost performance in some cases, such as sales personnel, but not others (policemen, say). This does not alter the underlying key principle that reward should reflect contribution. It just means that the principle may be applied in different ways according to the circumstances. It is worth remembering here the policy choice aspect of the Harvard model (Figure 1).

In fact, the DTI/CIPD (2005) report cited above found that different 'bundles' of high-performance work practices seem to be effective in different industry sectors (p.71):

> There is no 'one best way' or 'one best set of practices': this is not a tick-box approach. The crucial component is the business strategy, because this underpins the choice of practices, the way they are implemented and their effectiveness in improving performance. It is the business strategy that gives the high-performance working practices their dynamism and provides the framework against which performance can be evaluated and improved....

> The choice of which bundle of practices to use in order to achieve a given organisational outcome or objective is influenced by the type of sector in which the organisation or company is operating. Some bundles of practices are more effective in particular industrial sectors than others.

KEY THEMES IN HRM

The findings of these reports, together with those of the WERS survey series, especially the 2004 survey, allow us to build a picture of the key themes in HRM in the twenty-first century.

- The adoption of 'high-performance work practices' – also known as 'high-commitment' or 'high-involvement' work practices' – which are intended to achieve better individual, team and organisational performance by increasing employee commitment and involvement. These are typically thought of as comprising 'bundles' of sophisticated HR practices in the areas of employee involvement, resourcing (eg in recruitment) and rewards and commitment.

- A 'flexible organisation' with a 'core' of key employees (including non-managerial employees) with greater investment in these human resources; and a 'peripheral' workforce of other workers who typically enjoy less secure and less attractive terms and conditions of employment and less HR development. But in efficient organisations the barriers to the core will be permeable to hard-working and capable employees on the periphery.

- The organisation of work at a micro-level – teamworking, cross-training, multi-skilling, and problem-solving groups to increase functional flexibility, participation in the design of work processes, and the sharing of task-specific knowledge.

- Sophisticated HR practices in recruitment and selection – eg the use of psychometric testing and personality profiling and competency and performance tests for a wide range of key or core employees including non-managerial ones.

- Employee relations in a unitarist environment – trade unions are in a historically precipitous decline in most advanced economies, and especially in new industries, but all but the smallest employers have to find means of communicating with their employees and achieving perceptions of fairness and legitimacy in pay rates and conditions of employment.

- Change management: 'the only constant is change' has become a cliché but reflects the acknowledgement now that the competitive global economy and continuous increasing technological advances are realities. Physical resources are relatively easy to change; human ones are much more challenging. HRM is often tasked with taking the lead and coordinating change across the organisation.

- The 'learning organisation', defined as an organisation which encourages learning at all levels and thereby brings about continuous (and by definition often unpredictable) change to itself. This is a consequence of the realisation that employees are expected and encouraged to learn all the time, and should employ their learning by being innovative and enhancing performance; that 'to pay someone to work is to pay them to learn'.

- Knowledge management: 'using the ideas and experience of employees, customers and suppliers to improve the organisation's performance', in the words of a managing editor of the *Financial Times* (Skapiner, 2002).

- Leadership to initiate and effect change and to achieve high-performance working.

In all of these areas it will usually be the line or general manager who initiates action and carries responsibility to make it happen, but he or she will increasing rely on HRM specialists, who may have a lead role within the organisation in coordinating activities across the organisation.

SUMMING UP: WHAT IT'S ALL ABOUT

In July 2006, in an article entitled 'Technology dinosaurs', *The Economist* reported that exactly 25 years after the launch of the IBM 5150 – the famous IBM PC which led the personal computing revolution – many of 'Silicon Valley's former high-fliers' were in trouble. Dell's share price had hit a five-year low following a profit warning; Intel was still losing ground to AMD; Silcon Graphics had filed for bankruptcy; and Borland had laid off a fifth of its staff and was about to sell the best-known part of its business. Even Microsoft had just announced that it would buy back 8% of its shares for some $20 billion – 'a sign that its high growth days are behind it', according to *The Economist*. Noting that companies which start off with a successful product often fail to stay the course, the article concluded that having a great business idea often creates a false sense that the firm is stronger and more successful than it really is, and that 'failure to evolve leads to extinction'. Evolution means managing and developing people.

In today's and tomorrow's world, sustainable competitive advantage can only come from the skills, experience, creativity, imagination and brainpower of people. In the modern economy it is relatively easy to raise capital to fund a bright idea, but managing the human resources of an organisation to turn that idea into a business and achieve *sustainable* competitive advantage – how to create and build the next BMW or the next Apple – is the single most important management challenge in the twenty-first century, and that's what ambitious MBAs want to be involved in.

To do this, managers have to know about people. Of course they need to know about other things like strategy, finance and marketing as well, and they really do need to understand the technology underlying their businesses, but they *must* know about people. They have to understand HRM and be able to work with specialists in that field.

KEY ISSUES IN PM AND HRM

A consensus has evolved that post-Taylorist organisations require a new approach to managing people because in a technologically advancing, global economy sustainable competitive advantage ultimately can only come from the talents and efforts of an organisation's core employees. This approach is usually termed human resource management (HRM) and differs from more long-established personnel management (PM) in taking a strategic view of the use of human resources; in seeking to harness the willing commitment of employees rather than their coercion; and in favouring an individualistic rather than collective employment relationship.

All models of HRM should be regarded as 'ideal types' or 'normative models' which are unlikely ever to be found in entirety in real life. The 'Harvard model', one of the earliest such, which links situational factors and stakeholder interests to HR policy choices and outcomes, remains a useful first 'map of the HRM territory' for general managers, although it ignores crucial aspects of learning and of employee development.

Almost certainly no organisation practises absolutely pure HRM or PM. It can be helpful to think in terms of two traditions in people management: the older personnel management one, which tends to be pluralistic, bureaucratic and Taylorist; and the newer human resource management one – unitarist, non-bureaucratic and post-Taylorist. Many firms will have some mixture of these two traditions – but HRM is in the ascendant.

There has been considerable academic interest in HRM, much of it hostile both to its intent and its effects, but there is well-established empirical evidence that in the UK and other countries many HRM initiatives have become well established, without perhaps attaining the comprehensive changes in management philosophy and action that many early champions of HRM predicted. We may safely conclude that in the twenty-first century people management in developed economies in general far more closely resembles the HRM model than the PM one. One important consequence of this is that line and general managers are more directly involved in people management issues than previously.

We identified the current areas of key interest in HRM for managers as being:

- the adoption of 'high-performance' (or 'high-commitment' or 'high-involvement') work practices to increase employee commitment and involvement to achieve better individual, team and organisational performance

- a 'flexible organisation' with a 'core' of key employees and a supporting 'peripheral' workforce

- the organisation of work at a micro-level – especially teamworking and associated initiatives

- the use of sophisticated HR practices in recruitment and selection

- a unitarist environment in which trade unions have limited influence or are non-existent

- change management

- the establishment of a 'learning organisation' culture

- knowledge management

- leadership.

An HRM strategy for Caledonian Healthcare

CASE STUDY

You have been retained as a management consultant for Caledonian Healthcare (CH), one of the largest health insurance companies in the UK, insuring 435,000 lives and with a 6% market share. Following the acquisition of Acme Health Limited in June 2002, Caledonian Life renamed itself in April 2003 to become Caledonian Healthcare. It now employs 770 staff – 450 people in Guildford and 320 in Stockport. The ratio between female and male staff is roughly 60:40, and 20% of company employees are part-time staff. CH offers a range of products from traditional private medical insurance to self-pay options, which reduce premiums. It has also recently started providing healthcare solutions that aim to prevent health problems before they occur and manage absence for corporate customers.

The organisation is in major financial difficulties and has lost money in the financial year 2005/6. There is no clear business strategy and business focus was entirely on sales. This has resulted in poor customer service, with increasing numbers of complaints. Supporting the failing business is a poor culture characterised by 'siloed' management, poor leadership, blame and power struggles. Staff turnover is running at 20% a year. As a result, the HR strategy is simply focused on survival and is mainly reactive (focusing on recruitment). There is no support or resources for new initiatives, like job evaluation or appraisal systems. In 2006, a new chief executive joined the company with ideas to turn the business around. In particular, he sees an opportunity for HR to work closely with him to help achieve desired business outcomes, and he has hired you to produce an HR strategy aligned to the business needs of the company.

What would you recommend?

Caledonian Healthcare: resolution and outcomes

The new chief executive in fact did not hire a management consultant but instead worked with the existing HR team from the outset. He sought to combine commercial ideas with HR corporate values, including customer and quality focus, teamwork, communications and integrity.

The business needed, first, cost-cutting and then profitable growth. Changes were made at director level to 'refresh' the top team and create a new start. The chief executive and his new team quickly decided that the people needed were for the most part already in the organisation, but that they had not been supported, nurtured or encouraged to use their potential. Aligning HR and business strategy was focused on building trust and engagement with staff. As the chief executive put it,

'We expect a lot from our people and expect them to have their own demands in return. People want to be valued for what they do.'

The business aim was to increase market share from 6% to 15% over the next five years by differentiating through customer service, and HR had an important role to play in this. To make sure HR became, and continued to be, aligned with business objectives, HR staff were taken through business strategy documents at quarterly briefings.

There was an initial review of turnover and absence management policies, reward and recognition practices, and the company's approach to learning and development. There was also continual appraisal of HR policies and procedures in order to make sure that the policies supported the ethos of a 'great place to work' and did not inadvertently work against it.

The HR strategy focused on specified activities, with a designated member of HR to lead each one. The areas were: staff engagement; resourcing and retaining staff; reward and recognition; creating a learning organisation; and establishing a partnership with staff.

The company promoted staff engagement and created a staff consultative committee designed around the European Works Council model.

The chief executive and head of HR hosted two coffee mornings a month at which employees could speak frankly about any issues from any area of the business. People were encouraged to speak out if they thought their jobs were limited by business processes. It was the head of HR's responsibility to take notes and get back to individuals by email or letter with actions for improving the situation or an explanation of why the situation could not be changed. There was a 'back-to-the-floor' scheme where directors worked in all different parts of the organisation. The chief executive instituted a policy of meeting every new employee when they started, and to support this there was also a presentation, through which they were told three key messages:

1 Everyone's job is important to the success of the business.

2 Everyone is encouraged to contribute ideas.

3 It's important to enjoy work and get on well with colleagues, and a work–life balance is necessary to perform well.

Outcomes

Two years on, the business had moved into profit, and was looking sustainable with new business up by 26%. Staff turnover was at less than 10% at both sites (reduced by 60%), and sickness absence was around 3%. The company was in the top 25th percentile of companies in the UK for staff engagement and was finding that ex-staff were returning. Customer satisfaction was measured at 97% overall and customer retention was up by 2.2%.

The head of HR felt that the improvements were a 'virtuous circle' and the company was increasingly 'a great place to work'. The most positive outcomes for HR were showing how important it was as a function and the difference it could make to the company. The HR policies were now taken seriously. For example, when HR recommended that the company should only recruit the best people, the organisation stuck to this, even if it meant not filling a vacancy.

Based on the case of Standard Life Healthcare described in the Work Foundation Report *Achieving Strategic Alignment of Business and Human Resources* (2004).

ENDNOTES

1 The main elements of Frederick Taylor's *Principles of Scientific Management* (1911) were time and motion studies of work processes; standardisation of tools, implements and methods; and increased division of labour. This approach is often termed 'Taylorism'. Henry Ford pioneered the modern model of mass production by combining scientific management and moving assembly lines, first put into operation at Ford's Model T plant at Highland Park, Michigan, in 1914. 'Fordism' displaced a largely craft-based production process in which skilled workers exercised substantial control over their conditions of work.

2 'Paradigm' is a term that was popularised by Thomas Kuhn in his study of scientific revolutions and has become widely used in the social sciences. Kuhn defined it as 'the entire constellation of beliefs, values, techniques, and so on shared by the members of a given community' (1970; p.175).

3 Normative models. In the social sciences we have two types of description. One is the 'normative', which is prescriptive, telling us what *ought* to be; the other is the 'positive', which describes what *actually is*. Understandably, much of management literature is normative – readers want to know the 'best' way to do something. But if the nature of such descriptions is not made clear, confusion results when we assume that what the author is saying ought to happen is really happening.

CHAPTER 2

Looking ahead: HRM and strategy

INTRODUCTION

One of the key findings of Chapter 1 was the importance of strategy to HRM. Ulrich's first recommendation for the HRM function was that it should become a partner with senior and line managers in strategy execution (Ulrich, 1998; p.124). We also noted in that chapter that one of the reasons why HRM was supposed to be a better model for people management than either personnel management or personnel administration was because it was supposed to be 'strategic' – not only in itself but also in the sense that the HRM strategy would be consciously designed to support the overall business strategy.

LEARNING OUTCOMES

On completion of this chapter you should have acquired an understanding of:

- the importance of managers taking a strategic view of HRM
- the elements of corporate strategy which are relevant to HRM
- the relationship between organisational strategy and organisational structure, and the relevance of this for HRM
- some implications of organisational macro-structure for strategy and HRM
- 'best-practice' models of HRM and strategy
- 'best-fit' models of HRM and strategy
- the HRM strategy process.

We saw also in Chapter 1 that strategy was important in underpinning the choice of high-performance work practices (HPWPs) which were best suited to the organisation, how these work practices would be implemented, and how effective they would be in improving performance – according to the DTI/CIPD (2005) survey:

> It is the business strategy that gives the high-performance working practices their dynamism and provides the framework against which performance can be evaluated and improved.

There seems little doubt then of the importance of the topic. What might be less obvious to the reader is the role of organisational structure in the relationship between strategy and HRM. Not only are corporate strategy and corporate structure inextricably linked, however, but structure itself can affect HRM. For example, in a large company separate divisions might pursue different HR practices and policies as their particular business conditions demand – but this may then lead to difficulty in coordinating HRM strategy for the company as a whole.

The intimate relationship between strategy and structure was first clearly identified by Alfred Chandler:

> A company's strategy in time determined its structure … the common dominator of structure and strategy has been the allocation of the enterprise's resources to market demand.

And the importance of the human resource was evident in Chandler's account (Chandler, 1962/1991; p.383):

> Of these resources trained personnel with manufacturing, marketing, engineering, scientific and managerial skills often became even more important than warehouses, plants, offices and other physical facilities.

No MBA student will need to be reminded that the academic literature on business strategy is vast, complex and contentious. HRM has a particular perspective, of course, and it is this that we shall follow. We will not be reviewing the whole of the management literature on strategy.

THE UNIVERSALIST VERSUS CONTINGENCY ARGUMENT (AGAIN)

As we remarked in Chapter 1, the *universalist* ('one-best way') versus *contingency* ('it all depends on the circumstances') debate runs through all management literature, and HRM is no exception. So we should not be surprised to see this appear in discussions of HRM and strategy. There are three main positions:

- the 'best-fit' school of thought, which suggests that certain HRM polices and practices work best with particular company strategies (or in some cases specified strategy-structure combinations). Examples are Miles and Snow (1984) and Schuler and Jackson (1987)

- the 'best-practice' school is universalist and states that specified HRM policies and practices always give best results (ie best organisational performance) regardless of strategy or structure or any other factor. Pfeffer (1994) and Huselid (1995) are instances of this school

- strategic choice – the view that is implied in the Harvard model described in Chapter 1 and the one adopted in this text as the most useful for managers. The managers of an organisation can make choices in HRM and these may be *influenced* by contingent factors and prior decisions, but are not *determined* by either.

CORPORATE STRATEGY

A widely accepted definition of strategy in business and management is that given by Johnson and Scholes (1997):

> The direction and scope of an organisation over the longer term, which ideally matches its resources to its changing environment, and in particular to its markets, customers and clients to meet stakeholders expectations.

Armstrong (2001; p.32) describes 'strategic HRM' as follows:

> The defining characteristic of strategic HRM is that it is integrated – HR strategies are generally integrated vertically with the business strategy and horizontally with one another.

The term 'strategy' is usually associated with long-term decisions and is distinguished from short-term 'tactics' or 'operations' (Purcell and Ahlstrand, 1994; p.27). The principle is clear, but as Boxall and Purcell note, it is usually unhelpful to make too hard a distinction in practice between strategy on the one hand and either tactics or operations on the other (2006; p.28).[1] In real business life the distinction is often somewhat blurred.

But we can say that strategic decisions in management are likely to be concerned with:

- the long-term direction of the organisation

- the scope of the organisation's activities

- matching the organisation's activities to its environment (ie its business-social-political environment)

- matching the organisation's activities to its resources.

Most strategic decisions will differ from operational ones in that they will involve more uncertainty – and they will primarily be concerned with the organisation as a whole, or at least a significant part of it: a division or strategic business unit.

Echoing Miles and Snow's earlier concept of the adaptive cycle (discussed below), Boxall and Purcell (2006) argue that the strategies of firms are their attempts to deal with the strategic problems that they face – most fundamentally, their initial viability (ie survival) and thereafter sustaining competitive advantage – and that strategic management is best viewed as a process that is continually evolving and changing as the firm survives.

In their concepts of the adaptive cycle and the associated strategic typology, Miles and Snow (1978) produced two of the most elegant and economical ideas in the literature of business strategy. The 'adaptive cycle' is the process by which firms seek a fit between their markets, their technologies and their structures. The strategic typology identified four distinct outcomes to the adaptive cycle problem, three of which were particular, successful solutions while the fourth represented failure to achieve the necessary fit.

Miles and Snow saw the process of organisational adaptation as central to successful organisations. Not only must the organisation respond to its environment, it must where possible adapt the environment. In creating their own concept of the 'adaptive cycle', Miles and Snow embraced both Thompson's image of top management continually 'shooting at a moving target of co-alignment' (Thompson, 1967; p.148) and Child's idea of 'strategic choice' (Child, 1972; 1997). This complex and dynamic process of adaptation was seen (Miles and Snow, 1978; p.21) as being capable of analysis into three major problems which management needed continually to 'solve': 'entrepreneurial' (ie domain definition), 'engineering' (technology) and 'administrative' (structure-process and innovation).

Miles and Snow acknowledged that a huge number of possible organisational strategies and strategy-structure relationships theoretically existed, but argued (1978; p.29) that

> Patterns of behaviour begin to emerge which suggest that these organisational forms can be reduced to several archetypes. We have identified four types: the Defender, the Reactor, the Analyser and the Prospector.

'Defenders' were organisations which had narrow product-market domains. Top managers were highly expert in the organisation's limited area of operation but tended not to search outside their domain for new opportunities. Attention was mostly devoted to improving the efficiency of their existing operations rather than making major adjustments in their technology, structure or methods of operation.

'Reactors' were organisations in which top managers usually perceived change and uncertainty but were unable to make the organisation respond effectively. Lacking a consistent strategy-structure relationship, such organisations seldom made any kind of adjustment until forced to do so by external pressures.

'Analysers' operated in two types of product-market domain, one relatively stable, the other changing. Formalised structures and processes allowed the organisation to operate routinely and efficiently in the stable domain, while in the more turbulent one top managers scanned their competitors closely for new ideas, appropriating those which appeared to be useful.

'Prospectors' continually searched for market opportunities. They created change and uncertainty to which their competitors had to respond, but operating efficiency was often sacrificed in their strong concern for product and market innovation.

The primary and secondary literature on the Miles and Snow typology argues that strategic type will affect a firm's performance and its human resource management policies and practices (Miles and Snow, 1984).

Although the conclusion that Miles and Snow reached about the primacy of 'strategic choice', based on the work of John Child (1972, 1997), is widely accepted in the HRM-strategy literature (see, for example, Boxall and Purcell, 2006), and although their strategic typology of Defender, Reactors, Analyser and Prospector is very well known, the underlying logic demonstrated in the adaptive cycle is curiously neglected in the literature.

COMPETITIVE STRATEGIES

Michael Porter is arguably the most influential figure in business strategy. His book *Competitive Strategy*, which was first published in 1980, is, at the time of writing, reportedly in its 53rd printing (!) and is available in 17 languages.

The need for organisations to find sustainable competitive advantage is central to Porter's work. He distinguished three 'generic' competitive strategies: differentiation, cost leadership and focus.

- *differentiation* – setting the company's products or services apart from those of its competitors through, for example, advertising, features or technology to achieve a product or service which customers perceive as unique; and so achieving a premium price
- *cost leadership* – being the lowest-cost producer while achieving normal prices
- *focus* – concentrating on one or more niche markets and pursuing either differentiation or cost leadership in each niche.

Somewhat controversially, Porter maintains that a firm must choose one and only one of these strategies (or any rate each strategic business unit must) or it risks being 'stuck in the middle' with no sustainable competitive advantage and will be vulnerable to competitors.

Porter has his critics, of course, but an evaluation of his work is outside the scope of the present text. His relevance to strategic HRM is that one of the most influential 'best-fit' models of HR policies and practices – that of Schuler and Jackson (1987) – is based directly on his strategic prescriptions.

BEST-PRACTICE MODELS OF STRATEGY AND HRM

Best-practice models of HRM are universalist in nature and assert that regardless of context or internal factors there is one best way of managing human resources which, if applied, will lead to better organisational performance.

Pfeffer (1994) listed sixteen HR practices that would lead to what he termed 'competitive advantage through people': giving employment security; being selective in recruiting; paying high wages; using incentive-based pay systems; offering employee ownership of the enterprise; sharing business information with employees; encouraging participation and empowerment; team and job redesign; training and skills development; cross-utilisation and cross-training of employees; 'symbolic egalitarianism' (eg single-status working conditions); 'wage compression' – ie a relatively small range from highest to lowest basic pay; an emphasis on promotion from within the organisation; a long-term perspective in HR; measurement of HR practices; and, finally, an overarching philosophy that values people and their contribution.

Pfeffer later consolidated his list of practices to seven: employment security; selective recruitment; self-managed teams or teamworking; high pay which is contingent on company performance; extensive training; reduction of status differentials; and sharing information (Pfeffer, 1998).

Huselid (1995) in a large-scale study of US manufacturing companies across a range of industries and firm sizes reported evidence that the use of specified high-performance work practices was reflected in better firm performance as measured by reduced employee turnover, increased productivity and enhanced corporate financial performance.

The HPWPs were in the areas of personnel selection, performance appraisal, incentive compensation, job design, grievance procedures, information-sharing, attitude assessment, labour-management participation, intensity of recruitment (as measured by the selection ratio), average number of hours training per employee per year, and promotion criteria.

Huselid also specifically looked for evidence for internal and external fit in HR strategy (ie a coherent HR strategy for the former and a link between the HR strategy and the corporate strategy for the latter) but reported (1995; p.667) that

> despite the compelling theoretical arguments that better internal and external fit will increase firm performance, I found only modest evidence for such an effect for internal fit and little for external fit.

However, he acknowledged that the theoretical arguments in favour of both internal and external fit remain 'compelling', and he called for further research before a firm conclusion could be reached. It must be said that we still await such conclusive evidence that one way or the other would close the debate on best-fit or best-practice for good.

Huselid also made a final comment (1995; p.68) of significant interest, although it is seldom referred to in the HRM literature:

> Although traditional economic theory would suggest that the gains associated with the adoption of high-performance work practices cannot survive into perpetuity (because the returns from these investments will be driven toward equilibrium as more and more firms make them), the substantial variance in the HRM practices adopted by domestic [US] firms and the expectation that investment in such practices helps to create firm-specific human capital that is difficult to imitate suggest that at least in the near term such returns are available for the taking.

These are perhaps the two most widely known best-practice models, but there are many others, the most important of which is US Dept of Labor (1993), which Huselid based his work upon. Dyer and Reeves (1995), Becker and Gerhart (1996) and Youndt *et al* (1996) reviewed the field.

We can see from the above that best-practice models are typically universalist prescriptions for high-performance work practices. These models typically emphasise the importance of employee selection, training, flexibility, performance management and incentive-based pay, but they neglect issues of collective employee relations. This perhaps reflects their North American origins and arguably decreases the possibility of true universalism when applied to countries such as those of Scandinavia or Northern Europe which still enjoy a more vigorous tradition of employee representation and trade union influence than does the United States.

BEST-FIT MODELS FOR HRM AND STRATEGY

SCHULER AND JACKSON

Schuler and Jackson identified a set of twelve behaviours that were needed to make competitive strategies work. For each, the differentiation strategy required the opposite from that needed for cost leadership. These behaviours were: the degree of creative, innovative behaviour; the focus on long-term behaviour; the degree of independent, autonomous behaviour; concern for quality; concern for quantity; capacity for high risk-taking; concern for results; preference to assume responsibility; flexibility towards change; tolerance of ambiguity and unpredictability; range of skill application; and degree of job or firm involvement.

Schuler and Jackson then explicitly linked these HR characteristics of the workforce to Porter's generic competitive strategies (Porter 1980).

According to Schuler and Jackson (1987), if a firm pursues a cost leadership strategy in Porter's terms it will be sufficient that the employees show a preference for predictable and repetitive behaviour with a low degree of flexibility and a narrow application of skill. They need only have a low concern for quality of the product. Employees need show little desire for responsibility and will probably have low feelings of involvement with their jobs or organisations. To support these employee behaviours and attitudes the firm's human resource practices can exhibit low employee participation, with little job security and minimal training.

Conversely, if a firm follows a differentiation strategy, the employees will have to exhibit a high concern for quality and be creative and innovative, with a high degree of flexibility and wide application of skills. They will have to be willing to assume responsibility and will experience a high level of involvement with both job and organisation. To support these employee characteristics, human resource management practices will have to maintain a much higher level of employee participation. Employee relations will be cooperative rather than hostile, and job security is likely to be high. Rewards systems will be geared to individual and group performance.

One might almost say that for Schuler and Jackson a cost leadership strategy requires only personnel management whereas a differentiation strategy needs HRM.

MILES AND SNOW

Miles and Snow examined the sorts of HRM activities associated with their strategic types (Miles and Snow, 1984). They claimed to find quite consistent and distinct patterns of HRM in each of the Defender, Prospector and Analyser strategic types which in each case amounted to successful HR strategies. As might be expected, no consistent pattern could be found in Reactors.

According to Miles and Snow, the key HR strategy of Prospectors is to 'buy in' the personnel they require. They are 'poachers' who do not have time to undertake long-term training or development, so they attempt to lure experienced personnel from competitors. Similarly, they cannot afford bureaucratic management systems and so their HR practices tend to be informal and their reward strategies are highly geared towards performance. Employee relations will be unitarist and formal recognition of trade unions is unlikely.

Defenders, on the other hand, are doing very well out of the current business situation and so their HR strategies are geared to maintaining the status quo. With deep pockets they can afford to offer job security and long-term policies on development and training. Defenders aim to 'make' rather than 'buy' the talent they need. Their rewards systems are less likely to be performance-oriented, being geared instead to reinforcing loyalty and long-term commitment to the firm. Defenders are more able to afford pluralistic employee relations, and long-established Defenders are probably happy to recognise trade unions.

Analysers share characteristics of both Prospectors and Defenders, and their HR strategies and practices will reflect this.

Reactors by definition fail to achieve consistent and effective business strategies, and similarly with their HR strategies. Constantly reacting to crises and unforeseen events, their people management will be short-term and inconsistent and unlikly to be successful. Reactors are prone either to neglect HR or to be subject to shortlived fads and fashions.

HR AND PORTFOLIO ANALYSIS

Purcell (1989) combined the concepts of divisionalisation and those of portfolio analysis using the Boston Consultancy Group (BCG) Growth–Share Matrix. This matrix places firms (or each of their divisions or strategic business units) in a quadrant according to (i) their relative market share compared to their nearest competitors, and (ii) the rate of market growth. Each firm (or SBU) is classified as either a 'cash cow', a 'star', a 'dog' or a 'problem child'.

'Cash cows' enjoy a high relative market share in a low-growth market. Low-growth markets are usually mature, so the cash cow is similar to Miles and Snow's Defender – a large, mature, successful firm whose priority is to preserve the status quo. As the name implies, cash cows are very profitable and they provide funds for the wider corporation. They seek order, stability and predictability to continue to enjoy their dominant market position. They will tend to have well-established, rather bureaucratic HR systems and in older industries may well cling to the personnel management paradigm with a highly unionised workforce, structured systems of collective bargaining and traditional rewards systems.

'Stars' have a high relative share of a high-growth market. They are young firms in new markets. Although they have a good market share, they may not be immediately profitable for two reasons: the market, being new, may still be small in absolute terms and investment costs for the firm will still be high. But stars are the hope for the future, and as the market continues to grow and mature, the successful star may become tomorrow's cash cow. Stars are akin to Miles and Snow's Prospectors. This is the category of firm most likely to use sophisticated HRM.

'Dogs' have a low relative share of a low-growth market. They may be burned out cash cows of yesteryear. Dog status does not mean that the firm or SBU cannot be profitable in the short term, but their future is bleak and good management will sell them or close them before they slip into unprofitability. With little prospect of increasing market share, profit margins can only be improved by constantly cutting costs – including those for people. With low rewards and no development the people management in this category will be the opposite of the HRM model.

Firms classed as 'problem children' have low relative shares of fast-growing markets. Typically, they are young firms in new markets which are not fulfilling their potential. Better management might turn them into stars. They require a flexible operation with employees willing to be adaptable and who possess a range of skills. They cannot afford the high overheads associated with formal HR procedures and structures.

We can see that this analysis implies that because each quadrant of the BCG matrix requires a different business strategy, each also requires a different HR strategy. This has obvious implications for a large divisionalised business which seeks a consistent HR strategy.

REFLECTIVE ACTIVITY

Can you identify your own organisation within the BCG matrix?

If you can, does the HR strategy fit the description given above?

If not, why not?

Of course we should be sceptical of too mechanistic a 'fit' between HR practice and strategy (see Chapter 1 on HPWP bundles), but we can see in the match between HR practices and Porter's competitive strategies, in those with Miles and Snow's strategic typology, and in Purcell's matching of HR with strategic business units that there is some plausibility in these correlations. Perhaps it is best to regard these prescriptions as starting points in selecting appropriate HPWPs for a particular organisation.

THE HRM STRATEGY PROCESS AND STRATEGIC CHOICE

Boxall and Purcell (2006) are probably right to hold that neither the best-practice nor the best-fit approach is completely correct. Their solution – which seems sensible in principle – is to think in terms of (a) some underlying general or generic processes of managing human resources that are universal and which can be applied regardless of context; while there is also (b) a 'surface layer' of policies and practices in any organisation which are influenced by contingent factors. The difficulty, of course, is in identifying the generic processes. Boxall and Purcell suggest recruitment as an example of the generic processes – but they do not proffer a definitive list.

The empirical studies we cited in Chapter 1 – eg DTI/CIPD, 2005 – certainly imply that the optimum selection of HPWPs for any organisation is influenced by, and dependent on, the business strategy, and that both are the consequence of managers' making choices.

Purcell and Ahlstrand (1994) examined the relationship between corporate strategy and human resource management in multi-divisional companies, the organisational form which dominates large organisations in developed economies. According to Purcell and Ahlstrand (1994), three levels of strategy formation can be identified in the multi-divisional firm:

- first-order strategy – ie decisions on long-run goals and the scope of activities
- second-order strategy – decisions on the way the enterprise is structured to achieve its goals
- third-order strategy – decisions regarding the development of functional strategies (for example, those regarding human resource management).

These authors were, as we have said, principally concerned with strategy-making in multi-divisional firms, but the logic of their argument – that strategy decisions ultimately operate at three interlinked levels – can be applied to any firm large enough to have an explicit HRM strategy, whether it is divisionalised or not. We can take their account as a general model of the HRM strategy-making process.

We should not make the mistake of regarding this process as being overly mechanistic. The three-stage process features 'political' bargaining and trading between power groups (usually groups of senior managers) in an unclear and uncertain environment.

Of course, not all strategies are the product of wholly rational and objective evaluation – they may 'emerge' from streams of actions within the organisation (Mintzberg, 1978). Indeed, increasingly so, one might think, in 'knowledge economies'. However, even emergent strategies have to become articulated and visible, at least to some degree, at the point at which resources must be mobilised to support them. Business strategies will almost always be pretty fully articulated in terms of the first two levels of the Purcell and Ahlstrand model, and so will be largely a 'given' by the time the HR strategy is being planned or articulated itself. This is not to contradict the possibility of feedback from the third level to these higher levels. For example, a business strategy which requires certain HR resources may have to be modified or rejected if these resources prove to be too scarce or too expensive to obtain.

KEY ISSUES IN STRATEGIC HRM

The HRM function should be a partner with senior and line managers in strategy execution. The HRM strategy has to be internally consistent and must support the overall corporate strategy.

We took the model of strategy-making in divisionalised firms which was developed by Purcell and Ahlstrand, featuring three interlinked levels of decision-making to be a general model of the HRM strategy-making process in all firms. This model recognises the overriding importance of business strategy and the influence of structure.

'Best-practice' models probably contain a core of generic HR processes that are universal to all well-performing organisations, but these have not been definitively identified at other than a very general level. Best-practice models seem to miss important strategic, structural and contextual factors that in reality must be taken into account.

'Best-fit' models tend to be too mechanistic but probably offer a good first step in identifying strategies and HPWPs that firms should adopt.

HRM in action

CASE STUDY

It is all about getting people to realise they can change things.

People Management, 20 September 2007

Among his many talents, Sir Gerry Robinson is a master of understatement. 'I've generally found things reasonably easy to sort out,' says the boss who masterminded the turnarounds of Coca-Cola UK and Granada, where he is credited with stemming the TV company's losses in a year and posting returns 10% higher than expected.

'I think I get bored too early in jobs and I really enjoy something that requires a huge shake-up. My strength has been the capacity to sort out messes.'

Along the way, he has notched up chairmanships at Allied Domecq, The Arts Council, BSkyB and ITN, as well as snatching the Forte group from under its founders' noses. He is now chairman of

Moto service stations. Not bad going for a boy who led a cloistered life in a Catholic seminary in Lancashire until he was 17, before deciding not to become a priest.

After his first job at Lesney Products, makers of Matchbox toys, Robinson moved to Lex Service Group, then owners of the Volvo franchise, because, he says, he 'wanted a car'. From there he was promoted, then headhunted to Grand Met as finance director of Coca-Cola UK, ending up as chief executive of Grand Met's contract services division, before staging a management buy-out – the largest ever seen at that time – to create Compass Group.

A clue to Robinson's success may be his relentless enthusiasm for the nuts and bolts of business and for getting things right. Alongside an open and approachable charm, he is a stickler for efficiency and radiates a cut-to-the-chase, no-nonsense attitude to management that many have described as ruthless. He is impatient with those who believe management is complex or take a 'philosophical' approach.

'Business is essentially simple,' he says. 'The more you allow people to feel that things are complicated – and it's very tempting because it makes them feel clever – the less they are able to find out the answers. At the sharp end, people almost always know how to do it better. Good management is allowing them to find the answers and do it.'

Robinson is similarly dismissive of HR theories. 'I don't subscribe to over-sophisticated HR,' he asserts. 'In many ways it does itself a disservice. A genuinely important part of getting an organisation right is having people who know how to find the right people and having systems to encourage people to contribute.

'If you get into unbelievably complex philosophical analysis, or theoretical training, then it can become very costly and unhelpful.'

Robinson rejects the recent trend for management based on 'values'.

'There's no doubt that if you run an organisation that doesn't have decent values, you will be worse off,' he concedes. 'But everyone ticks the boxes and it begins to reveal a reverse correlation: the more talk there is, the less it is happening.'

Yet he is clear about HR's value to the business. 'It's the most important function to get right,' he says. 'You stand almost no chance of getting things right if you have the wrong people,' he adds. 'I cottoned on to that very early on.'

Consequently, he believes that the real task of HR is helping to choose the right people for the job and having the expertise to make sure they do the job they are meant to do. 'It is a skill that is much underestimated,' he points out. He is committed to training – nothing fancy, just 'good, solid, reliable training' for functional quality. It is a refreshingly pragmatic, straight-talking approach to HR.

Robinson can be equally disarming about his setbacks, citing the launch of the doomed ITV Digital project as his biggest mistake. 'In my heart of hearts, I knew it was wrong,' he admits. He is even on good terms with Greg Dyke, despite his leaving to take over LWT. 'I tried to persuade him to stay on,' says Robinson. 'And it was a disaster when he left the BBC. He's a good people person.'

Known as a supporter of the Blair government, Robinson denies he has any political ambitions under the new Brown regime. But there seems to be one task he is itching to get his hands on. Having recently returned to filming at the hospital in Rotherham, Yorkshire, where he controversially tackled waiting lists for a BBC2 TV series *Can Gerry Robinson fix the NHS?*, it's clear there is more he would like to be able to do.

'If someone asked me to run the NHS, the first thing I'd do would be to bring accountability back,' he says. 'People need to be held accountable directly for what they do.' As he warms to his theme, you begin to see how he must operate when tackling the thorny business crises he is renowned for sorting out.

'There are 600 hospitals. I'd have one person responsible for six hospitals. I'd build a management structure and get truly excellent people and pay what it takes. Running the NHS is the hardest job in the country. But have we really gone out and got [Tesco CEO] Terry Leahy? Have we, hell! I don't think management is taken seriously as a skill. If we got the right person to lead the NHS, they could release efficiencies of billions. The pay-off would be phenomenal.'

You can almost hear him rubbing his hands with relish as he continues. 'I'd take it out of government and create an independent health service – although it can never be completely independent because of funding. And I'd abolish the Department of Health – I'm not sure what it does, but there are a lot of people, and it is damned expensive.

'I heard that only 20p in the pound reaches operating level. If that's true, it is appalling. If you want something to happen, you have to manage it. It frustrates me.'

In Rotherham General Hospital, his trick to cutting waiting lists was to get the chief executive, Brian James, to walk around the floors and get a feel for what the issues really were. 'I think he thought I would come in with some amazingly clever idea – some sort of magic – and I think it was a disappointment to him to hear that if you want to change something you have got to do things,' Robinson says. 'But having people know that what they do is noticed is such a powerful thing. It's not very different from a family.

'There are rules and boundaries and everyone wants to have the security that people care about them and are following through.'

He is full of praise for staff who can see where change is needed. 'People in the NHS feel unhappy despite being totally committed. I believe it is all about people management,' he says. 'It is recognising people's need to contribute and be part

of something. Over the years, instead of promoting people who have achieved things, I think they have promoted people who told a good story, not those who took a risk and had ideas. You can see it in any government organisation.

'[At Rotherham] people weren't allowed to feel they could influence a damn thing. You had a management divorced from day-to-day operations. It is all about getting people to realise they can change and influence things. Success breeds success. If people start to see that things can happen, it's amazingly encouraging,' he says.

Making a difference in business, Robinson says, involves two things: 'One is being absolutely clear about what the hell you are trying to do. And then it is about the people.'

You can see why Sir Gerry is an inspiring leader. But you can also see why he has developed a fearsome reputation as an axe-wielder. Yet he complains that this image is unjustified. 'I have only ever fired five people, and only one [David Plowright, see below] was high-profile,' he claims. It seems Gerry Robinson would have you believe he is really a pussycat – but, as everyone knows, even pussycats have sharp claws.

Robinson's highlights

£17m profit in two years. Led management buy-out of Compass Group from Grand Met in 1987. Joined Granada in 1991 and stemmed its losses in a year. Knighted in 2003 for his services to arts and business.

Career low points

In the early 1990s, was widely criticised for his role in ousting the late David Plowright from the post of Granada TV chairman, after Plowright had completed 35 years' service and secured Granada's franchise. There was also ITV Digital (launched as ONdigital in 1998). Following a series of problems, including a disastrous £315m deal with the Football League, it went into administration in 2002.

REFLECTIVE ACTIVITY

What HR strategy would you recommend for the NHS?

ENDNOTES

1 Although I do not agree with all of their conclusions on the subject I am indebted to Boxall and Purcell's (2006) review of strategy and HRM, and in particular their discussion of 'best practice' and 'best fit' models, and recommend their text to any reader who wishes to undertake further reading on the topic.

CHAPTER 3

Designing work:
organising jobs and people

INTRODUCTION

Of course there has been division of labour in some sense since at least
the Stone Age, with women having to mind the home and hearth while
the men and boys went hunting and warring. Only Robinson Crusoe did
everything himself – and as soon as he found Man Friday, the latter did all
the servant stuff.

LEARNING OUTCOMES

On completion of this chapter you should:

- have an appreciation of the concept of division of labour
- know what is meant by job design
- understand the principles of scientific management
- know about developments in job design following 'scientific management', and especially the principles of the autonomous work group and the Toyota production system
- understand the principles of team formation
- appreciate the team roles required for effective teamworking
- see why organisations seek flexibility in work patterns
- have some appreciation of the organisation of work beyond the team level: by function, by product, the use of the matrix structure, and divisionalisation
- understand the role of HRM in change management.

What do we mean by job design? Michael Armstrong defined it (Armstrong, 2003; p.10) as follows:

> Job or role design: deciding on the content and performance and competency requirements of jobs or roles in order to provide a basis for selection, performance management and reward and to maximise intrinsic job satisfaction.

The recognition of the importance of organisation in the efficiency and effectiveness of work can be traced back at least to Adam Smith in his concept of the division of labour. The first sentence of Smith's great work of 1776, *The Wealth of Nations*, reads:

> The greatest improvement in the productive powers of labour and the greater part of the skill, dexterity, and judgement with which it is anywhere directed or applied, seem to have been the effects of the division of labour.

The necessity of the division of labour has naturally been hugely multiplied by the enormous technological advances which have been made, and the resulting complexity of products and services which are now possible, since Smith observed his simple pin-makers in eighteenth-century Kirkcaldy. For example, the modern motorcar is composed of more than 20,000 individual parts many of which require computer-assisted design and manufacture, while the computers and machines themselves each consist of many, many parts and software which needed many engineers and programmers to produce – and so on.

But, as the example of the car shows, to make anything work after division of labour must come re-integration or synthesis. The 20,000 odd parts of the modern car have to be assembled absolutely correctly if the car is to function at all.

So we can see that organisation of work is really fundamental to the modern technological world.

The task of management in any enterprise is to achieve the most effective combination of division and synthesis of work. That is why the organisation of work matters to executive management and investors. Why it matters to HRM is that unless the whole process, from conception through design to production, can be completely computerised, the division and synthesis crucially depends on, and intimately affects, human beings.

In this chapter we are concerned, first, with the 'micro-organisation' of work, from the level of the individual job to that of the group or team of related workers. We then examine the organisation work at levels above the team or group. After that we look at patterns of work and flexibility, and finally at some aspects of change management.

MICRO-ORGANISATION OF WORK: THE TASK, JOB AND TEAM

SCIENTIFIC MANAGEMENT

Fredrick Winslow Taylor presented a paper called 'A piece-rate system' to the American Society of Mechanical Engineers in 1895, giving him a claim to be the world's first management guru. He certainly became one of the most notorious. He is probably the only management writer whose works were the subject of an examination by a US House of Representatives Special Committee, which occurred in 1911 (Aitken, 1960).

Taylor (1911) established the following principles of what he termed 'scientific management'.

- a clear division of tasks and responsibilities between management and workers – management studying the work methods for each job, establishing the most efficient, and then dictating these to the workers
- 'scientific' selection and training of workers: matching suitable employees to the scientifically designed jobs
- the 'enthusiastic co-operation' of management and workers, secured by the use of economic incentives.

The use of this approach combined with high-speed, high-volume assembly lines at Ford's Highland Park plant in the USA led to typical work cycles of one to two minutes. This variant of 'Taylorism' came to be known as 'Fordism'. Scientific management produced remarkable increases in productivity, but was usually deeply resented by the workforce. It became associated with poor industrial relations and increased absenteeism, ill-health, employee turnover and sabotage. The 1911 House of Representatives hearing came about because of concerns that the intended use of scientific management techniques at a new US Navy arsenal would result in unacceptably hostile industrial relations in a vital military facility. In the event, Tayor's methods were not employed.

Despite these drawbacks scientific management was widely accepted and applied throughout the twentieth century. Braverman (1974) demonstrated how Taylor's approach had been extended to clerical work. Recent analyses of Japanese car assembly methods ('Toyota-ism') reveal some similarities with Taylorism, as we shall see later in this chapter.

CRITICISMS OF SCIENTIFIC MANAGEMENT

At least since the time of the Hawthorne Studies (Roethlisberger and Dickson, 1939) scientific management has been subject to criticisms that it assumed that the only motivation of the worker was economic; that it ignored workers' needs for feelings of achievement, job satisfaction and recognition; and that it neglected the importance of social relations and group psychology in the workplace.

However, it has been said (Buchanan, 1994) that:

> Modern techniques of work design have been developed and applied in the second half of this century as antidotes to Taylorism. The impact of these alternative techniques has not been as powerful or pervasive as the influence of scientific management on management practice.

THE INFLUENCE OF MOTIVATION THEORY ON THE DESIGN OF WORK

Psychologists have been studying the motivation of workers for over 100 years and the theories that have sought to explain employees' motivation have reflected the dominant psychological theories of their day. The earliest theories were based on the assumption that people had an 'instinct' to work. Later theories such as those of Maslow (1943) and Herzberg (1966) introduced the concepts of 'needs', 'drives' and 'motives'. Behavioural psychology brought an emphasis on reinforcement of behaviour – ie in this context, job performance.

The 'cognitive revolution' in psychology has been influential more recently. This approach reacted to extreme behaviourism, which had held that mental states were irrelevant to behaviour, by insisting that people's behaviour was affected by their conscious states and intentions. Goal theory provides managers with a workable technology to structure work – including more abstract and complex work such as management and professional activities – in a way that can apply the general lessons learned from the body of motivation theory.

It is fair to say that there is still no comprehensive and universally accepted theory of motivation, and our current understanding and practice of motivation and commitment are influenced to some degree by all of the various principal schools of thought since the time of Maslow at least. However, we must not doubt the immense influence that motivation theory has exercised on the organisation of work. Buchanan could comment (Buchanan, 1994; p.93) that:

> Maslow's influence is clearly stamped across the work design theories and practices of the latter half of the twentieth century.

For instance, the concept of the 'composite autonomous work group' or 'self-managing multi-skilled team', which was first developed by the Tavistock Institute of Human Relations in London, explicitly reflects Maslow's ideas.

A comprehensive discussion of motivation theory is beyond the scope of the present text. The interested reader may be directed to Landy and Conte (2007) for an up-to-date and accessible treatment of these theories.

SOME PRACTICAL CONCLUSIONS FROM MOTIVATION THEORY

Some useful general principles have been derived from the body of motivation theory:

- We should set goals whenever we can, and, where it is possible and sensible to do so, we should involve the employee(s) concerned in designing and agreeing the goals.

- Establishing agreed, specific and difficult goals ('stretch goals') leads to significant increases in employee performance.

- We should link rewards to performance wherever we reasonably can. The actual scheme or schedule of rewards is usually less important than having a clearly perceived link to performance.

- We should seek to increase employees' sense of self-confidence ('self-efficacy') that they can successfully perform the job or task.

- We should let employees know the level of performance that is expected of them, and give them accurate and timely feedback on their actual work performance.

- Giving positive rewards for good performance is more effective in motivating people then punishing them for poor performance.

- Perceived fairness or equity is important to the motivation of employees.

Practicalities of goal-setting

One of the first and best-known systems of goal-setting at work was 'management by objectives' (MBO). The phrase was coined by Peter Drucker. MBO was initially developed for organising managerial work, but it is now extensively used at all levels of organisations. When used properly it facilitates both the performance management and the development of individual employees.

Drucker stressed the importance of involving employees in the setting of goals for themselves rather than managers simply imposing goals upon them. From the manager's point of view the art of goal-setting is obtaining genuine employee input into the setting of goals which can 'stretch' the employee to improve their performance.

There is a widely known acronym that is helpful in reminding us how goals should be set at work: they should be 'SMART' – that is, they should be:

- **S**pecific
- **M**easurable
- **A**ssignable

- **Realistic**
- **Time-bound.**

In other words, people should know exactly what they are being asked to achieve (ie their goal is 'Specific'). Their performance should be capable of being assessed against some criteria or standard of success ('Measurable'), and this means looking for appropriate measures of performance whenever this is feasible. There should be no doubt or ambiguity about responsibility, whether individual or team ('Assignable'). No one should be asked to undertake responsibility for any action that is intrinsically impossible or for which they are not capable (goals must be 'Realistic'). All actions must be successfully completed by a stated time (be 'Time-bound').

Of course, as any manager will tell you, it is not always just as easy as that sounds. The great strength of the 'SMART' approach is that it compels the manager to seek clarity and realism in what he or she is asking people to do, and this can be hard, time-consuming work, entailing considerable interaction with other people. Moreover, this requirement works both ways, up and down the organisation – no manager should accept a goal or objective themselves until they are happy with its 'SMART' profile.

The degree of direction or participation which the manager employs in this process will depend on many factors, such as the degree of urgency, the complexity of the task and the expertise and knowledge of the individual or team undertaking the work.

REFLECTIVE ACTIVITY

Write down the last three things you were tasked to do in your work. How SMART were your goals?

Write down the last three activities you assigned to subordinates. How SMART were these?

HRM in action: the 'critical few'

When the present author was undertaking research into management development in firms in Scotland, one very well-known US technology firm explained to him their performance management and development system, which was known in the company as 'the critical few'. It was essentially MBO but with a neat twist relating to prioritising. It was described by the plant director as follows:

> A manager has to do 101 or maybe 1,001 things, but only a few – no more than half a dozen at most, and often less than that – are *really* critical at any time. If these 'critical few' are done well, then mostly the other ones either

fall into place or don't matter much. The smart manager learns to think that way and to spot his or her 'critical few'. If you can't learn to do that, you'll get buried in this place.

This illustrates the importance of prioritising one's own work as a manager, but competent managers also assist their people to find their own 'critical few'.

DEVELOPMENTS AFTER SCIENTIFIC MANAGEMENT

It should be remembered, even in a text on human resource management, that management's interest in work design is always primarily economic and not humanitarian. No doubt most managers, if everything else was equal, would choose a humanitarian work design over a less civilised method, but management will always pursue economic efficiency as the first objective. It is after all what management are there for. For instance, the renewed popularity of team-based approaches to work design in recent decades (discussed below) was stimulated by intensified competitive pressures rather than by attempts to improve the contentment of the ordinary worker.

The holy grail of job design has always been to get the technical efficiency of Taylorism without the costly human side-effects. The first remedy tried was job rotation, which entails moving workers from task to task at fixed intervals (say, 30 minutes). Job enlargement is the recombination of tasks which have been separated by scientific management techniques to lengthen the short 'Fordist' work cycle. Both job rotation and job enlargement are relatively simple to achieve and produced limited but positive results, such as reductions in turnover, absenteeism and sabotage.

Job enrichment or 'vertical loading' was popularised by General Motors in the USA in the late 1960 and 1970s. This consciously employed the theories of Herzberg (1966) to build 'motivators' into the work by giving more control and responsibility to the worker.

The autonomous work group

The principles of the autonomous work group are expressed in the 'Tavistock work organisation model' (Trist and Bamforth, 1951; Emery, 1963). This specified that work should be organised in teams and that individual jobs should provide variety, a meaningful task, an 'optimum' work cycle, the worker's control over work standards, feedback of results, preparation and auxiliary tasks, the use of valued skill and knowledge, and a perceived contribution to the end product. The teams should provide workers with the means for communication and also promotion. A very important aspect of the Tavistock model is its freedom from the technology that is used in the work, so it is applicable in virtually all work situations.

Autonomous work groups were extensively used in Scandinavia, especially by the car manufacturers Saab and Volvo (Gyllenhammar, 1977), and also elsewhere in Europe including Scottish and Newcastle Breweries in Edinburgh. There were some high-profile successes, but Valery (1974) estimated that over 1,000 autonomous work group experiments had been started in Scandinavia and that many of these failed. Autonomous work groups were not at first popular in North America, and in the 1970s job enlargement schemes were more accepted. The comparative lack of popularity of the autonomous work group with managers until the mid-1980s may be partly explained by its sophisticated theoretical basis and consequent complex language, and partly by its effect on the status and responsibilities of supervisors and junior managers. Until compelled to by the spectre of economic failure in global competition, most Western companies – workers as well as managers – were unwilling to make the revolutionary organisational and cultural changes that the adoption of the autonomous work group entails.

By the 1980s the increased competition from Japanese industries with team-based 'lean manufacture' reawakened Western, and especially American, interest in autonomous work groups. The management guru Tom Peters supported them (Peters, 1987; p.296):

> the modest-sized, task-oriented, semi-autonomous, mainly self-managing team should be the basic organisational building-block.

However, whereas the Tavistock work organisation model was a deliberate move away from Taylorist work principles and towards the self-actualising goal of the humanistic psychologists (Maslow, 1943; Herzberg, 1966), the Japanese team system explicitly contained some Taylorist aspects.

The Toyota production system

The Toyota production system (TPS) presents the paradigm case of Japanese work organisation – so much so that the word 'Toyota-ism' has passed into everyday management language. The TPS has been highly influential not only in manufacturing but also in services, including recently even the UK National Health Service, a work situation that you might think was about as dissimilar from a car manufacturing plant as could be imagined (see 'HRM in action' below).

There are four main principles of the TPS (Adler *et al*, 1997): 'just-in-time' production, flexibility, quality, and a combination of standardised work and continuous improvement.

'Just-in-time' production (JIT) aims to eliminate all work-in-progress (WIP) inventory. In addition to reducing the capital locked up in WIP, this helps to increase organisational learning by eliminating buffers of stock and WIP, and so exposing bottlenecks and problems in production. This then necessitates flexibility and participation from the team-workers because they must solve problems in real time.

To aid flexibility, workers are typically organised in teams of four to six, and tasks are rotated within the team. Team leaders train workers, cover for absent team members and handle administrative tasks. Clusters of from three to five teams typically comprise a group, and group leaders are the first level of management.

The *jidoka* quality principle dictates that the production process should be as error-free as possible. Traditional manufacturing processes rely on quality-control inspectors to catch substandard parts at the end of the assembly line, but managers trust the workers to inspect their own work in the TPS. Workers are expected to catch faulty parts immediately, to avoid waste, and to find the causes of production problems. Workers are empowered to stop the assembly line whenever they fall behind or see a fault they cannot repair.

Standardised work and *kaizen* or continuous improvement together constitute the fourth component of the TPS. Each task is analysed and the most efficient method is specified in motion-by-motion instructions describing exactly how each job should be done. This is the 'Taylorist' aspect of Japanese work methods which seems to sharply demarcate it from the Western autonomous work group. Despite the use of these methods, TPS is not Taylorist in the normal sense of the word, however. It is the team members and team leaders who identify the best procedures for each job, whereas in Western Taylorist production systems it is industrial engineers who would design the work process and observe and time workers at specific jobs. And as we have just seen, workers are empowered to stop assembly lines on their own initiative – a radically *anti*-Taylorist concept. Workers are also encouraged to engage in continuous improvement of their work process and constantly make advances in 'best practice'.

Autonomous work group versus Toyota-ism?

Hammarström and Lansbury (1991) compared the experience of Swedish car manufacturers which had adopted autonomous work groups with that of Toyota. Saab was forced to sell its car business in the late 1980s, and Volvo experienced troubles in the early 1990s that eventually meant it was bought by Ford – but their Japanese competitors thrived. No doubt the reasons both for the Swedish failures and for the Japanese success were complex and many-factored, but Hammarström and Lansbury concluded that for managers in many countries the Toyota approach appeared safe and more 'natural' than autonomous work groups as a means of production, and they questioned whether the Swedish model – and by extension the Western autonomous work group – could survive the impact of global competition.

TEAMWORKING

We can now say that teamworking is virtually the 'default option' in job design today. Only if there are compelling reasons not to organise people in teams will alternatives be considered.

We can define a work group or team as:

> A group of people collaborating in their professional work, or in a particular enterprise or task, who share common objectives and who need to work together to achieve them.

Tuckman (1965) studied the process of team development and identified four essential stages that all teams have to progress through if they are to be effective. He labelled these forming, storming, norming, and performing.

- *Forming*, the first stage, begins when the members meet. This stage is typified by anxiety and formality as members learn what behaviour is expected of them and how they should undertake the task. There is usually a greater dependence on the team leader at this time. Members typically will be asking themselves whether they will be able to do the task and fit in with the rest of the team.

- *Storming* is the second stage. Here the formality of the forming stage is dispensed with. There is often conflict between members and with the leader. There may also be resistance to the demands of the team task.

- Group cohesion appears at the third stage, *norming*. The 'norms' of the team emerge – how it will behave and go about its task, how it will solve problems, etc. Mutual support and cooperation are evident and views can be openly expressed without conflict. A team identity starts to be built.

- When the norms have been established, the team can start to *perform* effectively.

All effective teams have to go through these four stages of development. Many of the processes in the forming, storming and norming stages happen at a non-verbal, barely conscious, level. Virtual teams – ie those in which members operate at separate locations and use information technology for communication and coordination – have to go through the same development process as other teams if they are to be effective. It has been found that initial face-to-face meetings of the team greatly facilitate the development process – probably because the non-verbal and unconscious mechanisms seem to operate much more effectively face-to-face than when mediated by information technology. Geographical dispersion is no barrier to effective performance once a virtual team has reached the performing stage.

Tuckman and Jensen (1977) added a fifth stage to team development which they termed 'adjourning', meaning the end of the team as an effective unit. This may happen explicitly, as with the disbanding of a project team when the team has successfully completed its remit, but it can happen informally as the team starts to disintegrate. It will often not be immediately obvious to those outside the team. Production and service teams that are designed to operate without any defined end-point are susceptible to drifting into adjournment without management realising.

TYPES OF TEAMS

Not all teams are the same in terms of their functions and how they work. *Production or service teams* tend to undertake a limited range of standard activities and be highly interchangeable in terms of team members: everyone can do each other's job. This requires a high degree of cross-training, but yields very high flexibility. Such teams can be self-managing.

Project teams on the other hand are typically composed of highly skilled experts who are therefore not interchangeable with each other, and the team may have a very wide range of activities to handle, which might include solving hitherto unknown and unexpected problems. A designated leader is usually required.

Top management teams may have as wide a range of activities to deal with as project teams but will probably have some degree of interchangeability.

There are many other types of teams. Examples include cross-functional or cross-departmental teams, quality circles, functional teams, and problem-solving teams.

TEAM ROLES

After studying how management teams operated, Belbin (1981) identified a number of crucial roles that must be fulfilled by team members if the team is to be successful. Belbin's findings have been applied by many management writers to all teams, not just managerial ones. Belbin's work suggests that it is not sufficient to select effective teams solely on the basis of the functional skills of people.

Belbin labelled the eight roles he identified as being crucial to effective teamworking as 'chairperson', 'company worker', 'completer-finisher', 'monitor-evaluator', 'plant', 'resource investigator', 'shaper', and 'team-worker'. These are explained below.

The 'chairperson' role helps control the team and encourages all the members to participate. This role is often carried out effectively by someone who is neither the cleverest nor most creative in the team. What is important is that the 'chairperson' can identify team objectives clearly, can display a calm and confident manner, and stays in control.

The 'company worker' role helps the team to put proposals into practice. This requires self-discipline and the ability to organise. People who have a strong sense of duty and organisational loyalty, and who are dependable and predictable in their own behaviour, are well suited to this role.

The 'completer-finisher' role helps the team to finish the job and keeps a sense of urgency alive until it is done. This role needs someone who is good at the details of the problem or job in hand and is conscientious in seeing the task through to its end.

The 'monitor-evaluator' role enables the team to analyse problems and evaluate ideas and proposals. It requires the ability to make realistic and impartial judgements.

The 'plant' role encourages creative thinking within the team. It needs someone who is intelligent and perhaps unorthodox in their thinking – the good 'plant' can 'think the unthinkable'.

The 'resource investigator' function provides a link between the team and the rest of the organisation in order to obtain resources needed to complete the task. It needs someone who is extrovert and enthusiastic with good interpersonal social skills.

The 'shaper' role influences the way the team operates and is best performed by energetic and extrovert people who are not afraid to challenge the usual working norms and methods.

The 'team-worker' role helps support the individual team members and encourages team spirit and morale. This is best done by a 'people person' who can empathise with their fellow-workers and who is good at reducing interpersonal friction and defusing conflicts.

People can take on more than one role each, so it is certainly possible to have effective teams of fewer than eight members, but as the descriptions given above suggest, personality traits seem to play a part in determining which roles individuals are best suited to undertake or be most comfortable with.

REFLECTIVE ACTIVITY

Consider your own behaviour in a team in which you have worked. Which of the Belbin team roles do you feel most comfortable with?

Why did these particular roles/this particular role suit you, do you think?

HRM IMPLICATIONS ARISING FROM TEAM-BASED WORKING

People have to be given the skills and knowledge they require to work effectively in the team. Not only the technical skills to do the actual job, but the interpersonal skills required to work in a team, and also the presentational and communication skills necessary for the team to interface with other teams, with customers and with the rest of the organisation. The more autonomy the team has been granted, the higher the number, and the greater the complexity, of skills that are required.

Managers to whom autonomous teams are accountable will also require training to adapt to a supporting rather than a directing role in relation to the teams.

ORGANISATIONAL DESIGN

In this section we look at the organisation of work at levels above that of the team.

Contemporary thinking is that there is no 'one right way' to organise a business or other form of institution. As Lorsch (1970; p.1) has put it:

> The structure of an organisation is not an immutable given, but rather a set of complex variables about which managers can exercise considerable choice.

And to quote Drucker again:

> Organisation is organic and unique to each individual business.

The big difficulty for managers in trying to organise work is that activities can usually be ordered in a number of different ways, each of which might seem plausible. For instance, activities might be organised around the different functions of the organisation: production, marketing, finance, sales, etc. Or they might be arranged around the separate products, or by geographical location – the UK, Europe, North America, etc. Large multi-product firms can be organised into separate divisions or strategic business units (SBUs). Some of these different ways of grouping work activities might be used within the same organisation, and even combined, as we will see in our discussion of the matrix structure below. However, some general principles have been established.

BY FUNCTION OR BY PRODUCT?

We first consider the choice between organising by function or by product. A functional structure can give some real advantages where the organisation is concentrated on a single product or service and where the rate of change is relatively slow:

- The management structure can be relatively simple and all major decisions can all be dealt with by a small top management team.

- The functional structure allows specialist expertise to be built up and can offer a good career path for specialists.

- The simple structure makes it easy to obtain economies of scale as production rises.

So a functional structure is often the best for small, single-product organisations which operate with relatively simple technology in markets where change and risk are predictable and manageable.

Organising activities around products usually becomes more effective than a functional structure as a firm diversifies into multiple products. This advantage increases as competitive or technological changes increase in rate. In these circumstances the product structure is definitely superior to the functional structure in speed of decision-making by top management, in knowledge of customers and markets, in communication between specialists and managers, and in product development. It is also more effective at developing future general managers.

THE MATRIX STRUCTURE: THE BEST OF BOTH WORLDS?

Experience has shown that it is possible, and often desirable, to combine aspects of both the functional and product organisation. Project teams which comprise experts from different functions and departments who are all working on the same task (eg developing a new product) show this. Project teams are of fixed duration, but when the arrangement is long-term or permanent, it is called a *matrix structure*. The matrix structure is sometimes called 'the grid structure' when is applied over the whole of the organisation, as can be the case in knowledge-based industries.

In a matrix structure, functional specialists have two bosses: they report on project issues to the designated project manager but they are still under the overall authority of their functional managers (on whom their career progression might rely). Of course this can lead to stresses and tensions when the demands of the managers conflict. One of the most important advantages of a matrix structure is that it helps to preserve flexibility as successful organisations grow. It can also help to encourage delegation, which assists both motivation and the development of managers.

There are some acknowledged problems with matrix structures. There is inevitable conflict between product and functional managers over priorities of resources, time and costs. Functional managers often fear that their authority will be undermined by matrix structures, whereas functional specialists have concerns about loss of their specialist identity and the possible threat to their career progression. Individual stress will be increased by the conflict of dual reporting and ambiguity over what is demanded of people in the system. It has been said that in a matrix structure conflict and stress is the price that has to be paid for adaptability and change. Administrative overheads often increase because of more complicated managerial hierarchies and more managerial time being spent on handling conflict.

A matrix structure can be advantageous if an organisation is diversified, if it operates in a market where technical complexity requires the use of many specialists, and if it faces high competitive pressures. Indeed, in those conditions a matrix structure will probably recognise and improve a situation that has emerged anyway.

DIVISIONALISATION

Most large and diversified companies now follow a divisionalised structure with separate divisions or strategic business units (SBUs) based on different product ranges or the geographical locations of customers. This offers several advantages to larger organisations:

- Each division can concentrate on its own particular market, so major decisions are taken nearer to the point of action and corporate management is freed for more strategic matters.

- Profit responsibility is delegated to divisions, allowing business activities to be evaluated separately.

- The decentralisation of decision-making and responsibility is likely to motivate middle-level general managers and provide them with earlier training in general management.

There are some potential problems with divisionalisation, of course:

- The best basis for creating divisions may not always be clear – as between product and geographical location, for example.

- There will be conflict between divisions over investment resources and share of central services.

- The idea of divisionalisation rests on the assumption that a firm can identify a number of separate self-contained areas of business. So the greater the interdependence of the various parts of the company, the harder it will be to make divisionalisation work effectively.

- Even where the original divisional design was appropriate initially, fast growth of a division may alter its characteristics.

THE 'FLEXIBLE FIRM' AND HRM

As we will recall from Chapter 1, the 2004 Workplace Employee Relations Survey (2004 WERS) found solid empirical evidence that many UK organisations operated a 'flexible organisation' with a core of key employees and a 'peripheral' workforce of other workers who enjoyed less secure and less attractive terms and conditions of employment. A large majority of workplaces (83%) had part-time employees and these constituted more than half of the workforce in 30% of all workplaces. Just under one third (30%) of workplaces had employees on temporary contracts. The use of temporary agency staff, although less prevalent than fixed-term contracts, was still quite widespread, 17% of all workplaces employing 'temps'.

'Core employees' are those who are crucial to the organisation's success. These are not just top managers – anyone with critical knowledge or skills should be in the core. Core employees have high market value. They will be well rewarded and receive good development and career opportunities. The idea of 'talent management' was created for this category of employees. The core is protected from short-term fluctuations in market demand by several peripheral shells of employees who, as we move out from the core, experience increasingly less attractive employment conditions and rewards. The outermost shell typically comprises temporary staff and low-skilled labour recruited on a casual basis from the local labour market, or perhaps migrant labour (Atkinson, 1984).

The HRM content of the people management profile within the firm may drop rapidly from the core to the outer periphery. The people management applied to core employees will be HRM. These are the people for whom the 'war for talent' is waged. Those in shells close to the core will also probably enjoy the advantages of an HRM approach – many of them will become core employees in due course. But as we move further out from the core, the people management style will progressively resemble HRM less and less, employees receiving markedly fewer training and development opportunities, less secure employment and less attractive rewards. These people are more easily replaced from the local labour markets and figure much less in the 'war for talent'.

REFLECTIVE ACTIVITY

Does your employing organisation have the characteristics of a 'flexible firm'?

If it does, what are the criteria for becoming a core employee?

A FINAL WORD ON ORGANISATIONAL STRUCTURE

Inappropriate organisational structure can be expected to hinder organisational performance. However, good structure by itself cannot guarantee success. We should think of organisational structure as being able to make a necessary but not in itself sufficient contribution to performance. The performance of an

Figure 2 The flexible firm

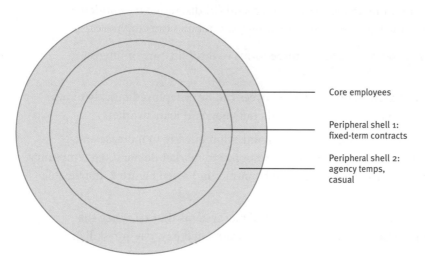

Core employees

Peripheral shell 1:
fixed-term contracts

Peripheral shell 2:
agency temps,
casual

Source: adapted from Atkinson (1984)

organisation is influenced by many factors. Structure cannot ensure that correct strategies are followed or correct decisions made. To quote A. P. Sloan, a former president of General Motors (Sloan, 1967):

> An organisation [ie structure] does not make decisions: its function is only to provide a framework, based upon established criteria, within which decisions can be fashioned in an orderly manner. Nor can structure compensate for lack of appropriate skills, the will to manage effectively, or the motivation to work together.

PATTERNS OF WORK: THE SEARCH FOR FLEXIBILITY

Peter Drucker once remarked that until the time of the Industrial Revolution 'only lunatics and criminals worked by the clock'. This may be something of an exaggeration but it serves to remind us how industrialisation and the factory system has accustomed us to the idea of a 'normal working week' something like 9 to 5, Monday to Friday. In fact this 'normal working week' has been showing a steady reduction in the number of hours it entails since the first Industrial Revolution. The purpose of this section is to explore the alternative patterns of work that are available.

Employers pursue flexibility in working patterns for three main reasons:

- to minimise human resource costs in both the short and the long run
- to protect the core from short-term fluctuations in market demand

- in response to the demands of an increasingly diverse workforce in terms of both (i) minimum legal compliance, and (ii) discretionary entitlement, surpassing the legal minimum, to attract and retain core employees.

In terms of economic efficiency, three forms of flexibility are of interest to employers:

- *functional flexibility*, by which employees can be redeployed quickly to new tasks and activities (eg multi-skilled craftsmen and team-workers)
- *numerical flexibility*, enabling the organisation quickly to increase and decrease the numbers employed in response to market demand (eg temporary employment, part-time working, subcontracting) – see Figure 2, the flexible firm, above
- *financial flexibility* – the establishing of pay systems that reinforce the requirement for flexibility (eg performance-related pay, pay-for-skills).

WORK–LIFE BALANCE

The diversity of the workforce both in the labour market and within establishments together with changes in aspirations of employees have implications for the way employers run their organisations

Kersley *et al* (2006; p.235)

There is evidence that both men and women are experiencing dissatisfaction with their work–life balance (White *et al*, 2004).

In addition to the need for compliance with equal opportunities legislation for all employees, employers are increasingly concerned in the 'war for talent' to be able to offer their core employees an employment package that not only is sufficiently attractive in financial terms but is able meet their requirements in terms of flexibility.

And there is evidence that many employers are prepared to offer more flexible working arrangements for at least some of their employees. According to the 2004 Workplace Employee Relations Survey, 70% of UK workplaces offered reduced hours to some employees, while 54% offered increased hours, 45% offered changed shift patterns, 31% job-sharing, 35% flexitime, and 26% home-working (Kersley *et al*, 2006; p.250).

ANNUAL HOURS

Organisations typically establish permanent manning levels that will cope with normal demand. However, fluctuations in demand can result in inefficiencies in that there may be overmanning at times of low demand and undermanning, requiring the use of temporary workers or overtime, at times of peak demand. For many organisations the demand for their goods or services fluctuates according to recognisable and predictable patterns, and in these cases the scheduling of employee hours according to annual hours should result in a better match between demand and hours actually worked in any period.

Annual hours arrangements are based on the principle that the number of hours that full-time employees must work is defined over a whole year rather than over a week or a month. Thus an average 38-hour week (with a total of five weeks' holidays per year) becomes 1,786 annual hours.

ALTERNATIVES TO PERMANENT FULL-TIME WORKING

Temporary working

The main purposes for employers in employing temporary workers are:

- to provide a more flexible alternative to full-time employees
- to cover for temporary peaks in demand
- to cover for holiday and sickness absence
- to protect the job security of core employees.

Most temporary workers are employed on short-term contracts of unspecified length or renewable from week to week. Typically, they receive the same basic pay and benefits as full-time workers but are usually excluded from fringe benefits.

Part-time working and job-sharing

Part-time working can cut down the need for overtime and/or unsocial hours payments to permanent staff and so be more cost-effective. It can lower unit labour costs where part-time workers earnings are too low to incur employers' tax liabilities and where part-timers are ineligible for fringe benefits.

Job-sharing is where two employees share the responsibilities of one full-time position with the salary and other benefits shared between them in proportion to the time each works. In principle any job could be shared in any way that was acceptable to the two parties involved and their employer, but the most common patterns are: split day, split week, or alternate weeks.

Home-working

Information technology has significantly increased the scope for home-working by employees. The 2004 WERS found that 26% of workplaces in the UK offered home-working to some employees.

CHANGE MANAGEMENT

Two of the least contentious statements in management literature are (i) 'Change is the only constant in management,' and (ii) 'The rate of change is ever-increasing.'

The CIPD has nonetheless stated (CIPD, 2006a) that:

> Organisational change is increasing, yet the high levels of failure indicate that effective management of these changes is still lacking.

We recall from Chapter 1 that the pace of change in competitive markets and in technology was a major factor forcing Western organisations to move from the personnel management to the HRM model of people management, and that Ulrich specified that HR should become an 'agent of continuous transformation', shaping processes and a culture that together improve an organisation's capacity for change. Torrington *et al* (2002) specified *change management* objectives as comprising one of the four main roles of people management.

Change is still being driven primarily by competition and technology, but organisational change can also be brought about by changes in business strategy, by the introduction of new management techniques, by internal organisational development, by changes in legislation, and by merger and acquisition activity.

RESISTANCE TO CHANGE

It is entirely rational for people to resist change when they are not directing it. Change may threaten their routines and methods of working, their conditions of employment and their established work groups and teams. It may bring economic fears if people think their jobs or earnings may be under threat. Uncertainty exaggerates these fears and undermines trust in management. Often, impending change brings threats to status and to existing skills and competences: people worry about whether their skills will be needed and whether they will be able to master new skills and competences that will be required.

So managing the human resource is perhaps the most crucial aspect of managing change in any organisation. Managers have to introduce and manage change and gain the commitment of their people, both during and after implementation. Successful management of change requires effective leadership and project management in addition to good communication skills.

There are a number of models of organisational change which are widely used in HRM. The best-known is that of Lewin (1951). This proposes a three-stage process:

- 'unfreezing' the status quo – this is achieved by creating a sense of dissatisfaction with the existing state of affairs, thus creating a climate which accepts that change is necessary

- 'changing' to the new desired situation
- 'refreezing' or establishing the new situation.

Beer, Eisenstat and Spector (1990) suggested that the most effective way to change behaviour was to concentrate on 'task alignment' where the new roles, responsibilities and relationships would 'force' new attitudes and behaviours on people. They advocated a six-stage change process to achieve this:

- Mobilise commitment to change through joint analysis and diagnosis of problems.
- Develop a shared vision of how to organise and manage the change.
- Foster consensus, competence and commitment to a new shared vision.
- Spread the word about the change.
- Institutionalise the change through formal policies, systems and structures.
- Monitor and adjust strategies and policies as needed.

THE ROLE OF HUMAN RESOURCES IN CHANGE

The CIPD recommends (CIPD, 2006a) that HRM specialists be involved from the initial stages in any major change initiative and be represented in the main project team. Their specialist expertise is useful in the following areas:

- advising project leaders on the skills available within the organisation – identifying any skills gaps, training needs, new posts, new working practices, etc
- negotiating and engaging with employee representatives
- understanding employee concerns and anticipating problems
- advising on communications with employee groups
- helping people cope with change.

REFLECTIVE ACTIVITY

Describe a recent organisational change that affected you. What was your role in it?

Did HR have a role? *Should* HR have had a role?

How might you have improved the management of the change?

KEY ISSUES IN JOB ORGANISATION

Except for the case of the single self-employed person, it is always necessary for people and work to be organised in some way in order to (i) achieve division of labour, and (ii) achieve the necessary synthesis of the outputs of that division. This is the basis of job design. 'Scientific management' represents the first systematic attempts at modern job design.

The autonomous work group developed from attempts to humanise work while still achieving technical efficiencies. The Toyota production system of 'lean manufacture' is highly influential and it combines both the teamwork and elements of Taylorism. We understand quite a lot about how teams develop and the roles that are necessary for effective teamworking.

Organisations seek flexibility and are increasingly structured with a core of key employees that is surrounded by peripheral shells of non-core workers.

Effective change management is vital for all successful organisations and HRM should have a crucial role in achieving effective management of change.

CASE STUDY

Job design in practice

Waiting times drop thanks to 'Toyota treatment'

The Scotsman newspaper (Monday 25 June 2007) reported that the National Heath Service in Edinburgh had adopted the Toyota production system in a pilot study which had resulted in significant improvements in services for patients. These included:

- Waiting times for patients needing CT scans were reduced from 21 weeks to four, which also allowed 20 extra patients a week to receive the service.

- The waiting time for a routine colonoscopy fell from 29 weeks to 18 weeks.

- A computer-based system to manage hospital beds saved more than 80 hours of staff travel time.

- And the 11 forms required to document rehabilitation patients were replaced with just one.

Following the principles of 'lean production', staff who dealt with patients 'on the front line' were asked to suggest improvements. These were not just doctors but included porters, nurses and drivers. The pilot has been so successful that the Health Service is to extend the programme to other areas of patient care.

A Health Service spokesman was quoted as saying: 'Our philosophy is that the person who is doing the job is the expert. They are the ones who know if something could be changed to make their job more efficient.'

From an article available online at http://edinburghnews.scotsman.com/index.cfm?id=992312007

FURTHER READING

Child, J. (1984) *Organisation: A guide to problems and practice*, 2nd edition. London, Harper & Row

CHAPTER 4

Managing the human resource flow

INTRODUCTION

In the opening chapter we noted that one of the key themes of HRM
in the twenty-first century was the use of sophisticated HR practices
in recruitment and selection. Recruitment and selection are two of the
most important HRM activities in any organisation. In this chapter we will
examine the general principles underlying these activities and also look
at some of the most widely used techniques. Oganisations also have to
manage the processes involved when employees leave the organisation,
and these too are studied in this chapter. We additionally introduce the
concept of 'talent management'.

LEARNING OUTCOMES

On completion of this chapter you should:

- understand the main models of recruitment and selection of human resources, and which of
  these are suitable for work organisations

- understand how recruitment and selection may be best viewed as particular stages in a larger
  process of 'managing and developing the human resource flow'

- have an appreciation of e-recruiting (ie how and why it is increasingly used in recruitment)

- have an awareness of the strengths and limitations of the techniques most commonly used in
  selection, and an appreciation of the use of assessment centres

- have an appreciation of the issues involved in managing the exit of employees from the
  organisation

- have an understanding of the concept of 'talent management'.

HR specialists often talk about recruitment and selection as separate activities – 'recruitment' meaning the process of attracting people to apply for the job, and 'selection' being the final choice of a particular applicant for a specific position. (The North American term 'hiring' covers both and is sometimes more useful.) It is important that we remember that recruitment and selection do not occur in isolation from other managerial and organisational processes. They are key stages in what Beer *et al* (1984; p.66) termed 'managing the human resource flow':

> The more dynamic the environment, the more a corporation must be concerned with managing the flow of people in, through and out of the organisation.

In the twenty-first century we can update this to say 'Managing *and developing* the human resource flow'. Table 3 illustrates the key stages in this process.

Table 3 Managing and developing the human resource flow

Strategic	Individual job/ person	Actions/outcomes
Long term	Short term	
Organisational development Human resource planning	Job analysis	Identifying the task requirements and criteria for job success
	Person specification	Identifying the attributes and experience the job-holder needs to achieve job success
	Recruiting	Attracting applicants for consideration for the position.
	Initial screening	Examining applications to identify those most suitable for further consideration
	Selection	Interviews, testing and obtaining other information to assess applicants' attributes
	Initial induction and training	Induction to the organisation. If necessary, additional testing, assessment and training to fit the person for the job
Continuous improvement	Performance management	Performance appraisal
	Learning and development	Knowledge and skill enhancement and development
Talent management		Promotion/transfer
Restructuring/ rightsizing	Employee exit and/or job restructuring/ elimination	Employee job exit: Employee *voluntary* organisational exit; resignation; retiral Employee organisational *involuntary* exit: redundancy; dismissal

Performance management and learning and development are dealt with in later chapters.

We can see that decisions on recruitment and selection are embedded in a process of managing and developing the human resource flow through the organisation, entailing a range of HR practices, from analysing the key aspects of the job through to managing the exit of the employee from the job or organisation. This process itself is further embedded in long-term HR decisions and actions, and HR experts often talk about 'strategic selection', at least for key employees.

In the twenty-first century it is no longer sufficient just to hire the right staff – the HR talent must be managed and developed to achieve and sustain competitive advantage. This is not bad news for HR departments: *The Economist* under the subheading 'The triumph of the HR department' could write (*A Survey of Talent*, 7–14 October 2006; p.6):

> Managing talent has become more important to a much wider range of companies than it used to be. One result has been that human resources departments which used to be quiet backwaters have gained in status. A survey by Aon, a consultancy, identified 172 HR executives who were among the five best-paid managers in their companies. That would have been unheard of a few years ago.

RECRUITMENT AND SELECTION

Before you can manage the talent of your human resources you have first to get hold of it. You must hire people with the knowledge, skills and attitudes you require. Taking the long-term aspect, you want core employees who can continue to adapt and learn, so that there is a better probability that your organisation can sustain competitive advantage in the future. And from that long-term perspective, attitude and capability or potential may be more important than current skills and knowledge.

How do organisations get the human resources they need? We might distinguish six possible theoretical models of personnel selection for organisation (Bass and Barratt (1981)):

- the trial or 'try it and see' model, in which everyone who is interested is allowed to 'have a go' at the job or role, and only some are kept on after their performance in the role has been assessed

- the 'lottery' model or random selection, in which a number of people are started on a chance basis

- the 'quota' model, by which it is required by law, or policy, that a fixed number or percentage of post-holders should be of a specific type – eg gender or ethnic group

- the 'common sense and experience' model, where selection is on the basis of the sort of people who have proved to be associated with successful job performance in the past

- *the 'matching attributes' model,* where selection is made on the basis of attempting to identify and to match attributes which the applicant possesses and which it is assumed predict job success
- *the 'competency' model* – a refinement of the matching attributes model – where emphasis is placed on the applicant's possession of certain particular traits or abilities, or the ability to perform to a specified standard (or some combination of both of these requirements).

Of course not all of these models are practicable in the real world of work.

The 'try it and see' model

No one would wish to be operated on a by a surgeon recruited under such a scheme, because he or she, however well motivated, might be completely unqualified. Clubs and voluntary organisations obviously work on this basis in acquiring new members and so there are no entrance criteria for the Girl Guides or Boy Scouts, for instance (other than age and gender). As far as paid employment is concerned, however, unless there are absolutely no skill or knowledge requirements for the job, this is a very costly method because there is no guarantee that anyone who wants to join the organisation can actually do the specified job. It is completely unrealistic for most organisations. A partial exception might be voluntary workers for charities – but even in that case there are usually some minimal requirements such as basic numeracy and literacy that not everyone in society meets.

We have to remember that ideally we want to be able to make quick and accurate decisions over whether an applicant can do the job effectively before committing the organisation to hiring them. Hiring is a costly business: the CIPD has estimated that the average cost of filling a vacancy in the UK is £3,600, rising to £8,200 when the associated labour turnover costs were also taken into account (CIPD, 2006b). A wrong hiring decision is of course even more expensive – not only do you have to do it all over again to get it right, you have to bear the consequences of incompetent performance until you do.

The 'lottery' model

This is where people are allocated by means of random selection to the posts or to the organisation. This will obviously be unsuitable for commercial and most other types of organisation for the same reasons that the 'try it and see' model is – there can be no guarantee of even minimal competence or qualification. It can be appropriate where the task or job is seen to be a necessary civic duty – eg jury duty or military service, although in the latter there will be minimum physical standards to meet.

The 'quota' model

Usually this would be dictated by law or organisational policy. For example, universities in the USA are required to take set quotas of students from specified ethnic groups. This can achieve desirable social goals but might obviously be at the cost of effectiveness in any particular instance.

The next three models are all variants on a general approach of trying to find in some systematic and objective way an individual who matches the job requirements.

The 'common sense and experience' model

Using experience would seem to be sensible but can lead to difficulties when employed crudely. For example, a highway maintenance job might involve an element of heavy manual work. Experience and 'common sense' might seem to dictate that men should be recruited rather than women because men are usually stronger. Leaving aside issues of illegal discrimination, this is misleading. It is strength not gender that will determine whether the job can be performed properly; and although on average men are stronger than women, some women are stronger than some men, and so some good applicants would be lost to the organisation if only men were hired.

The 'matching attributes' model

This is a model in which selection is made on the basis of attributes which the applicant must possess in order to do the job properly. It is assumed that these attributes can be assessed in some way prior to employment, and that these can reliably predict job success. This model should avoid the difficulties noted with the common sense and experience model because the selection of individuals should ignore factors that are not relevant to job success, such as age, race, gender, residence or occupation of parents. In the example given above, organisations following this model would find out the level of strength necessary to do the highway maintenance job, devise tests to measure the lifting ability of applicants, and then make the selection on the basis of the intrinsic abilities of individuals, not what group they belonged to. Of course, a corollary of using this approach is that the organisation has to know in some detail what is required to do the job properly – the skills, knowledge, attitudes and so forth – ie it must identify the *criteria for job success*. This approach has been refined and can be highly sophisticated using a battery of psychometric and other tests, and it is sometimes referred to as the 'selection paradigm' (Keenan, 2005), implying an ideal model of selection. However, as we will see shortly, it has not been refined to the point of becoming an exact science (and it is almost certainly impossible to do so) and no selection process, however sophisticated, is infallible.

The 'competency' model

In this model a 'competency framework' is established for the job to be filled. Depending on the type of competency model used, this framework will either be a list of aptitudes or characteristics or other inputs which are required (eg 'leadership') or it will consist of specific behaviours or other outputs that are necessary for job success (eg being able to read a balance sheet). Although the former is not so very different from the selection paradigm noted above, the latter specifies actual performance which must be achieved, and not just the potential to do so.

Competency models are increasingly popular with organisations.

HRM in action

CASE STUDY

Competency work pays off for council

Westminster City Council has introduced a competency framework, attracting interest from 25 other London boroughs and councils. Described as the 'golden thread running through the people management process', the framework is being used to drive the people management agenda, Tony Reynolds, organisational development manager, told *PM*.

The model was launched in January 2005, with 16 different competencies, each split into four levels, which correspond to the organisational structure. All positions at the Council have six to eight critical role competencies. 'These are the behaviours we want to recruit, develop, manage and reward,' Reynolds said.

More than 100 staff across the Council shaped the framework. After its launch, learning and development was restructured and a bank of self-development resources created. Feedback has been positive. A staff survey recently found that 80% of staff were already aware of the framework and 51% found it useful.

The next stage of the programme is talent management. 'We don't do enough,' Reynolds said. 'We want to work with our managers on talent identification and start to invest much more energy in developing and retaining these staff.'

People Management, 29 June 2006

REFLECTIVE ACTIVITY

Consider how people are recruited into your organisation. Which of the models above best describes the process involved?

Would another model give better results? If so, why?

This text is mainly concerned with the last two models of selection because they are the most appropriate ones for professional managers to operate. One of the key points to note is that in any systematic approach to selecting personnel, the selection decision is based on the organisation making a prediction whether or not a particular candidate could achieve job success.

JOB ANALYSIS AND PERSONNEL SPECIFICATION

The first step in the process of managing and developing the human resource flow (Table 3) is a decision about what the job is and what qualities are needed for its effective performance. At one extreme, job analysis may reveal that the requirements of the job are such that most of the employable population are capable of performing it adequately with appropriate initial training, and if so, hardly any effort at selection is warranted. At the other extreme – for example, the selection of astronauts – the job may call for a set of qualities that are rarely found in a single person within the population, and so demand a highly sophisticated (and expensive) selection procedure.

In any event, before hiring, the organisation should have identified the criteria for job success and the characteristics required of the job-holder in order to achieve this success. This is true whether the job is stacking cans on a supermarket shelf, being a member of a multi-skilled autonomous work team or, indeed, that of an astronaut.

The 'personnel specification' for the job – the list of the various attributes which successful candidates should have in order to achieve job success – can be usefully structured to assist the decision-maker(s) at the selection phase. Two frameworks often used in the UK are the Rodger's Seven-Point Plan and the Munro Fraser Fivefold Grading System. A basic outline of both frameworks is shown below.

Alec Rodger's Seven-Point Plan

- physical make-up
- attainments
- general intelligence
- special aptitudes
- interests
- disposition
- circumstances

The Munro Fraser Fivefold Grading System

- impact on others
- qualifications or acquired knowledge
- innate abilities
- motivation
- adjustment or emotional balance

RECRUITMENT AND SELECTION (HIRING)

If we remember that recruitment and selection are parts of a connected system of managing and developing our human resources (Table 3) we can appreciate that decisions taken in these earlier stages will impact on later stages. For instance, if after establishing the requirements for job success we then lower the specified standards in terms of skills, knowledge or attitudes for job success, we will inevitably have either to accept a lower level of performance in the job or take some form of remedial action at a later stage – eg initial training – either of which would incur additional costs to the organisation.

Decision-makers in the recruitment and selection process must try to make rational choices, for which they need information. Decision-makers ideally should limit their information-gathering to procedures in which the usefulness of the additional information justifies the cost of gathering it. However, this is not an exact science and organisations usually have no idea whether the cost of using, say, a particular psychological test, is justified. Common sense should be applied: a poor chief executive might destroy the firm, so nobody doubts the wisdom of gathering as much useful and relevant information as possible, even if this is expensive and time-consuming. But would you really spend as much time, effort and money in choosing a new janitor?

In essence, the information gathered in the selection process is used to predict likely success on the job if the individual is to be employed. All such predictions are liable to error, because no selection process can give wholly accurate predictions of future success.

Two kinds of decision error may occur in every selection process, however constituted:

- 'false positives' or erroneous acceptances, where applicants are selected but prove to be inadequate
- 'false negatives' or erroneous rejections, where applicants who would have performed adequately are rejected.

Employing organisations are more concerned about false positives because they lead to incompetent performance and expensive mistakes. Accordingly, it makes sense for such organisations to raise entry requirements to reduce the probability of false positives – even though this inevitably increases the probability of false negatives. The consequences of this is that a greater number of applicants who are actually capable of doing the job will be erroneously categorised by the selection process as not meeting the required standards and so be rejected.

In other spheres the question of false negatives may be of more significance – for example, in education where (ideally) there is concern that opportunities should be equitably distributed. Where there are no funding constraints a college might deliberately lower entrance requirements for a programme. This would result in increased failure rates overall if academic standards were kept at the same level as before, but would reduce the number of false negatives. It would give a greater number of capable applicants the educational opportunity, at the cost in this case of increased false positives – students who are accepted on the programme but who are discovered not to have the capabilities to succeed in it.

'STRATEGIC SELECTION'

The selection decision has always been important. We noted above that wrong selection decisions always incur costs to the organisation, both from the damage an incompetent employee might do, and of simply having to go through the process of hiring someone else. The more senior the employee, the greater the effects of incompetence: an office worker might lose data and even some customers, but an inept CEO could destroy the firm. The better an organisation's overall selection process, the better it should perform collectively, and this has obviously always been true. However, HRM literature suggests that the selection decision now has even greater importance for organisations:

- Changes in the labour market have brought about a more diverse workforce. This increases the pool of available talent but also raises questions of fairness and equality which must be addressed, not only to ensure legal compliance but to exploit fully the talent available in the market.

- In the light of the increasing need for multi-skilled flexible workforces and teamworking, selection becomes less a matter of matching an individual to the fixed requirements of a clearly defined job – immediate skills and experience may be less important than adaptability, willingness to learn and ability to work in a team. In a word, modern organisations typically need fewer employees, but these must be of a higher calibre than was often the case in the past. There are fewer and fewer unskilled and low-skilled jobs in advanced economies.

- The need to establish a close relationship between corporate competitive strategies and HRM has produced the concept of 'strategic selection' in which the selection system supports the overall current and future business strategies. As we saw in Chapter 1, this underpins the whole idea of HRM as an approach to managing people.

For these reasons organisations are now more likely than hitherto to use relatively costly techniques that previously would have been reserved for senior high-salary positions, such as psychometric testing or assessment centres, for selection for ordinary jobs (see the Asda example below in the next 'HRM in action' case study).

REFLECTIVE ACTIVITY

Think about how you were appointed to your present job. Clearly, the right decision was made! But as a professional manager, how would you rate the effectiveness of the process?

What could you do to make it more efficient in the future?

SOME COMMON SELECTION TECHNIQUES

The most common predictors used in the selection process are interviews, tests, information from application forms or letters, curricula vitae (CVs) or résumés, and references from previous employers (Beaumont, 1993).

The interview

The interview is widely used and heavily relied upon, probably because of low cost, high perceived applicability and just general familiarity. There is, however, a large body of evidence that its reliability and validity are surprisingly *un*impressive (example: Hakel, 1982). The difficulty is that although we can make real – and worthwhile – attempts to improve our effectiveness at interviews (see below), there are limits to what can be achieved. The problem is intrinsic to the technique: people are just not all that good at making decisions in such contexts.

Limitations of the selection interview process

Interviewers pay too much attention to first impressions, and information obtained early in the interview has a disproportionate effect on the final outcome. Interviewers tend to compare candidates to ideal stereotypes and are prone to falling for 'contrast effects' by which a candidate's performance is unconsciously exaggerated by the interviewer in comparison with that of a previous applicant (eg after a very good candidate the next one may look poorer than he/she actually is, or perhaps even better). Interviewers are also liable to be influenced by 'halo effects' by which one characteristic of the candidate overshadows others – eg what school or university they attended. This effect can be positive or negative.

Interviewers also make decisions very early. One classic study in Canada found that in a series of 30-minute interviews the interviewers made their decisions on the suitability of a candidate in an average of four minutes! This begs the question: what were they doing for the other 26 minutes? And the answer is almost certainly that they were seeking information to rationalise or support the decision they had already privately made.

Organisations will never abandon interviewing as a selection tool. No sensible organisation hires anyone without first seeing them in person, but many seek to improve its usefulness by using it in a more systematic way, and also by supplementing it with the use of tests or other techniques designed to obtain more relevant information about the candidate.

Some hints for interviewers

It is possible to improve the effectiveness of one's interview technique. Prior to conducting it, develop a 'game plan' for the interview to cover building rapport with the candidate, obtaining information, *providing* information (salary and other rewards, of course, but also main terms and conditions of employment; superannuation, sick pay, etc) and answering questions. This should be based on current job information. A plan is particularly important for panel interviews in which a team of people jointly conduct the interview.

- Outline the game plan to the applicant at the start of the interview.

- Try to put the applicant at ease.

- Follow a common format for all applicants.

- In general, avoid leading and closed questions.

- Provide a realistic and specific description of the job and organisation.

- The applicant should do most of the talking (aim for, say, 75%).

- Develop active listening skills.

- Develop skills to observe non-verbal communication.

- Make notes during the interview and complete your record of it immediately after it.

- Be fully informed of all relevant legal, policy and ethical issues.

- Get feedback on the subsequent job performance of successful applicants so that you have some basis for assessing the usefulness of your interviewing in predicting job success.

The information obtained from selection interviews may often be supplemented by information obtained by other means, which may include psychological tests.

Psychological testing

Psychological testing involves a varied set of instruments which are usually categorised as intelligence tests, ability and aptitude tests, and personality tests. The latter are the most controversial but are generally viewed as being popular, especially in the case of recruitment for 'greenfield sites' (ie completely new enterprises).

It has been estimated that there are over 5,000 psychological instruments available in the English language (Toplis *et al*, 1987). Pearn *et al* (1987) commented that the question of the usefulness of personality assessment was probably the most controversial subject in occupational psychology. A review of the available evidence in the USA (Schmitt *et al*, 1984) suggested that ability and aptitude tests have only a modest degree of predictive accuracy so far as job performance is concerned, personality tests being even less successful (although ability and aptitude tests could give better results than unstructured interviews).

In response to concern about the abuse of psychological tests, the Chartered Institute of Personnel and Development has issued guidance on the subject (CIPD, 2006c). This recommends the use of Chartered Psychologists to administer and interpret tests, invokes the observance of strict confidentiality, and stipulates the necessity to provide feedback for applicants.

Remember: a poor test, or a good test poorly administered, is much worse than no test at all!

Management assessment centres

An assessment centre is a procedure (not a location!) that uses multiple assessment techniques to evaluate employees for a variety of manpower purposes and decisions (Thornton and Byham, 1982). The assessment centre approach may use techniques such as tests, questionnaires and the use of background information. Information is gathered in a standardised and controllable manner on behaviour that is representative for future job behaviour. The assessment centre method is used with particular success as a method for potential evaluation and management development.

Assessment centres typically feature:

- the use of multiple assessment techniques
- the use of simulations and work sampling
- observation by multiple observers
- assessment by trained assessors
- the separation of observation and evaluation.

SO HOW EFFECTIVE IS SELECTION?

Muchinsky (1986) summarised the effectiveness of selection techniques as follows:

- No single method was simultaneously high on validity, fairness and applicability and low on cost: so a series of trade-offs was necessary.
- The single method that came closest to the ideal was biographical information ('biodata'), but while high on validity and applicability and low on cost, it was only moderate on fairness.
- Techniques that scored highest on validity were assessment centres, work samples and biographical information.
- Interviewing was low on validity, moderate on fairness, high on applicability and low on cost.
- Personality tests were moderate on validity, high on fairness, low on applicability and moderate on cost.

- Assessment centres were high on validity, high on fairness, low on applicability (beyond management grades) and high on cost.

RECRUITMENT AND SELECTION IN PRACTICE

The CIPD 2006 Recruitment, Retention and Turnover Survey of some 800 UK organisations (CIPD, 2006b) found that:

- The average recruitment cost of filling a vacancy per employee was £3,600, rising to £8,200 when the associated labour turnover costs were also taken into account.
- Local newspapers were the most common method used to attract candidates (79% of organisations surveyed), although three quarters of respondents also claimed to use their own corporate website to advertise vacancies.
- Employee referral schemes appeared to be gaining in popularity as a tool to find suitable applicants (47%).
- Interviews based on the contents of the CV/résumé or application form were the most frequently used selection method (66%).

Recruiting online

The CIPD 2006 Recruitment, Retention and Turnover Survey (CIPD, 2006b) found that:

- The trend for e-recruitment is growing – almost two thirds (64%) of the organisations surveyed used technology to aid their recruitment process during 2005.
- The greatest usage was email and online applications, advertising job vacancies and placing background information on corporate websites.
- Reducing recruitment costs was the main business objective for developing e-recruitment (71% of organisations).
- Nearly half of respondents (47%) strongly agreed that e-recruitment would replace paper-based applications in the future, *but* –
- The same number believed the trend towards e-recruitment was increasing the number of unsuitable applications.

As noted in Chapter 1, the findings of the 2004 Workplace Employee Relations Survey in the UK reinforced the view that many organisations operated a 'flexible organisation' with a 'core' of key employees and a 'peripheral' workforce of other workers. Most (83%) of workplaces had part-time employees, and in 30% of all workplaces more than half of the workforce were part-time employees. Just under one third (30%) of workplaces had employees on temporary contracts. The use of temporary agency staff was quite widespread, 17% of all workplaces employing 'temps'. About one fifth (22%) of workplaces gave preference to internal applicants when recruitiung, and the proportion was higher for the private sector (25%).

The selection process usually involved the use of interviews, application forms and references. Personality or competency tests, although used less often, had gained in importance in the search for greater objectivity in selection, despite continuing debate about their validity and reliability. Among workplaces using personality tests, three fifths (61%) of managers said that they used these tests when recruiting core employees. Performance or competency tests were routinely used in 46% of workplaces and were also more likely to be used when recruiting core employees, irrespective of their occupation. Overall, one third (34%) of all workplaces used such tests for these recruits.

TALENT MANAGEMENT

The consultancy firm McKinsey is credited with coining the expression 'war for talent', by which it meant the increasingly competitive market for key employees in the knowledge economy. 'Talent management' combines the traditional responsibilities of recruitment and selection with development activities which include 'succession planning'. In one sense it is the twenty-first-century version of an old description of the function of personnel management: 'getting the right person in the right job at the right time', but now the 'right person' is likely to possess key skills and knowledge, hold considerable market value and require (and demand) continuous development. Talent management is another of the HRM activities which applies to the core but probably not the periphery.

Definitions vary but within the UK HR profession the emphasis is certainly on the management development and succession planning areas, as revealed by the CIPD 2006 Learning and Development Survey (CIPD, 2006d), which found the following. Respondents were asked to identify the main objectives of 'talent management'. Responses are shown in Table 4.

We can see that talent management straddles both recruitment and selection, and learning and development, but is predominantly 'future-focused'.

Table 4 The objectives of talent management

Main objectives of talent management	Percentage of respondents
Developing high-potential individuals	67%
Growing future senior managers	62%
Enabling the achievement of strategic goals	42%
Meeting future skills requirements	38%
Attracting and recruiting key staff	36%
Retaining key staff	33%
Supporting changes	17%
Addressing skills shortages	16%
Assisting organisational resource planning	13%
Redeployment of staff to other roles	12%
Other	2%

Source: the CIPD 2006 Learning and Development Survey

CASE STUDY

HRM in action

Online tests boost jobs at Asda

Online personality testing at Asda has led to the supermarket chain running fewer assessment centres and making more job offers.

Judith Colbert, resourcing manager at Asda, said: 'The new process has ensured that we see the top 20% of candidates at interview stage, rather than 50%, as before.' She added: 'It's more consistent and we're getting a much better fit and are filling vacancies quicker.'

The online assessment – which was introduced for graduates last October and managers in January – is designed to match candidates' personalities with Asda's brand values. It involves a personality questionnaire, ability test and further questions about their CV and previous experience. Alan Redman, business psychologist at Criterion Partnership,

which worked with Asda on the online assessment, said: 'All of Asda's processes are about hiring people for attitude. Candidates who don't share their values won't enjoy working there.'

The online tests have also cut costs, he said: 'Generally, the most expensive part of recruitment is hiring assessment centres. By raising the calibre of people you are interviewing, you no longer see people who are clearly unsuitable.'

Redman added that the tool had helped to reduce HR's workload by weeding out the bottom 80% of candidates. Last year Asda had 15,000 applications for 750 manager roles and 8,500 applications for 60 graduate scheme places.

People Management, 13 July 2006

REFLECTIVE ACTIVITY

What do you think of Asda's process of selecting people via an online personality profile, as reported in *People Management*?

Would it work for your organisation?

Why/why not?

HRM in action

E-recruitment at Cancer Research

Cancer Research UK is the world's leading independent organisation dedicated to cancer research. It employs 3,500 staff and, due to its size and reputation, receives in excess of 16,000 applications and fills around 1,000 vacancies per year. To handle such high-volume recruitment activity, it therefore made sense for the organisation to introduce e-recruitment.

Cancer Research's move to e-recruitment was driven by many factors. Operating in an increasingly competitive market meant there was a need to reach applicants more easily and to develop a talent pool. By registering people's details, the organisation is able to keep in touch with potential candidates, and the 'job alert' system notifies individuals of relevant jobs when suitable positions crop up. Since September 2005, over 1,000 applicants have signed up for the automatic email 'job alert' system.

Rob Farace, Head of Resourcing at Cancer Research UK, explains that 'As well as overcoming recruitment difficulties and speeding up the recruitment process, there have been significant cost savings.' The e-recruitment solution has created more time for the resourcing team to focus on work that really adds value to the organisation. It has also enabled them to reduce the headcount of their resourcing team by one person.

To ensure proper implementation, the e-recruitment system was phased in gradually. In March 2005 internal jobs moved online. This was followed by external vacancies and graduate positions in September 2005. With recruitment devolved far down the line, it was essential to engage managers in the new recruitment system. Fortunately, feedback from them has been very positive. All data is real-time and can be found on the website, giving managers immediate access to candidate information. And gone are the days of waiting for applications to arrive through the post, which often created delays in appointing new members of staff. At the same time, when people apply from overseas, their applications are received instantly. However, the organisation is still accepting mail, telephone and email applications. Although most people now apply online, it believes it would be foolish to unfairly discriminate and risk losing potentially good candidates.

To date, there are no plans to use online testing to screen out unsuitable applicants. The reasons for this are that the charity is keen to retain a personal service, and prefers unsuccessful candidates to be clear about why they have been rejected. Naturally, as a fundraiser it would also like to encourage continuing support of its research. One of the biggest challenges of implementing the e-recruitment solution was the issue of branding. Reaching an agreement on the 'look and feel' of the new system proved challenging with so many stakeholders involved. While it was crucial for Cancer Research UK to uphold its reputation as a leading charity, it was equally important, as a recruiter, to promote the employer brand effectively.

In the future, the organisation is planning to link e-recruitment to the main HR personnel system as part of a move towards greater integration of resourcing activities with other areas of HR.

CIPD Recruitment and Retention and Turnover Report 2006. Information provided by Rob Farace, Head of Resourcing, Cancer Research

EMPLOYEE EXIT

GENERAL CONSIDERATIONS

The employee relationship may end voluntarily when the employee chooses to leave the organisation to take up a position elsewhere, or it may finish at the end of a person's career by retirement at an agreed age, or the person may have to leave involuntarily through ill-health, dismissal or redundancy. Some authorities argue (Armstrong, 2003) that employee exits are increasingly likely to be involuntary as competitive pressures from technological advances and globalisation continually force firms to reduce costs even when profitable.

All HR issues regarding employee exit must be dealt with in the framework of relevant current employment legislation. We do not deal in detail with employment law in this text but up-to-date guidance for both employees and employers in the UK may be found at the Government website http://www.tiger. gov.uk/ (TIGER stands for 'tailored interactive guidance on employment rights'). The Advisory, Conciliation and Arbitration Service (ACAS) website http://www. acas.org.uk is also helpful, especially on employee relations issues.

THE ROLE OF THE HR FUNCTION IN ORGANISATIONAL RELEASE

The HR function is normally given the task of managing organisational release. When this is dealing with involuntary release it can be a hard and stressful duty. There are ethical and professional considerations. Managers have no choice, of course, about taking part in organisational redundancy or 'downsizing' programmes, but they can make an important contribution to managing the process in such a way as to minimise both the individual distress and trauma that redundancy can cause and the organisational damage that can result from ill-considered or badly implemented dismissals. Professionally, HR managers are obliged to ensure that dismissal and redundancy policies and practices are in line with legal requirements, codes of practice and relevant company policies. They can also argue for policies and actions that minimise unnecessary redundancies, and can emphasise the need to handle dismissals and redundancies sensitively. They can advise line managers on the approach to adopt, provide training, help them communicate decisions to employees and other stakeholders, and provide counselling and outplacement services to the staff who will be affected.

DISMISSAL

Some degree of legal protection is afforded to employees in most developed economies, but the nature and degree obviously differ from country to country. One of the prime HRM functions is to ensure that the organisation is legally compliant in dealing with employee issues – and in none more so than dismissal.

Any society which allows legal protection to employees will also provide a means of redress through the courts, or quasi-legal institutions such as the UK's employment tribunals, to the employee who has been 'unfairly' or illegally dismissed. In investigating any allegation of unfair dismissal such bodies will typically seek answers to two fundamental questions: 'Was there sufficient cause for dismissal?' and 'Did the employer act reasonably in the circumstances?'

Dismissals are usually held to be fair when the employee acted in a way that constituted misconduct. Actions such as theft or fighting at work, or being drunk, are termed 'gross misconduct' and might justify summary (ie immediate) dismissal without any further warning. In most other cases, however, employers will have to show that they followed some reasonable procedure which informed the employee of his or her unacceptable misbehaviour and gave them some opportunity to respond positively. Poor work performance on one occasion is very unlikely ever to be regarded as reasonable grounds for dismissal, for instance. Other reasons might include the employee being unable to fulfil his or her contract of employment by reason of incapacity – and this can cover the employee's skill, aptitude and health (either physical or mental). This most often occurs when some change in a person's health renders incapable a previously capable employee. Effective recruitment and selection procedures should screen out all applicants who lack the capability to do the job in the first place.

REDUNDANCY

'Redundancy' is the term used when employees are dismissed not because of any issue with their performance or capability but because their jobs are no longer required by the organisation. As with the general case of dismissal most societies have legal requirements that organisations must comply with in terms of, for example, giving employees adequate notice, negotiating with trade unions, and paying compensation to employees who are made redundant.

There are other managerial considerations to note. One of the most damaging aspects of redundancy to an organisation is the effect on those who are *not* made redundant. The 'survivors' may feel very vulnerable to future job cuts and the most employable may well seek other work before that happens – so you can quickly lose a lot of your best people – just the ones you want to hold on to.

Managing the redundancy process

As noted above, 'downsizing' is one of the most demanding areas of people management. Managers should first ensure that legal requirements have been met – for example, requiring consultation with the employees concerned and/or their representatives. The information made available at any consultative meeting should cover the reasons for the redundancy, the steps the organisation has taken to reduce the number of redundancies to a minimum, and the arrangements that will be made for redundancy payments. There will probably be media interest in large-scale and/or sensitive redundancies and management should be prepared to deal with this.

Managers must also ensure that the redundancy selection procedure has been applied fairly and is legally compliant – eg is not discriminatory. Selection for redundancy on the basis of length of service – sometimes called 'last in, first out' or LIFO – is the easiest and most obviously objective method of selection for redundancy. Those with the shortest length of service in the organisation will be selected first. Until recently this was the most commonly used criterion for redundancy but its popularity is now declining as more employers become concerned that selection on length of service alone can have a detrimental effect on the firm's skill base. It is reasonable for employers to try to retain a workforce balance in terms of ability, so an individual's skill and knowledge are reasonable considerations, provided that they are assessed objectively and clearly defined from the outset of the selection process. The precise choice of factors and their relative weighting should be determined according to the current and future needs of the business.

All individuals affected by the redundancy process should be personally informed by interview, and managers should be appropriately trained and supported by HR specialists in handling this.

HRM in action

Redundancy

The lack of new orders for railway rolling stock caused ABB Rail Vehicles to announce the closure of their York plant in 1995. The company did not wish to use the LIFO principle because it was worried about its skills base.

Selection for redundancy was based on the following factors:

- service
- relevant qualifications
- attendance
- skills
- flexibility
- quantity of work
- quality of work

Assessment was based on an agreed points system with an appeals procedure.

KEY ISSUES IN HUMAN RESOURCE FLOW

In this chapter we have been concerned with 'employee flow' through the organisation; in particular, with how the organisation obtains the human resources it needs and how it manages the exit of employees. We first discussed some basic underlying principles involved in recruitment and selection, and two important findings soon emerged. First, that recruitment and selection should be seen as stages in a wider process of managing the human resource flow. This is because decisions made at the recruitment or selection stages will inevitably impact on later activities such as need for training and level of job performance. Second, that organisations should recruit using a model based on initially identifying the criteria for job success and then systematically seeking applicants with the necessary qualities to achieve that success. We noted that in the twenty-first century capability and attitude were often more important than the possession of particular knowledge or skills at the time of recruitment. A competency framework is often useful in recruitment and selection. Some of the most commonly used selection techniques were examined. We introduced the concept of talent management which in a sense bridges recruitment and selection and employee development.

All employees will eventually leave the organisation, and this process also has to be managed. After some general considerations of the question of dismissal we examined some of the issues surrounding redundancy and how that can be managed.

CHAPTER 5

Developing people

INTRODUCTION

In the HRM paradigm there is much greater emphasis on development than in the personnel management paradigm, and this is expanded to cover all core employees. The term 'employee development' (ED) or 'human resource development' (HRD) is often preferred to the earlier terms of 'training' and 'management development', and they cover both sorts of activity. Learning and development interventions span external education as well as both formal and informal in-house activities. There has been a cultural change in that the intention in ED/HRD is often to enable or facilitate learning and personal development rather than to impose training on individuals. There is also greater emphasis on informal learning at all levels, including self-development which might formerly in many cases have been occurring but was virtually never recognised. There are limits to this, of course, and it would be wrong to suppose that conventional structured training has no place in the twenty-first-century workplace.

LEARNING OUTCOMES

On completion of this chapter you should:

- understand the definitions of 'training' and 'learning'
- know how to undertake a training needs analysis, and its purpose
- appreciate the necessity to identify learning objectives
- understand the importance of the principles of learning
- have an appreciation of the main learning and development methods used in organisations
- understand the Kirkpatrick model of training evaluation
- understand the concepts of single- and double-loop learning
- know what is meant by the term 'learning organisation'.

Conventionally, in the personnel management paradigm (Chapter 1), learning at work was generally divided into more-or-less mutually exclusive domains for (i) managers (including other professionals) who might receive 'development', and (ii) non-managers, who were 'trained' (see Table 5). Traditionally in the UK firms did minimal training and development anyway, fearing that the money spent would be wasted because the employees would undoubtedly be 'poached' by competitors. Although there were some striking exceptions, until the late 1980s most UK firms did little or no management development at all, and – as noted above – the self-development that was in many cases occurring was virtually never recognised (see Table 5).

Table 5 The nature and scope of learning interventions under personnel management (PM) and human resource management (HRM)

People management paradigm	Class of employee	Nature of learning intervention/activity			
		Formal, external	*Formal, in-house*	*Informal, in-house*	*Self-development*
Personnel management	Non-managerial employees	Educational courses, usually vocational	Off-the-job training	On-the-job training	(ignored)
	Managers and other professionals	Development			(ignored)
Human resource management	All (core) employees	Learning and development			

Table 6 Types and natures of learning interventions and activities

Nature	Type	
	Formal	*Informal*
Off-the-job	Externally provided accredited education – eg MBAs, NVQs, professional qualifications	Voluntary accredited education
	Externally provided training courses	Voluntarily attended training courses

On-the-job		Learning partnerships
		   Coaching
		   Mentoring
		   Peer relationships
		Action Learning
		Self-development
		   Self-development groups
		   Learning logs

DEFINITIONS

Training is defined as a set of planned activities on the part of an organisation to increase job knowledge and skills, or to modify attitudes and social behaviour, to achieve specific ends which are related to a particular job or role.

Learning is a relatively permanent change in knowledge, skills, attitudes or behaviour that comes through experience. We may say that learning happens inside the person whereas training is something that is given to a person in the sense that it is a planned experience that is expected to lead to learning.

Development describes the continuing improvement of an individual's effectiveness in terms of their role or profession beyond the immediate task or job.

Education means the process of personal growth in abilities and attitudes which might take place independently of its application to work, and is therefore a broader experience than training or work-related learning and development (Morris, 1978).

The phrase *learning intervention* is now often used in the HRM literature to cover both training and work-related learning, reflecting the increased emphasis on active learning in the workplace.

Definitions of *management development* are given in the section on that subject later in this chapter.

A BRIEF OVERVIEW OF LEARNING PRINCIPLES

Detailed discussion of learning theory is outside the scope of the present text. The interested reader is referred to the relevant chapters of Landy and Conte (2007) for further reading.

On the basis of the research that has been conducted on the various theories of learning, certain rules or guidelines have emerged regarding efficient learning. These include:

- the principle of 'distributed practice' – ie breaking the learning experience up into manageable chunks for the learner
- praising the learner for correct responses, so reinforcing the learning
- training individuals to perform entire task units as a whole
- giving results of the training performance to the learners
- providing opportunities for practising the skills developed during training.

LEVELS OF LEARNING

There seem to be two levels of learning that occur in the modern organisation.

The first relates to obtaining knowledge in order to solve specific problems based on existing premises. The second is concerned with establishing new paradigms, mental models or perspectives. These two levels of learning have been termed 'single-loop' and 'double-loop' learning respectively (Argyris and Schön, 1978; after Ashby, 1940). The metaphor is drawn from the field of cybernetics. Single-loop learning is compared to the action of a thermostat which is used to control temperature (eg of a refrigerator), where the thermostat scans and monitors the environment (the temperature inside the refrigerator), compares the information it obtains with operating norms (the range of acceptable temperatures inside the refrigerator), and initiates any appropriate action (if the temperature is too high, the thermostat switches on the refrigeration unit to reduce the internal temperature until it is within the acceptable range). The thermostat then proceeds to scan the environment again, setting up a continuous loop of activity. In double-loop learning a 'single loop' operates as before, but here the 'operating norms' themselves are questioned and if necessary altered, thus creating a 'double loop'.

For example, firms should be constantly seeking to improve their product offerings, whether these are physical goods or intangible services (see Chapter 4 on job design). Quality circles and autonomous work teams encourage workers to seek improvements continually in production and design as they deal with the everyday problems of production and delivery. This should encourage continuous learning and result in steady, incremental improvements which we can think of as the outcomes of single-loop learning – basically, learning how to do the same things better and better. Every so often, however, a worker, or a team of workers collectively, might have a sudden flash of insight which leads not to an incremental refinement but to a radical rethinking of a process or feature of the product. This discontinuous change would be an example of 'double-loop' learning.

Radical innovation relies on double-loop learning, and in the 'knowledge economy' one of the key goals of the HRD function is to help a build a culture in which double-loop learning can flourish.

KOLB'S LEARNING CYCLE

Kolb and his colleagues (1971) identified a four-stage learning cycle which has been hugely influential in people development in HRM, especially in management development. The four stages are:

1 Concrete experience

2 Observations and reflection

3 Formation of abstract concepts and generalisations

4 Testing the implications of the concepts in new situations.

The learning experience runs in sequence from 1 through to 4.

1 The individual takes note of some concrete experience. This could be part of a planned learning intervention such as a skills demonstration, or it might be accidental – he or she may suddenly realise that something has occurred.

2 The individual thinks about, or reflects upon, the experience and its significance.

3 The individual constructs some mental model to explain what happened and why. This will allow the individual to generalise about where and how the experience may recur.

4 The explanation is tested out in some new situation.

LEARNING STYLES

The effectiveness of learning will vary from stage to stage of Kolb's cycle among different people. Some will learn most effectively at the first stage; others at the second, third or fourth. This has led to the concept of *learning styles*. Honey and Mumford (1989) identified a set of four learning styles, each of which suggested a preference for a particular stage of the Kolb cycle. The cycle should always be completed by the learner but the learning style will dictate which part of the cycle is most important for a particular person. These learning styles are:

- 'Activists' tend to learn best from the experience stage: they prefer to take action – eg hands-on learning or role-playing.

- 'Reflectors' tend to learn most from the second stage, observation and reflection.

- For 'Theorists' learning is most effective at the third, abstract conceptualisation stage.

- 'Pragmatists' learn best from trying out the new skill or knowledge in actual work situations, so they benefit most from the fourth stage of the Kolb cycle.

The theory of learning styles implies that, ideally, a trainer might design each learning intervention according to the learning style of the individual learner. Clearly, there are limits to this in practice, but learners can be encouraged to identify their learning style and thus increase awareness of the strengths and weaknesses in their own learning processes. Activists, for example, can be alerted to the fact that they may tend to skip abstract conceptualisation and might neglect full testing of their new skills or knowledge in the workplace. Theorists can be reminded to get 'hands on' in the learning intervention, and so on. Honey and

Mumford have produced a questionnaire which helps learners to identify their own particular learning style.

The theory of learning styles is not unproblematic: Coffield *et al* (2004) identified 71 different models of learning styles, 13 of which were judged to be influential. So caution is indicated, but the Honey and Mumford set of learning styles, as linked to the Kolb learning cycle, is certainly widely used and frequently cited in the HRD literature.

TRANSFER OF LEARNING

From the organisation's perspective, by far the most important issue is that of transfer of learning – ie whether the knowledge, skills, attitudes or behaviours learned will be available and used 'back on the job'. This is a critical issue in the evaluation of the effectiveness and utility of a learning programme, and for formal learning interventions such as conventional skills training where the intention is to impart specific knowledge or skills, or to develop certain attitudes, there can be little value from the organisation's point of view in learning which does not carry over to the job situation.

Some general rules have been established to increase the probability of transfer of learning:

- Maximise the similarity between the learning situation and the job situation.
- Provide as much experience as possible with the task being taught.
- Provide for a variety of examples when teaching concepts or skills.
- Label or identify important features of a task.
- Make sure the general principles are understood.
- Make sure that the learned behaviours and ideas are rewarded in the job situation.
- Design the learning content so that the learners can see its applicability.

EXPLICIT AND TACIT KNOWLEDGE

In almost all occupations, there are skills that will be picked up in the course of performing the job which cannot be acquired through training, only through experience. When training new staff it is important to distinguish what can be trained – such as the use of equipment and a fixed knowledge base – from what cannot. For example, medical students can be trained in how to take a patient's blood pressure correctly and effectively, but a good 'bedside manner' can only come with experience and observing skilled doctors dealing with their patients. To use the current jargon, we can train people by imparting 'explicit knowledge' but we cannot easily train people in 'tacit knowledge'. We discuss this later in this chapter in a section on knowledge management.

SOME COMMON LEARNING AND DEVELOPMENT METHODS

Action Learning was originally introduced for management development but is now widely used at all organisational levels. Groups of people work together to find practical solutions to real work problems. Instructors act as facilitators, encouraging participants to learn from each other and reflect on the experience.

Blended learning is a combination of multiple approaches to learning. Typically, a combination of technology-based materials and face-to-face sessions are used together to deliver instruction.

Case studies are detailed examinations of real-life situations written up and presented for educational purposes. Students typically work in groups to analyse each case and then to answer set tasks. They are very commonly used in management development.

Coaching is a non-directive form of development which focuses on improving performance and developing individuals' skills and giving feedback on a person's performance. Coaching should be delivered by trained personnel, who usually are drawn from outside the organisation.

Continuing professional development (CPD) is a continuous process of personal growth by which individuals improve their capability at work and realise their full potential. It is achieved by developing a range of knowledge, skills and experience which go beyond initial training or qualification, and which maintain and develop professional competence. Many professional bodies such as the CIPD now insist on CPD as a condition of continued membership.

'Corporate universities' have been established by some large companies for the delivery of management education. They are more than just in-company training departments and have been defined (Meister, 1998; p.38) as a

> centralized strategic umbrella for the education and development of employees [that] is the chief vehicle for disseminating an organisation's culture and fostering the development of not only job skills but also such core workplace skills as learning-to-learn, leadership, creative thinking and problem-solving.

E-learning is learning that is delivered, enabled or mediated using electronic technology for the explicit purpose of learning and development in organisations.

Instruction may be defined as the use of a highly structured teaching method to teach specific skills. Usually its format corresponds to a physical demonstration followed by supervised practice of the skills concerned.

Joint development activities are collaborations between employing organisations and academic institutions. They can include project work by which managers deal with work problems while receiving consultation/tutoring from the institution; consortia of companies running programmes with schools (eg 'company MBAs'); and reciprocal secondments between institutes and industry.

Lecturing is giving a structured talk, usually longer and more formal than a presentation, normally accompanied by visual aids and handouts of key points. A lecture may be combined with audience participation in a discussion, a question-and-answer session and/or group exercises/activities.

Mentoring is similar to coaching but the mentor is usually an experienced senior member of staff, though not the person's line manager. The emphasis in mentoring is less focused on the person's current job or role than in coaching, but more on his or her future development and career within the organisation.

Outdoor training comprises team exercises involving physical and mental tasks in challenging external environments. They are very popular in corporate team-building, believed by advocates to teach leadership and team- and self-development skills in addition to teamworking.

Role-playing is the enactment of roles in a structured context. This method is very useful for practising interpersonal skills.

Self-development is concerned with helping people to understand their own personal learning and development processes, and by doing so to assume greater control of, and responsibility for, their own development. There is an emphasis on longer-term development, as distinct from specific study or learning, and a stress on setting one's own goals and methods of achieving them. This technique can be applied to groups in which participants are encouraged to support each other. Self-development is frequently, but not exclusively, applied to managers and professionals.

Simulations/business games are group exercises or case studies, usually now computerised, in which the participants are asked to make certain choices and the computerised system gives them the 'result' of their decisions.

An example of a 'corporate university': the Boeing Company

The Boeing Company provides education for its employees through its Leadership Centre, and executive learning features highly in its curriculum. Newly promoted supervisory personnel must complete a computerised curriculum within 30 days. This training includes topics on company polices and procedures, finding and using resources, and understanding legal responsibilities. Entry-level managers spend one week at a local training site studying performance management, reviewing organisational structure and learning about regulatory issues for their industry. Managers are also required to take core leadership courses at the Centre at five specific turning points in their careers: when they receive their first management assignments; when they become managers of managers; to prepare them for executive responsibilities; when starting an executive role; and when they assume global leadership responsibilities.

Boeing's primary means of evaluating the success of its Leadership Centre is by conducting employee surveys on an annual basis.

Source: Vitiello (2001; p.42)

REFLECTIVE ACTIVITY

Outline a leadership programme for managers in a corporate university for a large organisation in your industry or economic sector.

THE PROCESS OF FORMAL LEARNING INTERVENTIONS

By 'formal' we mean a learning intervention that is wholly or mainly planned and structured. Of course, such an intervention may include areas in which informal learning is to be encouraged – eg managers may be encouraged to keep learning logs and CPD plans within a structured management development programme – but the overall intervention will be organised from the start with clearly identified learning objectives in terms of the knowledge, skills, attitudes or behaviours to be attained as a result of the intervention.

To assess the impact of a learning intervention we usually need to know something about the status of the learners' relevant knowledge, skills or attitudes (KSAs) before development takes place, so we should obtain baseline pre-intervention information. Similarly, after the intervention has taken place we need some post-intervention information. Finally, since the purpose of the intervention is to improve job performance, we should also seek information about how the learning and development has transferred to on-the-job-behaviour.

There is thus a four-stage process for any formal learning intervention:

1 Identifying the development need

2 Designing the development activity

3 Undertaking the development activity

4 Evaluating the development intervention.

This process is sometimes termed the training cycle.

The stages in the process are described in more detail below.

NEEDS ANALYSIS

We need to know the requirements of a job or role before we can know what constitutes good performance in doing it. In learning and development a particular form of job analysis is used which by convention was once termed *training needs analysis*. In the light of the changes in people development already referred to in this chapter, in this text we will use the terms 'needs analysis' (NA) or 'learning needs analysis' (LNA) to describe this activity.

The needs analysis provides a set of learning objectives for the development programme. These objectives might include adding knowledge, developing specific skills or helping to form specific attitudes – eg towards customers or clients. The objectives have a double role. Firstly, they guide us towards what learning principles and training methods should be used. Secondly, they provide a means for assessing whether the learning intervention has been successful.

The impetus for training is usually an identification of a need for improvement.

A job, task or occupational needs analysis is an examination of the actual duties and responsibilities that compose the job/task/occupation concerned. The question asked is 'What KSAs are required for successful performance of the duties?' In practice, a needs analysis consists of a combination of activities. Often there is a job description based on some earlier and perhaps less systematic job analysis. After reading this and any other relevant documentation relating to the job, the analyst will discuss the job with a supervisor or manager responsible for the staff concerned. This will allow the analyst to identify critical terminology, qualify important job dimensions, develop questions for interview and identify things to look for when observing the job. The analyst will typically observe several employees undertaking the task or job. Finally, the analyst may arrange interviews with other job-holders and/or distribute questionnaires for them to complete.

WHO NEEDS THE LEARNING INTERVENTION? PERSON ANALYSIS

There are usually two possible groups:

- present job-holders who are performing below standard

- new appointees who are about to take up the job or role.

For the first group the most obvious method for identifying weaknesses in job performance is via job appraisal or performance management.

REFLECTIVE ACTIVITY

Consider this: training current staff and training new staff are likely to be very different processes. Why is that?

ACTIVITY ANSWER GUIDANCE

Training new starts usually provides opportunities for new learning, but training experienced workers often involves eliminating old habits. So in addition to learning, the experienced incumbent often has to unlearn old methods or attitudes. When the Japanese car manufacturer Nissan built a car plant in the UK in the late 1980s, their recruitment policy was aimed at hiring people who had never worked in a British car factory.

THE IMPORTANCE OF LEARNING OBJECTIVES

On the basis of the needs analysis it should be possible to specify some objectives or goals for the training programme: what levels of KSAs would you like the trainees to have after the training intervention that they did not have before? Learning objectives for job incumbents are usually tailored to identified specific deficiencies in the employees' performance and they are often negotiated with the individual employee as a result of a performance appraisal. Learning objectives have several important uses. They represent information for both the learner and the facilitator about what is to be learned; they help to motivate the learner; and they allow evaluation of whether the learning intervention has been completed satisfactorily.

EVALUATING THE LEARNING INTERVENTION

The best-known model for evaluating a learning intervention is that developed by Kirkpatrick (1967). This operates at four levels: trainee reactions, learning reactions, behavioural change, and results.

Trainee reactions correspond to participants' evaluations of the usefulness of the learning intervention. It will be familiar to many readers from the ubiquitous 'happy sheet' or questionnaire doled out after company training events. The questionnaire typically asks the participant to rate their overall impression of the event, their perceptions of the trainer, and the extent to which the course and the trainee's own objectives have been met. Such an exercise clearly tells us nothing about how much has been learned, or whether what has been learned will be translated into better job performance, but it is not without some usefulness and is inexpensive and easy to obtain.

Learning reactions represents a level of evaluation that seeks to assess how much knowledge has been imparted to the trainee as a result of the intervention. This might be assessed by a written test, and again this can be inexpensive and relatively quick and easy to obtain.

Behavioural change is the third level of evaluation in Kirkpatrick's model. Specifically, the question is whether the training or learning intervention has resulted in observable changes in the trainee's behaviour in on the job. Such assessment cannot be quick, cheap or easy, although an effective performance management system should obtain the information required. Of course, changed behaviour will not always equate with improved job performance.

Results is the final level of evaluation. Has there been a measurable improvement in the trainee's job performance? This is the ultimate measure of the effectiveness of the learning intervention but it is often difficult to obtain, especially when the intervention has been in complex areas such as managerial or professional effectiveness. Even in more straightforward cases such as physical skills training it is often difficult to isolate the effects of the intervention from those of other extraneous factors.

INFORMAL LEARNING

So far we have discussed formal, structured learning interventions where the objective is to facilitate the acquisition of specific knowledge or skills, or the particular modification of attitudes or behaviour. Informal or experiential learning is quite different in nature, being unplanned and indeed unplannable in detail. It is the learning that the individual himself or herself acquires from the experiences of doing the job, from working in the organisation and from just thinking and reflecting on the work done. Informal learning may sound somewhat airy-fairy, but a US Bureau of Labor report published in 1996 found that people learned 70% of what they know about their jobs informally through processes which were not structured or sponsored by their employing organisation (reported in Armstrong, 2003; p.558).

To be effective, informal learning requires a level of employee motivation, confidence and capability. Employers who wish to encourage informal learning strive to create a climate which is supportive and to impart basic learning skills ('learning how to learn') to their people.

ORGANISATIONAL LEARNING AND KNOWLEDGE MANAGEMENT

The manufacturing-based industrial society of the postwar period has been evolving towards a more service-based society and, more recently, an 'information society'. The leading management thinkers of the late 1990s agreed that the manufacturing, service and information sectors would be based on knowledge in the future and that business organisations will evolve into knowledge-creators in many ways. Peter Drucker was one of the earliest writers to foresee this transformation, and he is credited with inventing the terms 'knowledge-work' and 'knowledge-worker' in the early 1960s. We are entering the 'knowledge society' in which the basic economic resource is no longer capital, or natural resources, or labour, but is knowledge, and in which knowledge-workers will play a central role (Drucker, 1993). The organisation has to be prepared to abandon knowledge that has become obsolete and learn to create new things through (i) continuous improvement of every activity; (ii) the development of new applications from its own successes; and (iii) continuous innovation as an organised process. Drucker (1993; p.24) recognised the importance of tacit knowledge when he argued that a skill (*technē* in ancient Greek) could not be explained in words but could only be demonstrated through apprenticeship and experience.

ORGANISATIONAL LEARNING

Theorists have long argued for the need for organisations to change continuously (see Dodgson, 1993) and to undertake 'organisational learning'.

The concept of the 'learning organisation' was defined by Pedler, Boydell and Burgoyne (1988) as:

> An organisation which facilitates the learning of all of its members and continuously transforms itself.

This leads to a continuous process of organisational transformation, the end-points of which cannot be planned with any certainty. The cumulative learning of individuals leads, over time, to fundamental changes in assumptions, goals, norms and operating procedures, not simply as a reaction to external pressures but based on the organic growth in knowledge of the people who compose the organisation.

Senge (1990) proposed the 'learning organisation' to overcome 'organisational learning disabilities'. To build a learning organisation managers had to (i) adopt 'systems thinking'; (ii) encourage 'personal mastery' of their own lives; (iii) bring to the surface mental models and challenge them; (iv) build a 'shared vision'; and (v) facilitate 'team learning'. Systems thinking was the key integrating 'discipline' of the five.

Nonaka and Takeuchi (1995; p.45) argued that Western organisational learning theories still used the metaphor of individual learning and failed to deal adequately with the idea of knowledge creation. They also considered that rather than relying on 'artificial' interventions such as organisational development programmes to implement double-loop learning, it should be a continuous activity of the organisation – not a special and difficult task that requires outside intervention.

In their theory of knowledge Nonaka and Takeuchi adopt the traditional definition of knowledge as 'justified true belief', but they add that whereas traditional Western epistemology has focused on 'truthfulness' as the essential attributes of knowledge and emphasises the absolute, static and non-human form of knowledge, they consider knowledge 'a dynamic human process of justifying personal belief towards the "truth"' (Nonaka and Takeuchi, 1995; p.58).

Most writers on knowledge management draw on Polanyi's (1966) distinction between tacit knowledge and explicit knowledge. Tacit knowledge is personal and context-specific and therefore hard to formalise and communicate. Explicit or 'codified' knowledge refers to knowledge that can be transmitted in formal, systematic language. Polanyi contends that human beings acquire knowledge by actively creating and organising their own experiences, and that knowledge that can be expressed in words and numbers thus represents only the tip of the iceberg of the entire body of knowledge: 'We can know more than we can tell,' as Polanyi famously put it (1966; p.4). In traditional epistemology knowledge derives from the separation of the subject and the object of perception: human beings as the subject of perception acquire knowledge by analysing external objects. In contrast, Polanyi contends that human beings create knowledge by involving themselves with objects – that through self-involvement and commitment, or what Polanyi called 'indwelling'. Scientific objectivity is not the sole source of knowledge, and much of our knowledge is the fruit of our own purposeful endeavours in dealing with the world.

Such arguments may not convince everybody, but it is certainly the case that the ideas of knowledge management have had an enormous influence on management thinking.

KNOWLEDGE CONVERSION: INTERACTIONS BETWEEN TACIT AND EXPLICIT KNOWLEDGE

Nonaka and Takeuchi assume that human knowledge is created and expanded through social interaction between tacit knowledge and explicit knowledge, a process they call 'knowledge conversion' (1995; p.59). They postulated four modes of knowledge conversion as these two types of knowledge are combined, which they termed respectively 'socialisation', 'externalisation', 'combination', and 'internalisation'.

Socialisation: **from tacit knowledge to tacit knowledge**

Socialisation is a process of sharing experiences and thereby creating tacit knowledge such as shared mental models and technical skills. An individual can acquire tacit knowledge directly from others without using language. Apprentices learn their trades from their masters, and on-the-job training uses much the same principle in business and management. Experience is thus the key to acquiring tacit knowledge.

Externalisation: **from tacit knowledge to explicit knowledge**

Externalisation is a process of articulating tacit knowledge into explicit concepts by means of metaphors, analogies, concepts, hypotheses or models. This utilises metaphor following Nisbet's (1969) argument that what Polanyi terms tacit knowledge may be expressible, to a degree, by means of metaphor. Successful creative design seems usually to work this way; Nonaka and Takeuchi give a number of interesting industrial design examples (1995; pp64–7).

Combination: **from explicit knowledge to explicit knowledge**

Combination is a process of systematising concepts into a knowledge system, combining different bodies of explicit knowledge. Nonaka and Takeuchi thought an MBA education one of the best examples of this (1995; p.67).

Internalisation: **from explicit knowledge to tacit knowledge**

Internalisation is a process of embodying explicit knowledge into tacit knowledge and is closely related to 'learning by doing'. When experiences through socialisation, externalisation and combination are internalised into individual's tacit knowledge bases in the form of shared mental models or technical know-how they become valuable assets.

IMPLICATIONS OF THE KNOWLEDGE-PRODUCTIVE ORGANISATION FOR HUMAN RESOURCES

Harrison (1997) has stressed the importance of these new developments in management theory and practice for human resource development (HRD). HRD can assist the knowledge-productive organisation in some crucial areas. It must help to build up the levels and kinds of educational and knowledge base, and the human competence, motivation and commitment which the business needs.

Specifically, it must help the firm to build its organisational capability by developing skills, awareness, knowledge and understanding to achieve the following: a real sense of purpose, good team-work, continuous learning, a willingness to embrace change, promoting learning relationships between internal and external customers, and ensuring that knowledge is both created and shared.

Natural learning processes in themselves will not be sufficient, nor will specific programmes, so additionally the human resource development function will have to help build a culture in which there is a strong base of education and training, and appropriate employee resource policies and systems for selection, deployment and rewards (Harrison, 1997; pp383–414).

CASE STUDY

Learning and development in action: Roadmap to success

Training programme leaves US mortgage company with $4 million worth of improvements

A programme to develop future high-performing leaders has resulted in improvements worth $4 million for one of America's major mortgage-lending companies.

Washington Mutual's (WaMu) Home Loans division developed the programme 'Roadmap' to address the issue of a shrinking internal talent pool during a time of significant growth and increasing competition within the industry. It was also hoped that the new learning opportunities would attract the best talent from outside the organisation.

'Learning opportunities became a competitive advantage for us,' Marian Anderson, assistant vice president of leadership development at WaMu Home Loans, told the ASTD Conference.

The nine-month programme involves a mixture of customised workshops, structured experiential job activity, action learning projects to solve real business problems, virtual meetings, 360-degree feedback and coaching from participants' managers.

Anderson described it as a 'holistic approach'.

Although the division, which has almost 14,000 employees, had previously offered many of the components as individual training sessions, Roadmap combined them in a more focused and cost-effective approach.

Participants, both managers of individual contributors and managers of managers, are selected for the programme based on their potential and talent. Key areas of focus during the training include self-awareness and job accountabilities, such as managing customer experience and deepening relationships. It also involves managing employees' performance and building sales and managing the business to ensure efficiency.

On top of the significant saving in operational costs after three years, the company has achieved its goal of hiring 70% internally, also saving money on recruitment costs.

Anderson also said that one of the most crucial aspects to the initiative is the 'coaches' kick-off', a pre-programme session with all managers of participants to ensure that they understand their role as a coach.

'The manager has a key role in the programme. We will not take a participant if the manager does not attend our coaches' kick-off programme. The coach as manager is an opportunity to help people apply lessons in their daily job,' she said.

Conference report, ASTD, Atlanta, USA, *People Management,* 11 June 2007

A learning intervention for the TRUST retail group

CASE STUDY

Background information

The following information has been extracted from the TRUST Group's website.

'TRUST is the UK's leading convenience store group with over 1,000 stores throughout the country. And we're still expanding! TRUST stores provide the ultimate in convenience shopping, trusted throughout the UK for our selection, quality and value. From a great range of fresh foods through to wine, beer, household products and store-cupboard essentials, our stores go far beyond providing for our customers' top-up shopping needs. One of our most attractive assets is the TRUST own brand range. This excellent quality label encompasses nearly 900 different products, from the innovative to traditional favourites, and we're constantly enhancing and enlarging the choices. Independent research reveals that 75% of our customers prefer to buy TRUST brand products.

'Because every TRUST store is at the heart of its community, delivering an essential service to the local area is our top priority. Each element is tailored to the needs of local shoppers – services, selection and facilities.

'TRUST stores may come in a range of sizes and formats, but every one is designed and laid out with local customers' preferences in mind, to make the shopping experience altogether easier and more enjoyable. Our aim is to provide the very best products at value-for-money prices. In particular, we focus on fresh, quality produce. Personal, friendly service is also very much part of the TRUST shopping experience. Add our range of convenient additional services such as hot food to go, fresh coffee, in-store cash machines, the National Lottery and electronic mobile top-ups, and you'll find everything you need at your local TRUST store!

'The first TRUST store opened in 1947, realising founder Adrian Wilson's vision to bring independent retailers together to benefit from increased buying power as a group. His vision has never been more relevant today in the face of tough competition from many quarters.

'Six regional distribution centres supply products and services to every one of our TRUST UK stores. The TRUST central office handles national marketing and buying services for the group, not only supporting our retailers with innovative and award-winning point-of-sale multi-media advertising and promotional campaigns, but also ensuring the best deals for our stores and our customers.

'Today, more than ever, independent retailers who affiliate themselves to TRUST benefit from an industry-leading and highly successful package. By helping our stores to compete and stay at the forefront, TRUST also ensures that each of our retailers can deliver the high standards and value discerning customers now demand.'

TRUST at a glance – key facts

TRUST is a 'symbol group', meaning that individual TRUST members remain independent but enjoy access to collective buying and marketing power and all the added benefits of operating under a strong corporate brand with back-up resources.

UK turnover is in excess of £2.7 billion and it is a market leader within the convenience store sector.

It has 2,700 UK stores and is the employer of over 50,000 people.

Average store size is 130 square metres/1,400 square feet.

TRUST owners have won more than 100 major industry awards in the past three years.

The TRUST Group can offer retailers financial packages and credit terms, equipment/leasing loans and licensing equipment/franchising agreements, and many other services.

'Our retailers have access to the latest industry developments, including professional merchandising and category management, store refurbishment, and training and development for both managers and staff.'

The following is list of competencies which a TRUST Group store supervisor is expected to possess. Each supervisor is responsible for the work of up to 10 sales assistants and reports directly to the store manager.

- Motivating, developing, and directing people as they work, identifying the best people for the job.

- Active listening, giving full attention to what other people are saying, taking time to understand the points being made, asking questions as appropriate, and not interrupting at inappropriate times.

- Service orientation: actively looking for ways to help people.

- Managing one's own time and the time of others.

- Teaching others how to do things.

- Monitoring/assessing the performance of oneself, other individuals, or organisations to make improvements or take corrective action.

- Understanding written sentences and paragraphs in work-related documents.

- Judgement and decision-making: considering the relative costs and benefits of potential actions to choose the most appropriate one.

- Active learning: understanding the implications of new information for both current and future problem-solving and decision-making.

- Critical thinking: using logic and reasoning to identify the strengths and weaknesses of alternative solutions, conclusions or approaches to problems.

REFLECTIVE ACTIVITY

Scenario:

Following an analysis of the annual performance appraisals of store assistants, management identified a persistent pattern of complaints of poor working relationships with the store supervisors to whom they reported. Supervisors were often described as being bad at communicating, poor at encouraging ideas and innovations, and insensitive in their relations with staff.

After careful consideration of these findings and further interviews with store assistants, supervisors and managers it was concluded that there was substance to the assistants' complaints. HRD were tasked with developing and implementing a skills improvement programme for store supervisors to alleviate the problems that had been identified.

Outline a formal learning intervention to deliver the required skills improvement programme.

ACTIVITY ANSWER GUIDANCE

Needs analysis

A needs analysis was conducted by analysing the job descriptions for store assistants, supervisors and managers, by interviewing a sample of assistants, supervisors and managers, and by observing work in a sample of stores.

It was concluded that there was a requirement for a programme of interpersonal skills training for store supervisors. A person analysis concluded that all existing store supervisors should participate in the proposed learning intervention, and that this should also become part of the entry-level management development programme

The learning objectives were identified as follows.

Interpersonal skills programme for TRUST store supervisors

After completing the learning intervention the participants should be competent in the following areas:

- Developing and maintaining rapport with others
- Listening to others
- Dealing sensitively with others
- Encouraging ideas from others
- Giving feedback to others.

Designing the skills programme

A set of five one-day workshops, one day for each of the five themes identified. A maximum of 25 supervisors could attend any workshop. The total resources needed to cater for all of the Group's store supervisors will have to be calculated and approved.

Methods:

- Instruction
- Video presentations
- Case studies
- Role-plays
- In-basket exercises.

Resources:

- One facilitator for each day
- Lecture theatre and break-out rooms in the company's central Development Facility
- Audiovisual PC equipment in the Development Facility
- Pre-programme written material for distribution to the learners prior to the programme
- Pre-intervention questionnaire on existing knowledge and skills levels
- Learning materials: videos, role-play materials, cases, materials for in-basket exercises
- Learners' feedback sheets for evaluation
- Test materials for evaluation
- Attendance certificates
- Completion certificates.

Evaluation

Trainees' reactions – questionnaires distributed at end of each day's workshop

Knowledge tests to be administered at end of the programme

Analysis of performance management appraisals

Staff attitude surveys.

MANAGEMENT DEVELOPMENT

The distinction between the development of managers and of non-managers is becoming increasingly blurred. The CIPD defines 'management development' (CIPD Factsheet on Management Development, 2007c) as:

> The entire structured process by which managers learn and improve their skills for their employing organisations.

Managers learn in many ways, including experientially, and many organisations combine formal and informal approaches. Handy *et al* (1988; p.12) proposed a clear distinction between 'business education' and 'management development'. By 'business education' is meant the formal or academic knowledge-base required for management, as is typically provided by an external source such as a university, business school or commercial college. The attainment of such education is primarily the responsibility of the individual manager. Business education cannot by itself qualify one for management but can only be a prelude to it. 'Management development' largely takes place within the organisation and should be seen as a combination of experience, training and education which, although usually initiated by the organiaation, requires the active co-operation of the individual, and for which both organisation and manager share joint responsibility. Twenty years on, Handy's distinction still has much to commend it, although organisations are very much more likely now to actively support their managers in acquiring business education, either paying the fees for external MBAs and the like, or setting up their own 'corporate universities'.

One of the key changes in management development in the UK and in many other countries in the past 20 years has been the growth in management education at university level. In North America this provision was evident for most of the twentieth century, but it was only in the latter decades of the century that most other countries took the academic education of managers as seriously as did the North Americans. Indeed, it was mainly the continuing success of the US managerial and entrepreneurial culture which brought about this change. The CIPD estimates that by 2006 there were over 100 higher-education institutions in the UK that offered undergraduate and postgraduate courses, around 20,000 first degrees and 11,000 higher degrees (mainly MBAs) being awarded every year. Over 80% of MBAs were awarded for distance-learning or part-time study. Some of these MBA graduates will have been sponsored by their employers, but others will have decided to study for themselves as part of their own programme of career development. Edinburgh Business School currently offers one of the largest distance-learning MBA programmes in the world with, to date, over 10,500 graduates working in over 150 countries (http://www.ebsglobal.net/).

Some large UK companies have followed the US lead in setting up 'corporate universities' which supply in-house many of the formal courses and programmes for their people development, including management development, which previously would have been supplied by external academic institutions (CIPD, 2007c).

THE OBJECTIVES OF MANAGEMENT DEVELOPMENT

The choice of management development approach and methods will depend on the strategic outcomes that the organisation is pursuing, such as performance, attitude and adaptability.

Improving managers' expertise in specific areas such as marketing, finance, production or HRM is usually highest on most companies' agendas for management development, followed by giving individuals experience to prepare them for senior management positions. Management development is also used either as a catalyst for organisational change or to help build a new culture following a major change such as a large-scale merger or acquisition. Management development can also be a key factor in building a learning organisation in which there is a climate for continual learning. In this case the emphasis is away from structured programmes and taught courses and towards enhancing opportunities for self-development via methods such as Action Learning, on-the-job training, career breaks, secondment to temporary 'taskforces' and e-learning.

METHODS OF MANAGEMENT DEVELOPMENT

It is recognised that a good deal of management development takes place on the job and that planned job experience and career succession can play vital roles in the process. Line managers should be involved in the development of their subordinates.

In the UK the most common formal methods of management development are external courses, attending seminars and conferences, attending in-company training to develop individual skills, attending in-company training to develop organisational skills, and pursuing external formal qualifications such as MBAs (Thomson *et al*, 2001; p.144).

The most popular informal methods in the UK are in-company job rotation, job observation, on-the-job training, mentoring, and coaching (Thomson *et al*, 2001; p.149).

CONDITIONS FOR SUCCESSFUL MANAGEMENT DEVELOPMENT

There is a consensus in the literature (Storey *et al*, 1997; p.43) that management development is most effective when:

- it is recognised by the organisation as a strategic business activity

- the design of management development programmes recognises the nature of managerial work

- the programme is tailored to fit the needs of the individual managers on it

- education, training, selection, career planning, reward systems and managerial evaluation are recognised as all being part of a connected system

- evaluation is itself a vital part of the system of development.

Mabey and Thomson (2000a) found encouraging signs of continuing progress in British management development. Compared to the findings of Thomson *et al* (1997), the fieldwork for which had been carried out in 1996, there was an increase in the number of organisations with a formal written policy for management development, from 43% in 1996 to 51% in 2000; and in those having a specific budget for management development, from 40% to 49%. Formal training had risen to an average of to 6.5 days per manager per year for larger firms (up 18%), and to 6.4 in small firms (up 25%). There was also found to be an average of 8.1 days for informal training. Half the organisations had or were pursuing Investor in People (IiP) status, and 63% confirmed their commitment to national vocational qualifications (NVQs) in management. However, only 14% were committed to Management Standards (MCI). It was found that 72% of firms were attempting to review management development (up 5% since 1996).

Mabey and Thomson (2000a) concluded that there was evidence that organisations were moving along a spectrum from 'weak' to 'strong' management development systems in which 'strong' systems were typified by planned structures, policy frameworks and effective management development processes. The authors also claimed that they had found evidence that firms with a strong policy framework (ie high amounts of formal training and a centralised management development policy) had better current benchmarked performance.

EXAMPLE: MANAGEMENT SKILLS DEVELOPMENT

Mintzberg's study of managerial work (*The Nature of Managerial Work*, 1973) identified ten management roles and suggested eight basic sets of managerial skills that might be taught:

1 Peer skills: the manager's ability to establish and maintain peer relationships. These include developing contacts and networks, negotiation – 'the ability to trade resources in real time', and consultancy – managing the expert–client relationship political skills (in connection with conflict and infighting in large bureaucracies).

2 Leadership skills: the manager's ability to deal with his subordinates – to motivate, train and help them.

3 Conflict resolution skills: interpersonal skills of mediating between conflicting individuals, and decisional skills for handling disturbances. Managers work under stress in both situations.

4 Information-processing skills: how to build informal information networks, find sources of information and use them.

5 Skills in decision-making under ambiguity: usually very little information is given to the manager and what is given is likely to be unstructured.

6 Resource-allocation skills: managers must choose between competing demands on resources, know how to allocate their own time, and determine and allocate the work of subordinates.

7 Entrepreneurial skills: searching for problems and opportunities and the controlled implementation of change in organisations.

8 Skills of introspection: the manager should thoroughly understand his or her job, be sensitive to his or her impact on the organisation, and be able to learn by introspection.

REFLECTIVE ACTIVITY

How do you think each of the eight basic managerial skills identified by Mintzberg could be taught?

ACTIVITY ANSWER GUIDANCE

1 Peer skills: peer skills lend themselves readily to learning from experience.

2 Leadership skills: leadership skills require participative learning, but most authorities consider that leadership abilities are closely linked to innate personality, and if this is so it may place limits on the degree to which leadership can be taught.

3 Conflict resolution skills: role-playing can be a useful teaching approach.

4 Information-processing skills: skills of finding and validating information can be taught by research assignments and model-building exercises; case studies and role-playing are useful in teaching dissemination skills. Managers must also be trained in obtaining unstructured and undocumented information, in how to use the telecommunication media, in using scheduled

and unscheduled meetings, and in using tours, 'the manager's prime tools' (Mintzberg).

5   Skills in decision-making under ambiguity: managers should learn the skills necessary for finding problems and opportunities, for diagnosing unstructured problems, for searching for solutions, for managing the dynamics of decision-making, and for handling parallel decisions and integrating them into plans.

6   Resource-allocation skills: in-basket exercises are a useful teaching method for these skills.

7   Entrepreneurial skills: it may be questionable how much such skills can be taught, but organisations should try to create a climate which encourages the use of these skills.

8   Skills of introspection: a manager's job itself can be the most important teaching resource, provided the manager knows how to learn from experience.

In summary, Mintzberg holds the view that formal education itself cannot make managers. The most successful educational and training processes will be those that can:

- best determine which candidates demonstrate potential or actual management skills; and

- improve significantly their performance of these skills.

CASE STUDY

Management development in action

Where are the Generation-X leaders?

Carol Glover reports:

HR has to start selling the concept of leadership and management development to Generation X-ers now to avert crisis, according to Heather Neely of Rainmaker Thinking Inc. It has to educate organisations about the realities of managing a cross-generational 'free agent' workforce, she said.

Rainmaker has studied Generation X-ers – those who were born between 1963 and 1977 – over the past eight years. They are, according to Neely, the most misunderstood generation ever. They are also the most cynical having hit the workforce during the global downsizings of the 1980s and 1990s which forced them to embrace the concept of career 'free agency' and not looking to organisations for job security. Neely uses the phrase 'just-in-time job loyalty' as the average tenure of a Generation X-er is just 18 months.

Neely urges HR to use a 'generational lens' when thinking about training. It must incorporate the needs of three very different cohorts: Baby Boomers born between 1943 and 1964, Generation X-ers born 1964 to 1977, and Generation Y-ers born 1978 to 1985. The one-size-fits-all training and development framework will no longer work.

HR also faces a huge organisational leadership crisis as the Baby Boomers are all due to start retiring in the next 15 years but Generation X-ers are few in number and are not interested in traditional management career ladders.

C2/Managing the New Workforce, *People Management,* 10 April 2003

CASE STUDY

Management development in action

Tailoring management development

A structured development programme has been the key to developing a culture that puts people first at West Sussex County Council, delegates were told.

Kieran Stigant, in charge of community engagement and organisational development at the Council, said that the organisation realised that its managers were seen as 'superior technicians' who could solve problems, rather than as developers of people who could unlock the potential of employees.

As a result, the Council put in place a management-development ladder aimed at 'achieving a focus on our communities – developing the organisation to be capable of delivering the services our communities need', Stigant said.

The four-stage programme begins with a basic 'Introduction to management' and finishes with 'Journey into the future', which focuses on behavioural change.

Implementing the development programme has required heavy investment from the Council – and high levels of commitment from the staff involved. The advanced management development stage of the programme, which is based on self-managed learning, costs £1,500 for each participant. Individual managers are required to put in around 600 hours over 18 months – and many put in twice that amount of time.

'When we started, I didn't have a clue whether it would work out or not,' admitted Stigant, who said that the response from managers had been outstanding.

David Burt, management development manager, Safeway

Kieran Stigant, assistant chief executive, West Sussex County Council

Personnel Management, 16 April 2002

CHAPTER 6

Employee relations

INTRODUCTION

'Employee relations' is the term now normally used to describe the policies and practices an organisation uses in dealing with its employees, and the systems of rules and mechanisms by which organisations and employees interact with each other. The term usually implies collective relations such as collective bargaining with trade unions (TUs) or staff associations (SAs), and the resulting agreements, but it also includes policies and procedures which operate at small-group or individual level – eg disciplinary and grievance procedures.

LEARNING OUTCOMES

On completion of this chapter you should:

- understand the nature and importance of conflict in employee relations
- understand the nature of negotiations in the context of employee relations
- understand the purpose and nature of both grievance and disciplinary procedures
- be able to describe the process of traditional collective bargaining and agreements
- be familiar with the main forms of industrial action
- understand the nature of 'new employee relations'
- understand the concepts of employee engagement and employee voice.

In Chapter 1 we introduced the idea of 'perspective' in people management and outlined the three most important for our purposes – namely, unitarist, pluralist, and radical or critical. We noted that the HRM model is really unitarist in its culture but that it is often successfully applied in a pluralist milieu. There is no doubt, however, that in countries such as the UK and the USA where trade union power has declined, employee relations are significantly less collectivised than was the case several decades ago. As we also saw in Chapter 1, as early as 1990 the Workplace Industrial Relations Survey reported a significant decline in trade unionism in the UK, accompanied by a considerable increase in HRM-style initiatives in participation and communication, such as team briefings, quality circles and newsletters, replacing the more traditional collective methods. There was also evidence of the increasing involvement of line managers in HR activities which had previously been reserved for specialist personnel management departments. The later Workplace Employee Relations Surveys have confirmed these trends in the UK.

Most countries have legal frameworks which give statutory rights to employees, both individual – eg protection against unfair dismissal – and collective – eg the right to trade union membership and recognition, and ensuring legal compliance on the part of the organisation is a vital responsibility for HR managers. The actual rights and responsibilities of both parties may vary widely from country to country – a point that multinational companies have to bear in mind when framing their HR strategies and policies.

Where traditional formal employee relations processes such as collective bargaining have declined, HRM initiatives in such areas as teamworking and more direct methods of communication between management and workers have often taken their place.

DEALING WITH CONFLICT

We use the term 'conflict' widely in employee relations. It does not always mean a breakdown in the working relationship, although that can be a consequence of conflict. We mean any situation where there is a significant difference in objectives or interests between management and the workforce, whether it is a collective difference about pay rates or major terms of employment, or individual differences about a particular work situation.

So the issue of conflict and how to deal with it is important for managers, both at the level of the individual or small group – eg by means of disciplinary and grievance procedures – and at the larger-scale handling disputes with trade unions or staff associations which represent collectively some significant section of the workforce.

The adoption of more sophisticated management models such as human resource management (HRM) has had implications for the conduct of employee relations.

GRIEVANCE AND DISCIPLINARY PROCEDURES

The 2004 Workplace Employee Relations Survey (WERS) found that nearly half (47%) of UK workplaces reported having had a formal grievance from employees in 2004. The most common types of grievance raised were those on pay and conditions (18% of workplaces), unfair treatment by a supervisor or line manager (16%), and work practices, work allocation or pace of work (12%).

The same survey found that 55% of managers reported using at least one disciplinary sanction in 2004, and 28% of workplaces had made at least one dismissal on disciplinary grounds (Kersley *et al*, 2006: p.229).

Most managers would agree that it is inevitable that there are issues of grievance- and discipline-handling in most organisations. Notwithstanding the unitarist culture of most HRM models, few managers really expect that the interests of both employers and employees will always coincide. These interests are expressed in the parties' respective legal rights and responsibilities, but also in the informal expectations they have of each other.

Employees expect that employers will treat them reasonably, fairly and consistently, and that action will be taken against them only on the basis of just cause and after proper and thorough investigation. Employees will feel they have a right to pursue a grievance if these expectations are not met.

Employers expect employees to perform their duties and tasks in a satisfactory manner in accordance with their legal obligations and organisational policies and procedures. If the employees' performance is not satisfactory, employers will consider that they have the right to apply disciplinary action.

HR has an important role in resolving such differences and so assisting the effective running of the organisation. Apart from ethical and legal considerations, if grievance and discipline cases are dealt with properly, we assume that employee dissatisfaction should be reduced and motivation increased, with consequent improvements in individual, team and organisational performance. If the employment relationship is working in any sort of reasonable fashion to begin with, it is usually seen by both sides as an ongoing relationship that should survive the resolution of any one dispute whether individual or collective.

As we saw in Chapter 1, a key characteristic of HRM is the devolution to the line manager of most day-to-day people management. This includes handling grievance and discipline with minimum HR specialist input, at least initially, so it is now perceived as crucial that all line managers be trained to handle grievance and disciplinary cases properly.

If an employment tribunal investigates the dismissal of an employee, it will test the issues of fairness and reasonableness by considering whether the procedures that were applied by the employer conformed to the concepts of natural justice. From the employer's point of view the main purpose of procedures is to ensure that standards are maintained and legal compliance adhered to.

Good grievance and disciplinary procedures typically are set in stages, and on the principle that issues should be dealt with as close to their origin as possible. Not all actions have to go through all these steps, however, since the first instance of severe misconduct may merit disciplinary action much more punitive than that of, say, a verbal warning. For example, fighting in the workplace and being drunk at work are both classed in almost all circumstances as 'gross misconduct' deserving immediate dismissal, as may be the refusal to carry out a reasonable and legitimate instruction from a superior. But the general principle is always to deal with issues at the lowest level possible given the nature of the inappropriate behaviour.

It may be surprising but it is a fact that in the UK employment tribunals still report cases in which the employer has failed to conduct a proper and fair investigation before taking disciplinary action against an employee (Earnshaw and Cooper, 1998; p.15). It is the employer's responsibility to ensure that any disciplinary action is taken only after a full and proper investigation of the facts has been conducted. Line managers need appropriate training in handling grievance and disciplinary matters. HR experts are still usually involved in both, but not necessarily in person, at least at initial stages. The line managers will need access to expert HR advice, however, whether or not HR personnel themselves are present.

REFLECTIVE ACTIVITY

Find out what the disciplinary and grievance procedures are which operate at your place of employment (or some other workplace with which you are familiar). If there are neither, outline what you think the procedure(s) should be.

ACTIVITY ANSWER GUIDANCE

If an organisation lands in court or in some legal sub-forum (such as the UK system of employment tribunals) to defend its actions in respect of any grievance or disciplinary matter, there are five tests that will be applied to the employer's actions: fairness, reasonableness, consistency, operating with just cause, and operating within the law. Grievance and disciplinary issues are usually regarded as linked and often share common procedures to avoid the perception that one is being given greater status or importance than the other by the organisation. Useful advice on the handling of grievance and disciplinary matters, both from the employee's point of view and that of the employer, and also advice on employee relations issues more generally, can be found at the Advisory, Conciliation and Arbitration Service (ACAS) website: http://www.acas.org.uk/

NEGOTIATION AND BARGAINING IN EMPLOYEE RELATIONS

'Negotiation' – which comes from the Latin *negotiari* 'to carry on business' – is defined (*The New Shorter Oxford English Dictionary*) as:

> a process or act of conferring with another or others to arrange some matter by mutual agreement, a discussion with a view to some compromise or settlement.

To 'bargain' – which is derived through an old French verb meaning 'trade', 'dispute' and 'hesitate' – is defined (*ibid.*) as being:

> to discuss the terms of action, negotiate, seek to secure the most favourable terms, haggle.

These dictionary definitions give a good flavour of what we mean by negotiations or collective agreements between an organisation and a trade union.

Negotiation has also been defined (Kennedy *et al*, 1984; p.12) as:

> a process for resolving conflict between two parties whereby both modify their demands to achieve a mutually acceptable compromise.

And in the field of collective bargaining in employee relations (Farnham and Pimlott, 1995; p.412) as:

> Negotiation ... is a power relationship between managerial and trade union representatives. It is an activity by which the two sides make agreements regulating pay or market relations and managerial or authority relations between them.

Collective bargaining is the traditional term for the process by which pay, terms of employment and working conditions are mutually negotiated between employees, as collectively represented by trade unions or staff associations and employers. Collective bargaining can also take place at industry level where the employers are also represented collectively. In this case industry or national agreements will typically be supplemented by local agreement negotiated subsequently with individual employers.

We have already noted several times in this text that as human resource management has superseded traditional personnel management there has been a shift from collective towards more individualist work relations – and we discuss this later in this chapter in a section on the 'new employee relations'. We also saw in Chapter 1 the empirical evidence which shows a marked decline in trade union membership and influence in the UK over the last 20 years. Far fewer employees are now covered by collective bargaining in the traditional sense in the UK. In fact, most employers who recognised trade unions in the 1980s and who are still in existence today still recognise trade unions, but increasingly union influence is confined to the public sector and to traditional industries, and where it is present it is very much weaker than in the decades immediately following World War II. This has been the trend in the USA and many other countries also, although there are international variations – for example, trade unions remain relatively strong in continental Europe and Scandinavia.

But having said all that, even in the UK in the twenty-first century, collective bargaining remains an important part of the management process in some industries and many parts of the public sector. Where there has been a tradition of collective bargaining, it lends legitimacy to agreements on pay and conditions of employment.

Certain conditions are necessary for collective bargaining to operate:

- Both management and the workforce are organised. This implies the existence of trade unions or some other sort of association representing the employees.
- There is formal recognition of the trade unions or other employee association(s) by management.
- There is mutual agreement to negotiate in good faith and to keep agreements that are reached.

And even in the USA some traditional large industries are still engaged in very large-scale collective industrial relations, for example the car manufacturing industry. But increasingly this looks like the past and not the future.

There are some particular characteristics of the negotiating process in employee relations that should be kept in mind:

- The parties are not involved in a one-off negotiation (like, say, buying a car) and usually need, and want, to continue working together after the negotiation or bargaining has been completed.
- The negotiation is usually about more than one issue – eg basic pay *and* some aspect of working conditions or some other benefits.
- Negotiations are actually conducted by a small number of representatives from each side and agreements reached by them will require endorsement from the

parties themselves. So when trade union negotiators reach agreement with management on some issue, they normally have to seek approval from the wider membership of the union by means of a ballot. Similarly, management negotiators may have to seek endorsement from their board of directors.

- On each side, priorities, strategies and tactics must be established before the negotiations start with the opposite party, so there is always the possibility of internal conflict on each side.

- Once an agreement has been reached, there is joint responsibility to make it work.

THE NEGOTIATION PROCESS

Negotiators normally want to reach an agreement. In every negotiation there is a 'negotiating continuum' incorporating the 'bargaining range' of each side.

An effective negotiation enables each party to identify the 'bargaining parameters' between them and to reach an agreed settlement within these parameters (see Figure 3).

Management's bargaining range in a given negotiation runs from its ideal settlement point (what it would ideally like) to its resistance point (the point beyond which it will not go), with a target point of favourable and realistic expectation somewhere between the two. Similarly, the unions also have a bargaining range between their ideal settlement and resistance points (and also with a target point). The two bargaining ranges are not identical (different resistance and ideal settlement points), but if negotiations are to be at all possible there will have to be an overlap, and this overlap is bounded by the two sides' resistance points, which thus form the bargaining parameters.

Figure 3 Negotiation bargaining parameters

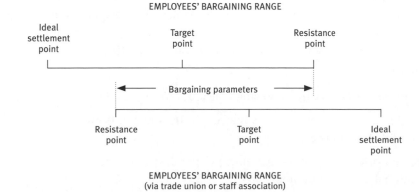

Source: Farnham and Pimlott (1995; p.414)

Example

Acme Widgets plc, a mid-level technology manufacturer, starts its annual pay negotiations with the Widget Engineer's Union. Acme management would ideally like to give no pay rise to its employees because the market is becoming increasingly competitive and although Acme is profitable, it is suffering continuous pressure on its profit margins and is always seeking to cut costs. However, it knows that this would be completely unacceptable to the workforce who will expect a pay rise at least equal to the rise in the cost of living as established by the Government's published rate of inflation for the previous year, which is 3%. Management know that they could just afford a maximum pay rise of 10%, but this would adversely affect the balance sheet and be extremely difficult to sell to shareholders. Benchmark settlements in comparable industries are running at 4% to 5% on average. Management have therefore privately set a target of 4%.

In this case, then, the bargaining range will be between 3% – which is the resistance point of the union side – and 10%, the resistance point of the employer.

The more equal the balance of power between the two parties, and the more skilled the negotiators, the more likely it will be that a settlement is reached somewhere between the two sides' target points.

Negotiation is not confined to traditional pay bargaining. Managers who have no responsibility for pay often still have to negotiate with trade unions or other employee groups on issues related to work (CIPD, 2005).

SOME TYPES OF COLLECTIVE AGREEMENT

SINGLE-UNION RECOGNITION

The existence of a number of unions within one organisation was frequently criticised in the 1980s because of the increase in the complexity of bargaining arrangements and the danger of inter-union demarcation disputes. One answer to this problem is representation of all employees through a single union. These single-union agreements had a number of characteristics that were advantageous to management.

Single-union deals have the following typical features:

- a single union representing all employees, with constraints put on the role of union full-time officials
- flexible working practices – agreement to the flexible use of labour across traditional demarcation lines

- single status for all employees – the harmonisation of terms and conditions between manual and non-manual employees

- an expressed commitment by the organisation to involvement and the disclosure of information in the form of an open communications system and, often, a works council

- the resolution of disputes by means of devices such as pendulum arbitration, a commitment to continuity of production, and a 'no-strike' provision.

Single-union deals have generally been concluded on greenfield sites, often by Japanese firms such as Nissan, Sanyo, Matsushita and Toyota. What cynics have termed a 'beauty contest' is often held by the employer to select the one union from a number of contenders.

PARTNERSHIP AGREEMENTS

A partnership agreement is one in which both parties (management and the trade union) agree to work together to their mutual advantage and to achieve a climate of more co-operative and therefore less adversarial employee relations. A partnership agreement may include undertakings from both sides. For example, management may offer job security linked to productivity, more involvement and better communications, and the union may agree to new forms of work organisation or work practices which offer more flexibility on the part of employees.

Five key values for partnership have been set down by Roscow and Casner-Lotto (1997):

- mutual trust and respect
- a joint vision for the future and the means to achieve it
- continuous exchange of information
- recognition of the central role of collective bargaining
- devolved decision-making.

Their research in the United States indicated that if these matters were addressed successfully by management and unions, companies could expect productivity gains, quality improvements, a better motivated and committed workforce, and lower absenteeism and staff turnover rates.

The Department of Trade and Industry and Department for Education and Employment report on *Partnerships at Work* (1997) concluded that partnership was central to the strategy of successful organisations. A growing understanding that organisations must focus on customer needs has brought with it the desire to engage the attitudes and commitment of all employees in order to effectively meet those needs, says the report. The five main themes or 'paths' identified by the report are:

- shared goals: 'understanding the business we are in'
- shared culture: 'agreed values binding us together'
- shared learning: 'continuously improving ourselves'
- shared effort: 'one business driven by flexible teams'
- shared information: 'effective communication throughout the enterprise'.

NEW-STYLE AGREEMENTS

As described by Farnham (2000), a major feature of new-style agreements is that their negotiating and disputes procedures are based on the mutually accepted rights of the parties expressed in the recognition agreement. The intention is to resolve any differences of interests on substantive issues between the parties by regulations, pendulum arbitration providing a resolution of those issues where differences remain outstanding. New-style agreements will typically include provision for single-union recognition, single status, labour flexibility, company council and a no-strike clause to the effect that issues should be resolved without recourse to industrial action.

DISPUTE RESOLUTION: CONCILIATION, ARBITRATION AND MEDIATION

The aim of collective bargaining is, of course, to reach agreement to the satisfaction of both parties. Negotiating procedures provide for various stages of 'failure to agree', and often include a clause providing for some form of dispute resolution in the event of the procedure's being exhausted. The standard processes of dispute resolution include conciliation, arbitration and mediation.

Conciliation is the process of reconciling disagreeing parties. It is carried out by a third party, in the UK often an ACAS (Advisory, Conciliation and Arbitration Service) conciliation officer, who acts in effect as a go-between, attempting to get the employer and trade union representatives to agree on terms. Conciliators can only help the parties to come to an agreement. They do not make recommendations on what that agreement should be. That is the role of an arbitrator (see below). The incentives to seek conciliation are the hope that the conciliator can rebuild bridges and the belief that a determined search for agreement is better than confrontation, even if both parties have to compromise.

Arbitration is the process of settling disputes by getting a third party – the arbitrator – to review and discuss the negotiating stances of the disagreeing parties and make a recommendation on the terms of settlement which is binding on both parties. The arbitrator is impartial, and employee relations academics or other figures recognised as experts in the industry concerned are sometimes asked to act in this capacity. Arbitration is the means of last resort for reaching a settlement where disputes cannot be resolved in any other way. Procedural agreements may provide for either side unilaterally to invoke arbitration, in which case the decision of the arbitrator is not binding on both parties. The process of arbitration in its fullest sense, however, only takes place at the request of both parties who agree in advance to accept the arbitrator's findings. ACAS will only act as arbitrator if the consent of both parties is obtained, conciliation has been considered, any agreed procedures have been followed to the full, and a failure to agree has been recorded.

The number of arbitration cases referred to ACAS declined significantly during the 1980s and 1990s. Some authorities such as Kessler and Bayliss (1992) attributed this decline to management dominance, which has meant that arbitration was regarded as pointless because managements were confident that their final offer would be accepted. In the prevailing climate, unions, if dissatisfied and denied arbitration, would in most cases be unwilling to take industrial action.

Pendulum or *final offer arbitration* increases the rigidity of the arbitration process by allowing an arbitrator no choice but to recommend either the union's or the employer's final offer – there is no middle ground. As defined by Millward (1994), the features of pendulum arbitration are that the procedure has to be written and agreed by management and the union (or unions), and it has to provide for arbitration that is independent, is equally accessible to both parties, is binding on both parties, and involves finding wholly in favour of one party or the other. The adoption of pendulum arbitration can be viewed as a concession by management, since it means giving up the power to impose a settlement on employees.

Mediation is an approach to finding a result in a dispute which can be thought of as something midway between arbitration and conciliation – being weaker than arbitration but somewhat stronger than conciliation. It takes place when a third party (often ACAS) helps the employer and the union by making recommendations which, however, they are not bound to accept.

INFORMAL EMPLOYEE RELATIONS PROCESSES

The formal processes of union recognition, collective bargaining and dispute resolution described above provide the traditional framework for employee relations in so far as this is concerned with agreeing terms and conditions of employment and working arrangements and settling disputes. But managers should always remember that within that formal framework, informal employee relations processes are taking place continuously, whenever a line manager or team leader is handling an issue in contact with an employee representative, an individual employee or a group of employees. The issue may concern methods of work, allocation of work and overtime, working conditions, health and safety, achieving output and quality targets and standards, discipline or pay. Line managers and supervisors handle day-to-day grievances arising from any of these issues and are expected to resolve them to the satisfaction of all parties without involving a formal grievance procedure. The thrust for devolving responsibility to line managers for human resource matters has increased the onus on them to handle employee relations effectively.

Creating and maintaining a good employee relations climate in an organisation may be the ultimate responsibility of top management, advised by HR specialists. But the climate will be strongly influenced by the behaviour of line managers and team leaders. The HR function can help to improve the effectiveness of this behaviour by identifying and defining the competences required, advising on the selection of supervisors, ensuring that they are properly trained, and encouraging the development of performance management processes that provide for the assessment of the level of competence achieved by line managers and team leaders in handling employee relations.

HARMONISATION

Harmonisation is the process of introducing the same conditions of employment for all employees. It is distinguished by Roberts (1990) from single status and staff status as follows:

- Single status is the removal of differences in basic conditions of employment to give all employees equal status. Some organisations take this further by putting all employees into the same pay and grading structure.

- Staff status is a process whereby manual and craft employees gradually receive staff terms and conditions of employment, usually upon reaching some qualifying standard – for example, length of service.

- Harmonisation means the reduction of differences in the pay structure and other employment conditions between categories of employee, usually manual and staff employees. The essence of harmonisation is the adoption of a common approach and criteria to pay and conditions for all employees. It differs from staff status in that, in the process of harmonisation, some staff employees may have to accept some of the conditions of employment of manual workers.

According to Duncan (1989), the pressure towards harmonisation has arisen for the following reasons:

- *new technology*: status differentials can obstruct efficient labour utilisation, and concessions on harmonisation are invariably given in exchange for an agreement on flexibility. Moreover, technology, by de-skilling many white-collar jobs and enhancing the skills of former blue-collar workers, has made differential treatment harder to defend

- *legislation*: equal pay, the banning of discrimination and employment protection legislation have extended to manual workers rights that were previously the preserve of staff. The concept of equal value has been a major challenge to differentiation between staff and manual workers
- *improving productivity* by the more flexible use of labour
- *simplifying HR administration* and thereby reducing costs
- *changing employee attitudes* and so improving commitment, motivation and morale.

INDUSTRIAL ACTION

The term 'industrial action' is ordinarily used to describe the sanctions which employees may resort to if bargaining or negotiation does not produce a result acceptable to them. The term is usually associated with strike action by employees against their employer – but that is only one form of industrial action. It should also be noted that employers/management have a range of sanctions that they too may resort to.

We will first consider industrial action in the sense of employee action.

There can be individual, unorganised forms of industrial action such as high labour turnover, deliberately poor time-keeping, high absenteeism, withholding of effort, inefficient working, time-wasting, sabotage and complaints. All these may of course occur with particular individuals who are dissatisfied with their employment regardless of the general employee relations situation in the organisation, but when they are exhibited by a large number of employees they may constitute deliberate, although unorganised, industrial action. Such behaviour is most likely to occur after collective industrial action has failed and employees have been obliged to accept an unpopular settlement.

Organised, collective action by employees can take a variety of forms. At its mildest, collective action could be 'going slow' or 'working to rule'. A 'go-slow' might involve workers in a breach of their contract whereas normally a 'work to rule' will not. In this form of industrial action employees obey the letter of managerial instructions, exploiting the fact that very often in full production rules may be bent and corners cut.

Overtime bans are rather tougher actions, exploiting management's use of overtime to provide flexibility in labour resources and costs. Very often an overtime ban can have immediate and pronounced impact on production. It is a double-edged sword, however: it immediately hits workers' earnings.

Often work-to-rule, go-slow and overtime ban action are used tactically by employees and unions early in a dispute or negotiation to put pressure on management to modify their position.

The ultimate sanction possessed by employees is to strike – ie to withdraw their labour.

Strikes are described as 'unofficial' when they take place without the support of the union concerned, and 'unconstitutional' when they occur without the agreed negotiating procedure having been followed.

The number of strikes and the proportion of days lost through strike action have diminished significantly in the UK since the 1970s. Arguably, this reduction has been caused more by economic pressures than by the legislation (Armstrong, 2001). Unions often had to choose between taking strike action, which could lead to closure, or survival on the terms dictated by employers with fewer jobs.

Another form of industrial action by employees is the 'sit-in', which is a mass occupation of employers' premises, perhaps to protest at the proposed closure of a plant and/or to physically prevent removal of machinery or other property. A similar action is a 'work-in' in which, in addition to occupying premises, the employees continue production without management, perhaps in defiance of them. All forms of unauthorised occupation are likely to be illegal, however (although employers may prefer in certain circumstances not to go to law about the matter – for example, when they wish to preserve or restore better employee relations in the future: such considerations are unlikely to be considered in the case of proposed closure, however, where the employers' concern will be disposal of property and equipment).

THE NEW EMPLOYEE RELATIONS

In 2005 the CIPD could report (CIPD, 2005; pp3–4) that from the manager's viewpoint,

> in general [the Employee Relations agenda] is no longer about trade unions. There is more emphasis on direct communication, managing organisational change and involving and motivating staff. Issues about work–life balance and the war for talent reflect a changing workforce with changing expectations. Employers have to come to terms with these changes in managing the employment relationship.

The same CIPD report (p.1) stated that:

managing the employment relationship remains central to good HR practice. The emphasis of employee relations continues to shift from institutions to relationships, but employee relations skills and competencies are still critical to achieving performance benefits. The focus now needs to be on gaining and retaining employee commitment and engagement.

These comments from the CIPD recognise that trends we have referred to in the text about the increasing dominance of the HRM paradigm of people management, combined with the simultaneous decline of traditional collective employee relations, have brought about a new form of employee relations in many sectors of the modern economy. One of the the key components of this new employee relations is 'employee engagement'.

HRM AND EMPLOYEE ENGAGEMENT

'Employee engagement' is a term now widely used in HRM literature to encapsulate management's attempts to motivate staff and focus their commitment to the organisation. The CIPD defines it (CIPD, 2007a) as follows:

> So what is employee engagement? It can be seen as a combination of commitment to the organisation and its values plus a willingness to help out colleagues (organisational citizenship). It goes beyond job satisfaction and is not simply motivation. Engagement is something the employee has to offer: it cannot be 'required' as part of the employment contract.

> Employers want engaged employees because they deliver improved business performance.

The idea is to encourage employees to choose to exercise 'discretionary behaviour' and exceed the literal requirements of their contracts of employment. Clearly, there are links to the psychological contract, which we touched on in Chapter 1. The idea of the 'employer brand' is also relevant here. A strong employer brand will help in attracting and retaining employees, and engaged employees will help promote the brand and protect it from being damaged by poor levels of service or product quality.

We might say that engagement puts the 'commitment' into high-commitment work practices.

The Institute of Employment Studies (IES) concluded that from the employees' point of view the main driver of engagement is a sense of feeling valued and involved, which comes from (Robinson *et al*, 2004):

- involvement in decision-making – having opportunities to feed views 'upwards'
- freedom to voice ideas, to which managers listen

- feeling enabled to perform well

- having opportunities to develop the job

- feeling that the organisation is concerned for employees' health and well-being.

According to the CIPD, engagement can result when an employee has job autonomy, support and coaching, feedback, opportunities to learn and develop, task variety and responsibility. The CIPD recommends regular attitude surveys of employees on the drivers of engagement. It warns (CIPD 2007a), however, that:

> Engagement levels are influenced by employees' personal characteristics: a minority of employees are likely to resist becoming engaged in their work.

EMPLOYEE VOICE

Employee voice is an employee relations concept that is closely linked to and underpins engagement. It comprises two-way initiatives which directly involve employees in exchanging information with managers, replacing or supplementing traditional, indirect means of communication such as joint consultation. It seeks to promote engagement and higher performance at work.

The mechanisms that provide employee voice can be classed as 'upward problem-solving' and 'representative participation' (CIPD, 2007b).

Upward problem-solving techniques are initiated by management and operate directly between managers and employees rather than through employee representatives. Such techniques include:

- electronic media, such as email, to spread and share information

- two-way face-to-face communications between managers and employees – for example, by regular meetings every few weeks

- suggestion schemes, under which employees put ideas to management, who then reward those whose ideas are implemented

- attitude surveys, to measure staff satisfaction with particular aspects of work

- project teams, which are groups of employees brought together to discuss practical work issues such as quality or work organisation.

Representative participation refers to schemes in which employee representatives meet managers on a regular basis, and range from partnership schemes to some 'traditional' employee relations vehicles such as European Works Councils, joint consultation and collective representation (which may be – but which is not necessarily – trade union representation).

These are the main mechanisms of employee voice. All these mechanisms are formal. But informal mechanisms – in effect, simply having a word about a problem to a manager who listens and takes action if necessary – can be a very effective form of voice. Informal mechanisms may be relatively more important in smaller organisations where fewer formal structures are needed.

Employee engagement in action

Engaged staff are vital for performance at B&Q and First Direct

'Employee engagement is a lead measure of business performance, with around 25% of employees in a typical organisation actively disengaged,' said Martyn Phillips, HR director for B&Q. 'As such, firms can be paying millions of pounds in salaries and bonuses to people who are actively destroying value in their businesses,' he warned. He added that an alarming number of leaders neither understand nor believe in engagement.

'There is a 100% correlation between non-believing and crap leadership,' said Phillips.

In 2005, after an 8% fall in sales, Phillips headed a drive to raise engagement at B&Q, making all managers – including the board – accountable for their team's engagement. Everyone was measured on their performance as a leader or manager, and the results published.

'You could be a high-performer in your particular area, but if you didn't reach a certain engagement score we were tough,' recalled Phillips. 'If you don't get good engagement scores, you shouldn't get a good pay award, and if you fail repeatedly, then you should probably leave.' He added that engagement should go up, not down, in periods of change. 'Using change as an excuse for low engagement is not acceptable. During difficult times you should work harder to help people through.'

Jane Hanson, HR director at First Direct, said she believed that staff engagement was the key factor in the recent success of the bank, which has seen profits grow by 30% in five years. But the factors that kept staff engaged were sometimes surprising.

'Research showed that what mattered most to our people was things such as having fun at work, making good friendships, our brand identity and values, and the way we support families,' said Hanson.

Its benefits include concierge services, an on-site crèche and flexible working options – but perhaps most importantly, lots of opportunities to have fun.

'We find every reason we can to celebrate, from weddings and births to customer compliments,' said Hanson.

Source: *People Management,* 19 September 2007

New employee relations in action

Employee relations at Dell

Dell is a US company that has grown rapidly since its formation 20 years ago, and currently ranks number 3 on Fortune's Global Most Admired Companies list. It seeks to deliver value to customers through its direct business model, by focusing on the customer experience and taking out cost from the production process.

The company is data-driven. Managers report on the achievement of targets on a daily basis. Its employee relations climate is strongly influenced by its aspiration to be a 'great company and a great place to work' through the adoption of a 'winning culture'.

The focus is on the team and on individual contributions to the team. People/line managers are expected to interact with individuals, and their performance in this area is closely monitored. Both people managers and individual contributors are measured on the way in which they deal with people as well as on their technical proficiency. There's a consistent emphasis on how people do their job, not just what they do, including, for example, support for colleagues and behaving ethically.

The company makes a conscious effort to recruit people who will have a good 'fit' with its values – people who are open, direct and who focus on getting the job done rather than engaging in office politics. The company runs a leadership programme each year, which in 2005 is focusing on personal development planning.

Employee engagement is driven by the relationship between individuals and their manager. The expectations of people managers are clearly defined:

- Set a performance plan.
- Work in each team on individual development plans.
- Undertake mid-year review.
- Undertake end-year review.
- Undertake monthly review with each individual (30 minutes to 1 hour).
- Give feedback to improve performance.

Dell measures people managers' compliance with their performance management targets, tracking what has been done at each stage. In addition, senior managers are expected to take regular opportunities to engage with more junior staff, for example, at 'brown bag' lunches with different groups, or while visiting operations in other countries, to help embed a common culture.

Other methods of encouraging dialogue include quarterly results meetings across the business at which senior managers take questions. 'Tell Dell' surveys every six months cover core areas suggested by statements such as 'Management is doing a good job positioning the company to win in the marketplace,' 'My manager is effective at managing people,' 'I receive ongoing feedback that helps me to improve my performance,' 'My manager sets a good example of ethical business behaviour,' 'I would recommend Dell as a great place to work,' etc. The surveys provide a broad measure of employee engagement.

The data is analysed to identify trends. Managers are then tasked with sharing their results with their teams and developing team action plans to address issues and drive improvements.

Source: extract from CIPD (2005)

CASE STUDY

New employee relations in action

Employee relations at ITV

The company's approach to employee relations is based on engaging with its employees. It does this by a combination of methods: collective bargaining, consultation with elected employee representatives, and direct engagement with individuals. Engagement is regarded as being critical to the success of the company, which is developing a balanced scorecard containing different measures of engagement.

ITV uses a wide range of direct communication methods to engage with individuals. ITV's intranet, known as the Watercooler, provides a daily online update on news affecting ITV, and there's a weekly Watercooler for employees who are not online. Other methods of communication include the *60-Second Update* – produced monthly by central communications and setting out what's going on in the business – individual development reviews, briefing meetings, workshops and using individual relationships with line managers. The effectiveness of the process is monitored through employee opinion surveys.

The company also engages in collective consultations through elected representatives because unions represent only 15% of employees and the employer wants feedback from the whole workforce. ITV needs to consult employees frequently because of the scale of change within the organisation. It has 15 communication/consultation groups centred on different businesses/locations.

ITV uses collective bargaining as a means of securing employee agreement on new working practices. It believes that collective relationships deliver significant change management benefits to the company and help to reassure employees that their interests are being respected. However, they rarely deliver engagement, which is built on the role of line managers, HR policies and effective employee communications.

The distinction between negotiation and consultation can be quite subtle. In practice, the company uses a similar approach in dealing with recognised unions (collective bargaining) and elected employee representatives (consultation): management sets out its proposals, it takes account of the response, and it decides what action to take.

Language is important. It's simply impolite to say, 'We're not here to negotiate.' Management's line is, 'We'll listen to everybody.' Negotiations can lead to industrial action if they break down, but this is less likely with the process of consultation. However, the critical issue is the same: are employees willing to support what you're proposing?

Communications with recognised trade unions:

15% workforce in membership; 50% coverage for collective bargaining purposes.

Communications with democratically elected employee representatives:

15 different communication groups; 250 directly elected employee representatives; frequent use of twin-track consultation.

Watercooler: *60-Second Updates*; management cascade; surveys; engagement in change projects.

This case, also extracted from CIPD (2005), is an example of a company which retains some aspects of traditional employee relations while simultaneously embracing the new employee relations.

KEY ISSUES IN EMPLOYEE RELATIONS

Some degree of conflict occurs in all organisations whenever the objectives or interests of management and employees fail to coincide. The issue for managers is really one of how conflict is managed rather than how it can be eliminated. Organisations try to manage conflict at the level of the individual and the small group by means of grievance and disciplinary procedures, and at the collective level with employee relations systems and agreements. Negotiation can be seen as a process for resolving conflict between two parties whereby both modify their demands to achieve a mutually acceptable compromise. Within any formal framework, informal employee relations processes are taking place continuously. Traditional collective employee relations has been in decline for nearly a generation. It remains important in some sectors, especially the public sector, but for many parts of the modern economy there is a new employee relations dealing with a much more diverse, individualised workforce. HRM initiatives such as direct communications and employee engagement have nearly eclipsed traditional collective employee relations.

CHAPTER 7

Rewarding people: the management of rewards and performance

INTRODUCTION

Rewards, both financial and other, are of obvious importance to employees and employers. One of the central changes that HRM has brought about in management thinking is that it is no longer enough for employers to think in terms of the old common-law principle of 'a fair day's pay for a fair day's work'. Employee commitment and motivation are so important in today's competitive knowledge-based world that rewards have to be actively managed to secure the maximum utilisation of human assets, and to attract, motivate and retain core employees. Reward management seeks also to encourage skills development and to reinforce both organisational culture and business strategy.

LEARNING OUTCOMES

On completion of this chapter you should:

- understand the importance of pay in HRM
- appreciate the significance of perceptions of fairness in rewards
- have an appreciation of the main types of payment systems including performance-related pay
- understand the importance of fringe benefits
- understand the concepts of pay for competence or skills
- have an appreciation of the 'cafeteria' approach to rewards
- understand the principles of job evaluation and why it is still important
- understand the principles of performance management.

One of the most significant changes in reward management in the UK in the last 20 years has been the extension of performance-related pay beyond the shop floor to white-collar and professional staff, who traditionally were paid straightforward salaries. Another profound change has been the emergence of performance management, which is often, but not necessarily, linked to rewards, and again directed at non-managerial as well as managerial groups.

Both employees and employers are always concerned about issues of reward and performance. In respect of rewards, employees are most concerned about perceived fairness. Employers seek control and minimisation of costs combined with the capacity to offer attractive packages to core staff. These objectives are not incompatible with an HRM viewpoint from management: performance-related pay, at least in principle, should allow reward and motivation for the employee and cost control at the same time. However, there is no perfect reward system for all situations and no payment system can continue to operate satisfactorily indefinitely.

This chapter reviews some traditional and more contemporary pay systems and discusses fringe benefits and 'cafeteria' systems. Job evaluation and its continuing importance in the context of equal pay are considered. Finally, performance management is examined.

REFLECTIVE ACTIVITY

How do you think the following people should be rewarded?

a) casual agricultural workers employed seasonally to pick fruit

b) skilled electricians employed on maintenance duties in a power station

c) university lecturers

Note your answers down now. After reading the chapter, look at the next Reflective Activity, which features the same categories of people, and answer the questions.

MONEY MATTERS

Despite some interpretations of motivation theory which seem to play down money as a motivating factor at work, most organisations behave as if they believe that money certainly does motivate people. Even Frederick Herzberg – usually viewed as the leading advocate of the view that money is not a motivator – is reported as having admitted that 'It sure as hell helps me sort out my priorities!' (Child, 1984; p.188). Most people appear to be interested in making money if they have the opportunity to do so. This would seem to apply just as much to those who are fortunate enough to have jobs which are already high in financial and intrinsic rewards as to those who face genuine hardship. For example, hospital consultants and dentists working for the NHS in the UK are often keen to increase their earnings by taking private patients, and the remuneration of top executives in industry and commerce regularly causes scandals in both the USA and the UK because many seem to reward themselves excessively. Pay and fringe benefits remain central features in contracts of employment and are always prominent issues in collective bargaining.

The value that individuals put on pay compared to other rewards can vary according to personal circumstances over which management have no control. An employee's domestic situation may dictate the extent to which he or she would be willing to trade pay off against other benefits, for example.

Pay is expressed in monetary terms which make it easy to calculate. This gives a clear scale of measurement and a link to measures of performance or output. It also means that it can be easily costed.

FAIRNESS

Any pay system will fail if it is perceived to be unfair by the employees. Fairness of pay is a comparative concept, not an absolute one, and it may vary from society to society, industry to industry and workplace to workplace. Convention seems to be the usual basis for accepting the fairness of a pay differential, and so changes in the status quo always provoke anxieties about unfairness (Wootton, 1955; cited in Brown and Walsh, 1994).

Collective bargaining, by which management and trade unions jointly agree pay rates, usually reinforces the perception of fairness because the use of traditional comparisons provides both employers and trade unions with a basis that is seen to be reasonable.

TYPES OF PAYMENT SYSTEM

Payment systems may be classified initially as

- payment by time schemes, in which the amount of pay awarded is principally determined by the time spent at work – eg an hourly rate or a monthly salary

or

- performance-related pay (PRP) or 'incentive pay schemes', in which some element of the total pay is variable and depends on some assessment or measure of the employee's performance. There are two main types of PRP:
  - payment by results (PBR), in which the variable element is determined by some objective measure of the work done or its value.

– merit-based systems in which the variable element is related to an assessment of overall job performance by a supervisor or manager.

The 2004 WERS survey found that 40 % of UK workplaces had incentive pay schemes (Kersley *et al*, 2006). These were more popular in the private sector than in the public, and there were significant variations from industry to industry. For example, 82% of workplaces in the financial services sector used incentive pay schemes. Incentive schemes were more common generally where product market competition was higher (*ibid.*, p190). There appears to be a rising trend: PRP schemes were much more likely to be used in the UK in 2004 than in 1998.

PAYMENT BY TIME

This means a fixed rate per hour, per shift or per week (all usually termed 'wages') or per month, per quarter or per year (all termed 'salary'). The simplicity of the time rate system is usually considered to be its main virtue. However, this simplicity is often compromised in practice by additional payments, 'grade drift' and proliferation of grades (Brown and Walsh, 1994).

Additional payments are normally linked to some extra factor concerning the work or employment, such as length of service, dirty working conditions, unusual difficulty of work, responsibility for training others, working away from home, etc. However fair they may be, additional payments complicate the simple time rate system and, at an extreme, risk undermining general perceptions of fairness if the system becomes too opaque to employees. Each complication also adds to the administrative costs of running the system.

'Grade drift' is the tendency for individual job grades to 'drift' with time into the higher levels of a grading structure, usually as a result of appeals for regrading or the consolidation of additional payments or bonuses into regular pay. Over time grade drift can add significantly to total pay costs without guaranteeing any corresponding increases in performance. Good job evaluation procedures should reduce this problem, but it is difficult to eliminate it altogether.

New job grades with marginally higher pay rates are often introduced to encourage employees to accept new work practices, new technology or new allocations of work and responsibility. The cumulative effect of such decisions again complicates the time rate system.

PERFORMANCE-RELATED PAY (OR INCENTIVE PAY)

With performance-related pay, remuneration becomes more complex and expensive to administer.

Performance-related pay: payment by results

In payment by results (PBR) systems, part of the employee's pay (usually between 10% and 20%) is variable and is dependent on the output of the individual or the individual's group. The purpose is to give an incentive for the employee to work harder, or more efficiently. PBR systems of some sort have been used since industrial work began and simple piecework schemes (see below) have certainly been used for very much longer (Brown and Walsh, 1994).

For individual PBR systems there are two main types:

- piecework
- incentive bonus schemes.

In *piecework*, the employee is paid a standard price for each piece or unit of output. Pure piecework schemes are rare. Most include a time rate element, a fall-back rate guaranteeing a minimum weekly wage, and some payment for interruptions to work which are not the fault of the employee.

In *incentive bonus schemes* the employee is paid a basic time rate with a standard time set for completing the job. A bonus is paid either for time saved against standard time for the task or for the extra production obtained in the time allowed.

At their best incentive bonus scheme systems give an inexpensive, popular and effective way of maintaining effort. However, at their worst they can have very damaging effects on industrial relations.

Because the purpose of the incentive bonus scheme is to encourage and reward effort, it is necessary to have some way of linking the rate of work to the level of output, and traditionally this has been done by using Work Study techniques. Though often unpopular with employees and trade unions, Work Study has two main justifications (Brown and Walsh, 1994):

- In the right circumstances it can be sufficiently accurate for its purpose in serving as the basis for satisfactory incentive schemes.
- Sometimes there is no other practical way of predicting levels of output, and so it is often necessary to use Work Study for production engineering and cost-control purposes, quite apart from the matter of pay.

Incentive bonus schemes sometimes fail for either of two reasons:

- Social pressure among the workers may act to reduce individual performance to the extent that the scheme so longer provides an incentive and enhanced performance is not achieved.

- In any incentive bonus scheme management must maintain its obligations to monitor performance. Failure to do so is a common reason for the failure of schemes.

Individual incentive bonus schemes are most suitable in jobs with a high manual content and repetitive short-cycle operations, and where product demand – and therefore output – is not subject to sudden changes.

Group incentive bonus schemes can be operated when the production process is such that it is difficult to attribute job performance or output to individuals. Group schemes can also be a way of encouraging team-work and co-operation. The bonus is earned on the performance of the whole group and allocated to each individual according to a predetermined formula.

Performance-related pay: merit-based pay

Although the traditional payment systems of payment by time and PBR continue to be used, in recent years an increasing number of private and public organisations have been using some form of merit-based performance-related pay for key employees. As we noted above, in merit-based systems the variable element is related to an assessment of overall job performance, and the detailed work measurement used in incentive bonus schemes is not applicable. Merit-based pay is therefore much simpler to operate than incentive bonus schemes and is suitable for a very much wider range of jobs.

Some general conditions have been established as being necessary for successful merit-based pay. These include:

- Employees must be able to influence work performance or output.
- The reward should be obtained as soon as possible after the accomplishment that generated it, and this connection should be clearly perceived by the employees.
- Targets and standards of performance required must be clearly understood.
- It must be possible to measure work performance or output in a way that is perceived to be both valid and reliable.
- The formulae used to calculated bonuses must be clearly defined and be understood by the employees.

For obvious reasons, merit-based pay works best, and is most easily accepted by employees, in performance-oriented and entrepreneurial organisational cultures.

Profit-sharing

In profit-sharing schemes employees receive bonus payments or share issues related to the firm's profits. It is argued that share ownership provides employees with a stake in the company with beneficial effects on motivation and commitment. Of course, problems may arise when a firm's profits are low or negative, particularly if workers' expectations have been raised.

Gain-sharing

Gain-sharing schemes are an attempt to involve management, unions and employees jointly in improving a company's productivity and profitability through agreed methods including, for example, better utilisation of labour, materials and energy. Resulting gains are shared between the company's employees according to a predetermined formula. These schemes are much more common in the USA than in the UK.

Pay for skills or competence

Skills-based pay is a payment system in which pay is linked to the level of skills used in the job and/or the acquisition of new skills which are recognised by the organisation as useful (Armstrong and Murlis, 1998).

Typical features of a skills-based pay system are:

- They are based on defined, recognised blocks or modules of skills.
- The successful acquisition of skills blocks gives the worker an increment to basic pay.
- The organisation may dictate the order in which the skills must be attained so that progression and development can be effectively managed.
- The training and acquisition of skills must be certified by the organisation and may require to be accredited by a reputable independent agency.

A similar approach can be taken to the acquisition of individual competences within an organisationally defined competency framework.

Skills- and competence-based systems can be bureaucratic to administer and expensive to introduce and maintain.

NON-PAY BENEFITS

'Non-pay benefits', which are also called 'fringe benefits' or 'employee benefits', are elements of remuneration that are additional to cash pay.

The main objectives of offering employees non-pay benefits are:

- to ensure that a competitive total remuneration package is provided to attract, retain and motivate staff, particularly core staff

- to increase the employee's commitment to the organisation
- to take advantage of tax-efficient methods of rewarding employees (ie where the employer can reduce its tax liability by offering some benefit instead of cash).

We can divide non-pay benefits into two broad classes: direct and indirect. Direct non-pay benefits can be costed exactly in monetary terms and, in principle at least, cash could be offered in place of any particular benefit without changing the monetary value of the total rewards package for the individual concerned.

Indirect benefits cannot be readily equated to exact financial measures. They make the organisation a more attractive place to work and can help to reinforce the psychological contract. They include status, power, recognition of achievement, training opportunities, career progression, good working conditions, recognition of the need to balance work and family responsibilities, and flexibility.

PRINCIPAL TYPES OF DIRECT NON-PAY BENEFITS

The main types of direct non-pay benefits include the following (Armstrong and Murlis, 1998):

- *pension schemes*, which are usually regarded by employees as the most important employee benefit
- *benefits relating to personal security*, which include sick pay and maternity pay and benefits which exceed the statutory level that employers are legally obliged to provide, benefits to partners and families following death in service, personal accident insurance cover, medical insurance, health screening, permanent health insurance (long-term disability cover), business travel insurance, and career counselling
- *benefits relating to financial assistance*, which include company loans, season tickets for travelling to and from work, assistance with house purchase (eg mortgages at rates more generous than market rates), relocation assistance, discounts, and fees to professional bodies
- *benefits relating to personal needs*: holidays, compassionate leave, career breaks, counselling, fitness and recreational facilities
- *other direct benefits* might include a company car and petrol, subsidised meals, clothing allowance, telephone costs and credit card facilities.

PUTTING IT ALL TOGETHER: THE 'CAFETERIA' APPROACH TO MANAGING REWARDS

This allows employees a degree of choice in their total remuneration package – for example, by permitting them to take fewer fringe benefits and more pay, or vice versa. The total overall value of their compensation remains the same whatever choices they make. This allows individuals to tailor their rewards to their particular needs and, importantly, allows them to alter their rewards as their needs change. For example, a working mother might choose to reduce her superannuation contributions in favour of more take-home pay for a number of years, whereas a middle-aged employee might wish to increase his superannuation payment to improve his eventual retirement package.

Typically, a cafeteria system features a core package of benefits topped up by a percentage of gross pay available for additional components.

Armstrong and Murlis (1998) described the advantages and disadvantages of the cafetaria approach.

The principle advantage of cafeteria systems are:

- employee satisfaction
- the communication of the real costs of benefits to employees and employers
- the identification of the popularity of various benefits.

The disadvantages are:

- the complexity of costing out non-pay benefits
- potentially greater administrative costs
- potentially considerable tax complications for employees.

JOB EVALUATION

As Rosabeth Moss Kanter has put it, the basis for determining pay is changing 'from position to performance, from status to contribution' (Kanter, 1988).

This would seem to be inevitable for organisations operating in increasingly uncertain and competitive markets. In fact, we should expect employees' pay to be determined by the market worth of their skills, knowledge and experience, and their actual performance in the job. Increasingly, these factors are becoming important in the UK, but the fact remains that many employers feel the need for some method of establishing the relative internal value of jobs. There are two main reasons for this (Armstrong and Murlis, 1994; IDS 1992):

- If a hierarchy of jobs can be determined in as independent and objective a manner as possible, decisions about actual grades – and so, pay rates – should be more consistent and defensible.
- In many countries equal-value pay legislation decrees that women are entitled to equal pay with men (and vice versa) where the work is of equal value in terms of

demands made in areas such as effort, skill and decisions. In Britain the case of *Bromley v H&J Quick Ltd* (1988, IRLR 249 CA) established that a job evaluation scheme can only provide a defence in an equal-value claim if it is analytical in nature. This implies that it should be a points scheme based on factor comparisons (see below). So employers who feel that they may be vulnerable to equal-value claims are easily persuaded that such schemes are essential.

THE JOB EVALUATION PROCESS

In this text we are for the reasons given above concerned only with analytical job evaluation schemes. Such schemes are complex and expensive to install and maintain, and they can give a misleading impression of objective accuracy, but as indicated earlier they are the only type of job evaluation scheme that can provide a defence in equal-value cases. We should note, however, that critics argue that important skills such as judgement and initiative cannot be properly evaluated by analytical means and that the contribution of 'knowledge-workers' cannot be validly or assessed by such approaches (IDS, 1992).

There are some general points relevant to any attempt at job evaluation:

- Job evaluation is a comparative process that determines grades but not actual rates of pay, which must be established by some other mechanism.
- Job evaluation is normally conducted by a panel on the basis of information obtained by means of job analysis.
- It is a systematic but not infallible process.
- It is the job, not the performance, of any particular job-holder that is evaluated.

In *points-factor job evaluation schemes* an analytical technique is used in which jobs are compared in terms of a number of separate characteristics or 'factors' such as skills, knowledge, decision-making, responsibility, and so forth. It is assumed that all factors are present in most if not all of the jobs being evalauted. Each factor is weighted to reflect its relative importance, and is allocated a range of points. Evaluation is based on an analysis of the job in terms of the factors. Decisions are made on the level at which the factor applies to the job; the points for each factor are added to give a total points score.

See the Scottish Softronics case study at the end of the chapter.

PERFORMANCE MANAGEMENT

Management is essentially concerned with performance: this has always been true, and the aim of management studies in all disciplines has ultimately always been to help managers harness employees' performance for the good of the organisation as a whole.

As we saw in Chapter 1, the 2004 Workplace Employee Relations Survey found that the use of performance appraisals had increased in the UK, 78% of managers in workplaces reporting that performance appraisals were undertaken. Two thirds (65%) of all workplaces conducted regular appraisals for most (60% or more) non-managerial employees (48% in 1998). Although, as we will see, there is more to performance management than just appraisal, the 2004 Survey provides strong empirical evidence that performance management is in widespread and increasing use in the UK.

Performance management has been defined as 'a means of getting better results from the organisation, teams and individuals by understanding and managing performance within an agreed framework of planned goals, objectives and standards' (Armstrong and Murlis, 1994).

So performance management is a systematic approach to management which uses goals, measurement, feedback and recognition as the means of motivating people to achieve. It is a more comprehensive concept than simply performance-related pay or performance appraisal – although the latter is certainly an essential component of any performance management system – giving explicit reference to the organisation's mission, vision and values. Performance management in this sense can be seen as almost a management philosophy rather than just a set of techniques.

A TYPICAL PERFORMANCE MANAGEMENT AGREEMENT

- It defines a performance agreement between individual and manager, setting out objectives but also development needs.

- Performance is to be continually monitored and assessed: high performance is reinforced with praise, recognition and the opportunity to take on more responsible work; low performance is responded to by means of coaching and counselling. In both cases management response is immediate rather than being deferred.

- Provision is made for the regular formal review of performance against objectives, and the setting of any new performance agreement.

PERFORMANCE MANAGEMENT AND PERFORMANCE-RELATED PAY

Performance-related pay is a natural adjunct to a performance management system that can reinforce performance. However, some organisations seem to have introduced performance management without PRP (Armstrong and Murlis, 1994).

REFLECTIVE ACTIVITY

Outline a pay-for-performance reward system for:

a) casual agricultural workers employed seasonally to pick fruit

b) skilled electricians employed on maintenance duties in a power station

c) university lecturers.

ACTIVITY ANSWER GUIDANCE

We might recommend that for (a) the seasonal agricultural workers, a simple piece-rate system by weight of fruit gathered (provided quality was maintained – eg by means of inspection at the point of weighing) might be both the most motivating and fairest in terms of workers' perceptions. It would also give the employer tightest control of pay costs.

The situation is more difficult for both (b) and (c). In both cases clear criteria for job performance would have to be established – eg for (b) the electricians, the number of inspections carried out in a given period and/or the average number of breakdowns/emergencies dealt with in a representative period; for (c) the lecturers, some carefully defined combination of teaching, research and administration. In these cases additional objectives might be agreed, opening up the possibility of additional pay for skills/competence.

KEY ISSUES IN REWARD MANAGEMENT

Rewards have to be actively managed to secure the maximum utilisation of human assets, and to attract, motivate and retain core employees.

Despite some interpretations of motivational theory, we cannot ignore the importance of money in rewards packages. Payment systems may be based on time, or may be variable where an element of total pay is dependent on some measure of output or an assessment of overall performance.

A 'cafeteria' system of rewards allows employees, within limits, the flexibility to decide the particular make-up of their total rewards package and gives them scope to alter this as their personal needs and requirements change. This can be very attractive to core employees – but such schemes are administratively complex.

Performance management is really a management philosophy rather than just a set of techniques. It is a more comprehensive concept than simply performance-related pay or performance appraisal, and uses goals, measurement, feedback and recognition as the means of motivating people to achieve.

Job evaluation is some ways a bureaucratic throwback to the days of traditional personnel management, but since only an analytical job evaluation scheme can provide an employer with a legal defence in equal pay cases at tribunals, its importance is actually growing in the twenty-first century.

Job evaluation in action

Scottish Softronics plc

Background information

Scottish Softronics is a small high-technology engineering firm located in a greenfield site in the Scottish Central Belt which specialises in providing complex electronic/mechanical engineering products that interface with state-of-the-art software engineering. Its major clients are leading software producers in the financial services industry. It has grown in size rapidly in the last few years after creating a number of new product lines. The firm prides Itself on its reputation for being a well-managed, technologically competent, high-quality supplier. The firm recently won Its first Queen's Award for Exports. Trade unions are not recognised by the firm, but management acknowledge the importance of employee relations and there is a staff association which employees are encouraged to join and with which management regularly consult over pay and main conditions of employment.

Concerns about equal pay issues in the industry combined with more general worries that the pay/grading structure is becoming unwieldy as a result of rapid growth and fast-changing work practices have prompted the managing director to ask the human resources director to brief him on the advisability of using job evaluation in the firm.

The HR director responded with a confidential memorandum the contents of which may be summarised as follows.

Job evaluation (JE) is widely used in British industry, partly – as the MD perceived – to protect employers against equal-value claims from employees at tribunals.

Job evaluation has a tendency to become bureaucratic and to encourage a multiplicity of rigid grades. Such developments would not be helpful to Scottish Softronics, which has invested considerable time, effort and expense in introducing flexible work practices on the shop floor and lower management. If JE is to be introduced, every effort should be made to avoid these potential difficulties.

Job evaluation should not be used to set the actual pay rates far each grade, but rather to set the general structure.

Scottish Softronics has recently introduced performance-related pay (PRP) for all employees. The company would have to ensure that any JE scheme it adopted would not interfere with PRP. The HR director added that through his membership of the Chartered Institute of Personnel and Development he was acquainted with several organisations which shared Scottish Softronics' general business philosophy and which appeared to be able to combine JE and PRP successfully. The HR director's recommendation was that JE should be adopted.

If this was accepted, a small steering committee should be formed, consisting of seven working members, four from management and three nominated from the staff association. The HR director would chair the committee and report to the MD on progress.

The MD responded that the board accepted the HR director's recommendation, and he instructed the director to proceed.

The job evaluation exercise

Scottish Softronics employs approximately 400 people, of whom just over 300 are shopfloor staff.

At the first meeting of the steering committee it was agreed that there should be no more than four general grades: associate (ie shopfloor), senior associate, administration, and management. An inspection of the payroll and personnel records revealed that there were something like 80 different jobs. The HR director indicated that although he would expect to see that number reduced, he was not too concerned about job titles or the number of jobs in total so long as the proposed system of four grades could be made to work.

At two further meetings of the committee, ten existing jobs were selected as benchmarks. A list of ten factors was drawn up: skill, effort, job complexity, responsibility, diplomacy, job conditions, supervision received, contact, dexterity, training.

Consider the ten factors listed above.

Would you make any changes to them?

Would you weight any of them – and if you would, how?

Scottish Softronics: resolution and outcomes

CASE STUDY

The original factors were provisionally weighted in points terms. The benchmark jobs were then analysed and scored by the committee. From this process it was concluded that some factors overlapped and others were hard to define clearly. The factors were redesigned working on the basis of four generic factors: skill, effort, responsibility, and job conditions. The factors were then re-weighted.

The benchmark jobs were then re-evaluated. The committee agreed that the results gave an acceptable grading structure and that the process should be applied to the remaining jobs in the firm.

Generic factors	Job factors	Points range	Weighting
SKILL	Education	1–5	3
	Experience	1–5	3
	Initiative	1–5	3
EFFORT	Physical demands	1–5	1
	Mental demands	1–5	3
RESPONSIBILITY	Process/equipment demands	1–5	1
	Material/product demands	1–5	1
	Responsibility for the work of others	1–5	3
	Responsibility for the safety of others	1–5	3
JOB CONDITIONS	Working conditions	1–5	1
	Unavoidable hazards	1–5	2

REFLECTIVE ACTIVITY

1 **Outline a performance management and rewards scheme package for schoolteachers.**

2 **Now read the extract from *People Management* 'A lesson in how not to' below, and answer the questions afterwards.**

A lesson in how not to

The HR profession can learn much from the way in which ministers have mishandled performance-related pay in schools, says Michael Armstrong, an independent consultant and author.

The Government is pursuing policies that are designed to raise educational standards, but it has had a bumpy ride in trying to support this laudable mission by introducing performance-related pay into schools. This culminated in an ignominious defeat in the courts where, as the result of an action brought by the National Union of Teachers, the Department for Education and Employment was judged to have acted unconstitutionally in forcing through its proposals.

Before that, there had been a huge negative reaction to the PRP concept not only from the teaching unions but also from informed academics such as David Guest, now at Kings Colleg, London, and Ray Richardson of the London School of Economics. Respected management consultants, such as Towers Perrin's Duncan Brown, also criticised the approach.

Education ministers made three major mistakes in introducing the scheme. First, they referred to it as performance-related pay, which was guaranteed to provoke the teachers' hostility. Rightly or wrongly, PRP has had a bad press, especially when it has been applied in the public sector. As far as the teachers were concerned, it implied that they would be rewarded as individuals on the basis of quantified outputs – namely, their pupils' progress. But, as Ray Richardson commented in his report to the NUT, attributing any performance differential to the skill or dedication of an individual teacher is problematic simply because teaching is, to a considerable degree, a collective activity. Successful education, he wrote, 'rests significantly on the contribution of a number of teachers'. In the final version of the payment scheme produced by the DfEE, judgements on eligibility are indeed to be based on competency assessments, following a study by Hay McBer, yet one fifth of the assessment is still related to pupil progress, a feature that the NUT still resists.

The second mistake was to follow blindly in the footsteps of the many private sector companies that have adopted PRP on the doubtful assumption that it will offer a performance incentive. There is no reliable evidence that PRP provides direct motivation and, as John Purcell, Professor of HRM at the University of Bath, pointed out in *PM* ('Pay per view', 3 February 2000), the belief that people need incentives to encourage them to behave in an acceptable way is worrying. Ray Richardson's final comment in his report was that the exercise 'rests on shoddy and disingenuous analysis. It is unlikely to achieve its publicly-stated objectives of materially improving teacher recruitment and morale.'

The third mistake was the failure to consult properly. Initially, opinions were canvassed, but the largely hostile nature of these opinions was ignored. The DfEE then proceeded to force through its proposals. Perhaps the Government has learnt something from the debacle that ensued. It now wants to introduce some form of additional payment for high-calibre teachers in further education, but this time it is doing this in consultation with the Association of Colleges, the sixth-form colleges and the unions on a 'partnership' basis.

What can personnel practitioners learn from this sorry story? The concept that it is right and proper for people to be rewarded according to their contribution is still valid. The alternatives are service-related pay or team rewards. Basing pay on service means that people are rewarded simply for being there, irrespective of their performance. Team pay sounds more attractive, but such a system is difficult to apply, as its low take-up in the private sector indicates.

There are two other lessons. First, the problem of agreeing criteria for teachers' pay is replicated in any PRP scheme. You can pay for performance only if you can measure performance, and it is often difficult to apply appropriate measures that can be used fairly and consistently. When PRP fails, it is often because the assessment process is flawed. Second, it highlights perhaps the main reason for the failure: inadequate consultation with the employees and their representatives, and little or no attempt to involve them in designing the scheme. I hope that the same mistake will not be made in further education.

People Management, 12 October 2000

Would you now modify the scheme you proposed for Question 1?

If you would, how?

CHAPTER 8

HRM and competency

INTRODUCTION

Armstrong (2003; p.147) defined competency-based human resource management as being 'about using the concept of competency and the results of competency analysis to inform and improve the processes of recruitment and selection, employee development and employee reward'. As he noted, the language of competency has dominated much of HR thinking and practice in recent years, largely because it is essentially about individual performance and consequently organisational effectiveness.

LEARNING OUTCOMES

On completion of this chapter you should:

- understand what is meant by management competencies
- be able to describe how the concept of competence developed in management thought
- recognise the differences between work-based and person-based competency statements
- appreciate the idea of meta-competency
- understand the definition of 'personal competency'
- understand the concept of a hierarchy of managerial competencies.

GENERAL DEFINITIONS OF SKILLS AND COMPETENCIES

The *Concise Oxford English Dictionary* defines 'skill' as 'the ability to do something well; expertise or dexterity', deriving through Middle English from the Old Norse *skil*, 'discernment' or 'knowledge'. The same source defines 'competency' as the quality or extent of being 'competent', which in turn is described as 'having the necessary ability or knowledge to do something successfully', from the Latin *competere* in the sense of 'being fit and proper'. It is interesting that there is the basic notion of 'knowledge' in both terms.

Although previous usage of the term 'skill' in management literature often covered what we would now define as 'competence', the latter term is often favoured now. Statements of competence tend to be both fuller in detail and broader in scope than most descriptions of skills, and therefore give more precise meaning. They are also usually more explicitly focused on the achievement of acceptable performance in the job, rather than on mere possession of the capability to perform properly. So, for example, whereas a *skilled* bricklayer will possess the knowledge and ability required to do his or her job properly, in any particular case he or she may not actually work well, for whatever reason – but a *competent* bricklayer not only has the knowledge and ability needed but in fact performs proficiently. This use of the terms 'skill' and 'competency' may seem to be the converse of normal usage: 'skilled' normally suggests a high level of capability whereas 'competent' can imply 'mere competence' – ie the ability to achieve a minimum acceptable standard – but it reflects the managerial imperative for people actually to achieve effective performance and not just to possess the capability to do so.

The Cannon Working Party Report into management education training and development in the UK (1994) gave a general description of the notion of management competency in the following way:

> The term 'competency' is taken to mean the ability to perform effectively functions associated with management in a work-related situation.

SPECIFIC DEFINITIONS OF COMPETENCIES IN THE MANAGEMENT LITERATURE

The term 'competency' first came to widespread managerial attention in the USA following the publication of Richard Boyatzis' study *The Competent Manager* (1982), which followed earlier work by Klemp (1980). Mangham and Silver (1985), explicitly citing Boyatzis, introduced the term to the UK debate on management development, reporting that many UK organisations and managers at that time lacked even the vocabulary to describe or define properly what they meant by 'competent managerial performance'. At around the same time vocational education in the UK was undergoing a revolution in which traditional examinations and tests of work skills were transformed into 'competence-based' awards. This brings us immediately to a key point in our definitions of 'competence'.

Boyatzis described competency as the 'capacity that exists in a person that leads to behaviour that meets the job demands within the parameters of the organisation environment and that in turn brings results'. The UK Training Agency defined 'competence' as 'actions, behaviour or outcome that the person should be able to demonstrate'.

These subtly different definitions actually show that there are two distinct models of competence. The first, following Boyatzis' definition, is what can be termed an 'input model'. That is, it is mainly concerned to define and describe what a competent person brings to the task or job – for example, knowledge or skill, such as the ability to read a balance sheet, or some other attribute such as a personality or character trait, like empathy or hardiness, and so forth. This model is sometimes referred to as 'person-related'. The second, exemplified by the UK Training Agency definition, is an 'output-model' and is predominantly concerned with actual performance – eg undertaking the task of totting up a balance sheet correctly, thus demonstrating that the task can be competently done. This is also described as a 'work-related' model.

In practice the distinction is not always clear-cut, and descriptions of output-based competencies may include, for example, some specified knowledge requirements in addition to the observable behaviours that lead to effective demonstration of the stated tasks. For instance, the CIPD Standards competency framework (see below) is essentially an output-based model but one that also has stated knowledge requirements.

COMPETENCY-BASED HUMAN RESOURCE MANAGEMENT

As noted earlier, the language of competency has dominated much of HR thinking and practice in recent years, largely because it is essentially about individual performance and consequently organisational effectiveness. Although there is often confusion between individual and organisational competencies, these are linked, and another reason for the interest in individual competencies is undoubtedly the importance attached to organisational 'core competencies' (Hamel and Prahalad, 1994). Because these are usually dependent on the organisation's attracting, retaining and motivating key personnel, the HR profession can perhaps be forgiven for jumping on this particular bandwagon.

COMPETENCY FRAMEWORKS

A competency framework is essentially a structured collection of competencies used by an organisation to frame and underpin activities (managerial or non-managerial). Professional bodies also may use competency frameworks to show the requirements for their qualified practitioners. The use of competency frameworks has become an increasingly accepted part of modern HR practice. Rankin (2004) reported that 76% of responding UK companies when surveyed used competency frameworks or were about to introduce them. The use of competency frameworks has also extended to senior levels of the organisation (top and middle management) in addition to clerical, administrative and non-office roles (CIPD, 2007d).

It has been found empirically that employers' competency frameworks typically contain between 10 and 20 basic competencies which relate to a spectrum of roles across the organisation (IDS, 2001). In addition, some organisations have developed role-specific or technical competencies to address the problem that occurs when the basic competencies turn out to be inadequate for particular roles or jobs. More recently, some organisations have established organisational-cultural competencies which seek to reflect the ethos of the company itself, and these are concerned with ensuring that employees work in a way that is consistent with company culture.

Competency frameworks are now widely used to help select, appraise, train and develop staff. For example, in the recruitment process competencies can contribute to the content of job or role profiles, any written or practical tests, and the job interview itself. Banks of potential interview questions can be developed which are directly linked to a role's competencies. Competencies, together with personal objectives or targets, can form the basis of the appraisal systems used by organisations. In this way, employers can measure how staff carry out their work through assessing their performance against personal objectives and the role's required competencies.

The CIPD's 2007 *Learning and Development* survey (CIPD, 2007e) found that the use of competency frameworks was well established in the workplace, 60% of the respondents having a competency framework in place, and of those who hadn't, almost half (48%) intending to introduce one. In those organisations that had a competency framework, on average almost four out of five employees (78%) were included, and 50% of those organisations had a single competency framework across the organisation.

Table 7 shows the subjects included in competency frameworks as reported by respondents (CIPD 2007e; p.19).

The same survey (2007e; p.19) reported the main uses of competency frameworks as in Table 8.

Most competency frameworks (85%) were designed in-house (although often with the help of consultants). A small proportion (8%) used frameworks produced

Table 7 Subjects included in competency frameworks

Skills area	Percentage of respondents
Communication skills	63
People management	59
Team skills	58
Customer service skills	54
Leadership/decision-making	53
Problem-solving skills	50
Technical skills	45
Results-orientation	42
Other	9

Table 8 Main uses of competency frameworks

Main uses	Percentage of respondents
Performance reviews/appraisals	56
Employee effectiveness	47
Organisational effectiveness	44
Training needs analysis	36
Career development	36
Recruitment	28
Customer satisfaction	26
Job design	19
Other	3

Source: CIPD annual Learning and Development Survey Report, 2007

and made available by an external organisation – eg a professional association or government body.

According to the CIPD (2007e), the main benefits of a competency-based system are:

- Employees have a set of objectives to work towards and are clear about how they are expected to perform their jobs.
- The appraisal and recruitment systems are fairer and more open.
- There is a link between organisational and personal objectives.
- Processes are measurable and standardised across organisational and geographical boundaries.

The following criticisms are often made of competency-based systems:

- They can become overly elaborate and bureaucratic.
- They can become out-of-date very quickly due to the fast pace of change in organisations, and it can therefore be expensive and time-consuming to keep them up-to-date.
- Competencies are often based on what good performers have done in the past.
- Competency frameworks can institutionalise discrimination against women and minorities.

PERSONAL MANAGERIAL COMPETENCIES

DEFINITION OF PERSONAL MANAGERIAL COMPETENCIES

Bearing in mind the description of managerial competency given by the Cannon Working Party cited above, for the purposes of the present text we define 'personal managerial competencies' as:

> The competencies that must be mastered by the individual manager rather than being shared among a group or team.

They include both purely self-related competencies, such as time-management, and competences which deal with working with and managing other people, such as team-building. They do not include those competencies which are shared amongst managers and other staff which constitute 'organisational competencies' or 'core competencies' in the sense used by Hamel and Prahalad (1994). Unlike 'core competencies' these personal competencies are very largely independent of the organisation or professional grouping to which the manager belongs: all effective managers should possess them.

A HIERARCHY OF PERSONAL MANAGEMENT COMPETENCIES

There is a logical hierarchy of competencies, in that complex management tasks such as, for example, negotiating, require the application of a combination of less complex competencies. But underlying all management activities there is a small set of what we term here 'meta-competencies'.

There is also a set of competencies that we term 'intermediate competencies', and this includes, for example, interviewing, scheduling the work of others and creating budgets. These competencies lie between the meta-competencies and the competencies exercised in complex management tasks.

The meta-competencies in themselves are not necessary simpler than 'complex' or intermediate ones. For example, we suggest that leadership – one of the most difficult and important management activities – is actually a meta-competence. Leadership is not simpler than, for example, interviewing or bargaining, but the idea of a hierarchy implies that relevant competencies at a 'lower' level in the hierarchy should be acquired before 'higher' ones can be mastered. So, for instance, it might be possible for managers to learn something about how to negotiate or to conduct bargaining without having mastered leadership competencies, but not only would they certainly be less effective all-round managers without leadership competencies, they would also be much less successful at these particular management tasks.

Accordingly, we first identify a relatively small set of 'meta-competencies'. We then specify a set of 'intermediate' or 'basic management' competencies and a set of 'complex management competencies', which, in both cases, require the application of one or more meta-competencies. The basic management competencies are intermediate in nature and complexity so the application of the complex competencies will typically require some use of these competencies in addition to one or more of the meta-competencies.

The meta-competencies are listed in Table 9.

The set of meta-competences described above is not itself 'uni dimensional'; two of the meta-competencies – leadership/influencing and self-awareness/reflection – are in an important sense of a higher order than the others (numeracy, communication, interpersonal competencies, decision-making and organisation and planning) in that

- each has a complex interaction with the others, and
- each has a greater impact on the effective delivery of the other intermediate and complex management competencies.

A hierarchy of competencies is shown in Table 10.

REFLECTION AND COMPETENCIES

The conventional view of professional practice held that professionals operate by applying formally learned specialist or technical knowledge. This was challenged in an influential work by Schön (1983; 1987). He argued that this was not actually the way that professionals usually solved problems. Rather they used a form of tacit knowledge linked to specific activities, which he termed 'knowledge-in-action'. They also developed what he called 'repertoires' of solutions and learned how to reinterpret difficult problems so that they were more easily solved by the

Table 9 The meta-comepetencies

Meta-competencies	comprising
Basic business numeracy	Handing basic statistics Interpreting financial statements
Communication	Writing competencies Speaking competencies Presentation competencies (including using IT)
Interpersonal competencies	Listening skill Understanding non-verbal communication (NVC) Obtaining rapport Eliciting responses from others
Decision-making	Identifying problems Generating and evaluating alternatives Making decisions Implementing decisions
Organising and planning	Setting goals and objectives Prioritising activities Scheduling work and project planning Monitoring and reporting
Leadership and influencing	Actioning Managing work Motivating Managing performance Supporting
Self-awareness/reflection	Skills of reflection – eg reflective writing Learning skills Constructing and maintaining a personal development plan (PDP)

use of these repertoires. Schön argued that for initial development, for day-to-day practice and for continuous improvement, 'reflection' was the crucial competence. He distinguished between two types of reflection: 'reflection-in-action', which took place during the event, and 'reflection-about-action', which took place after the activity. Schön's work has been highly influential and has led directly to the concept of the 'reflective practitioner' or 'reflective professional' which has become central to the continuing development programmes of many professional bodies including management ones (the CIPD, for example).

Cheetham and Chivers (1996, 1998) proposed a model for professionals which integrated reflection and competency frameworks. The model of personal competencies in this text draws on the Cheetham and Chivers model – but one

Table 10 A hierarchy of competencies

Meta-competencies	Examples of intermediate management competencies	Examples of complex management competencies
Basic business numeracy Communication Interpersonal competencies Decision-making Organising and planning Leadership and influencing Self-awareness/reflection	Gathering and analysing data Creating budgets for resources Presentation competencies (formal, high-level) Formal report-writing Scheduling work of others Supervising work of others Handling (local) discipline Handling (local) grievances Interviewing Identifying own training and development needs Time management Stress management	Team-building Team-leading/-motivating Managing resources Bargaining Negotiating Dispute resolution Coaching Developing others Self-development

fundamental difference is that *leadership* is a meta-competence within this model but is absent from the Cheetham and Chivers one.

The process of reflection links (i) professional competence to the meta-competencies and also (ii) the professional competencies to each of the knowledge/cognitive, functional, personal/behavioural and values/ethical levels of competence.

Thus possession and mastery of the meta-competencies first drives the acquisition of professional or managerial competence via the development of knowledge/cognitive, functional, personal/behavioural and values/ethical levels of competence. But thereafter continuous loops of reflective learning refine these levels of competence to continually improve the quality and application of professional/managerial competence.

Henderson and Dowling (2008) developed a learning process model for the development of managerial competencies (Table 11).

ORGANISING THE LEARNING PROCESS FOR COMPETENCY DEVELOPMENT

Whetton and Cameron (1991) developed an approach to teaching management skills based on social learning theory (Bandura, 1977; Davis and Luthans, 1980) which combined conceptual knowledge with opportunities to practise and apply behaviour. Their original learning model consisted of four steps:

1 The presentation of behavioural principles or action guidelines, generally using traditional instruction methods

2 Demonstration of the principles by means of cases, films, scripts or incidents

3 Opportunities to practise the principles through role-plays or exercises

4 Feedback on performance from peers, instructors or experts.

These authors added a fifth, pre-assessment stage to the model, since they found from experience that in order to benefit from the model individuals must be aware of their current levels of proficiency in a specific competency, and be motivated to improve on that level. The resulting five-stage learning model was adopted by Quinn *et al* (2003) in their text *Becoming a Master Manager: A competency framework*, and termed by these authors the 'ALAPA' model from the acronym for the five stages: Assessment, Learning, Analysis, Practice and Application. These authors have continued to employ this model – eg Whetton and Cameron (2005).

The framework for teaching management skills devised by Fandt (1994), which in many respects independently echoes the Cameron and Whetton learning architecture, was also influential in the approach taken in this text, especially in identifying some of the components of what we term 'meta-competencies'.

Henderson and Dowling (2008) built on the work of the above noted authors and added a significant development by incorporating a final reflective stage to encourage and enable future self-development in the competency concerned. This represents a crucial development of the learning model. The resulting five-stage learning process for managerial competencies is shown in Table 11.

Table 11 A five-stage learning process for managerial competencies

Learning stage	Means of achieving learning
1 Assessment of existing competence level	Via self-assessment test
2 Understanding the competence	Via study of the theory underlying the competency
3 Applying the competence	By analysing case studies and illustrations
4 Feedback on performance	By comparing performance to supplied answer guidance
5 Reflection and further development	Via keeping a diary/log

Source: Henderson and Dowling (2008)

CASE STUDY

Competency-based HRM in action

A competency framework at the English Football Association

The Football Association (FA) is the governing body for football in England and has a high profile in sporting and public life. Some 290 staff are employed and the key focus is the development and regulation of the game at all levels, from international football to grassroots. The FA is a not-for-profit organisation, which means that all the surpluses it gains from its commercial activities are invested back in the game at all levels. The diversity of the organisation's remit necessitates a diverse range of skills and staff. Although everyone is driven by different motivations and needs, all share a common 'love for the game'.

Tom Harlow, who was appointed to his position as Learning and Development Manager in June 2006, made one of his top priorities the establishment of a competency framework to cover all staff. A competency framework had been in place but the system was in disrepair, with different competency categories applied in different parts of the organisation. This made the system overly elaborate, it commanded little respect, and was seen to add little value to the framework of the organisation.

New organisational priorities suggested that a unified approach to performance management was desirable. Both in employee surveys and informal feedback, the FA staff expressed a discomfort with silo working and a desire for career development across functions. A key part of the need to devise and introduce a new framework was the need to recognise the commonality of tasks across the different roles in the workplace and to ensure that these were rewarded fairly.

The new framework was delivered in October 2006. It is based on six behaviours – 'the standards that staff are required to demonstrate to achieve high performance':

- teamworking
- communication
- leadership
- customer service
- delivery, and
- fairness and inclusion.

For each of the six behaviours there are four levels of indicators that correspond to the FA's four hierarchical grades.

The framework was derived internally and Harlow drew on his awareness of best practice and his experience in his previous role. The design activity was also aligned to two major business initiatives. The first was a working group looking at the strategy for football development; the second was a group supporting internal communications. The expertise of participants in both groups was used to facilitate the definition of desirable behaviours at all levels in the framework.

The tight timetable applied to complete the framework design was driven by the need to use it as the basis for the 2007 performance review process. In Harlow's view, while they are good at setting objectives, 'Managers are struggling to find a way of dealing with very good or poor performance.'

In this sense, competencies are a tool to facilitate effective performance management. There is a danger of managers' taking the indicators too literally and using them as a checklist for every individual. All managers have been briefed and given detailed support. They are encouraged to consider 'What is important for the individual and the role?' in interpreting and applying the framework. This approach has been stressed and reinforced in a one-day workshop delivered by external consultants.

The priorities for the next stage of the framework are to audit the understanding and ensure that it is embedded effectively, to integrate it into other HR activities, and to make sure it evolves effectively. The framework will shortly be extended into recruitment activities. So far, it has been well accepted and welcomed by managers and employees, who see it as a clear and concise way of setting standards and measuring performance. They also believe it brings consistency across the organisation and gives clear goals for development. It will have to evolve further and constantly be reinforced and remain fully aligned to the changing needs of the organisation.

Information provided by Tom Harlow, Learning and Development Manager; CIPD, annual *Learning and Development Survey Report*, 2007 (2007d)

Competency-based HRM in action

An example of a competency framework: the CIPD Professional Standards

The set of Chartered Institute of Personnel and Development (CIPD) Professional Standards is an example of a competency framework.

The Practitioner-Level Standards are in four parts under the following headings:

Specialist and Generalist Personnel and Development

People resourcing standards

Learning and development standards

Employee rewards standards

Employee relations standards

People Management and Development

Leadership and Management

Managing information for competitive advantage

Managing in a strategic business context

Managing and leading people

Managing for results

Applied Personnel and Development

Management report

Continuing professional development (CPD)

Format and level of CIPD Standards

The Standards indicate the Institute's expectation for performance under the headings of 'performance indicators', which have two parts; in the first, 'operational indicators' define what the practitioner must be able to *do*; in the second, 'knowledge indicators' define what the practitioner must *know*.

CASE STUDY

Competency-based HRM in action

The need for managerial competencies: Acme Electronics

Acme Electronics plc was founded in 1924 by Bill Hoyle, a pioneering electrical and electronic engineer, and over the last 50 years has been something of an icon of British high technology. For the period from the end of World War II to the end of the Cold War (1945 to 1989) the company was highly dependent on UK government defence contracts. Until the mid-1980s these large projects were carried out on a cost-plus basis by which the firm charged the UK Ministry of Defence the total cost of the project and then added an acceptable profit margin. This allowed the firm to pursue engineering excellence to produce the best possible defence products.
One of its major achievements was the development of world-beating sea radar for UK fighter aircraft such as the Sea Harrier jump-jet, which the US Navy declared to be 'twenty years ahead of any thing we have'. Much of the firm's work during that period remains classified for security reasons. The firm had a reputation for employing some of the very best engineering and science graduates in the UK, who were attracted by the technical challenges of its defence work.

The large government projects and the cost-plus basis of contracting insulated the firm from the commercial realities of a competitive, global market and the firm's reputation for management never quite equalled that for its technology. In the mid-1980s the UK government, keen to inject more efficiency into the defence industry, stopped the practice of cost-plus contracting and the market for defence contracts became much more competitive.

Acme found it difficult to compete. Its technological competencies were as impressive as ever, but increasingly it seemed to observers that the firm was lacking managerial and strategic skills. This impression was confirmed in the early 1990s when an American partner who had been brought in to sharpen up its business skills was found to have embezzled over $100 million from the company. The partner went to jail and the firm went into bankruptcy.

It was bought by the Universal Electric Company (UEC), the biggest UK engineering conglomerate, which already had a considerable presence in the defence industry. UEC had been created and was still managed by the formidable Lord Portis, who practised a particularly aggressive type of financial control which included, among other practices, his telephoning every divisional MD every month and asking for personal explanations for all discrepancies between performance and budget. Personal accountability at all levels was the keynote of the UEC managerial culture.

Acme was rationalised by its new owners (or 'ruthlessly asset-stripped', according to some company insiders) but UEC valued its core competencies which were retained in a new division called Acme Defence Solutions (ADS). After a full review of ADS' physical and human resources, UEC concluded that its new acquisition contained significant managerial potential in its engineering project managers, which, if developed could benefit UEC as a whole.

These engineering project managers were typically highly experienced in managing complex, long-term and valuable projects, but due to the culture and working structures of Acme their portfolios of management skills were somewhat lopsided. As one senior Project Engineer put it:

'I never had to deal with people issues. We worked in a matrix structure where the firm had large departments of technical specialists who were seconded to projects under people like me. Projects typically lasted for years. If someone didn't match up or fit in, I just got a replacement the next day. The performance on the project was everything, and my job was to make the project succeed physically – to get the radar or the rocket guidance systems or whatever to work. Cost or efficiency or productivity were never the issues. I suppose these did matter somewhere, but these were for what we called the "bean-counters" – the accountants – to worry about, not us. Technological excellence was our only requirement. We felt we were fighting the Russians – who were better engineers and scientists than you might think – and we simply had to beat them. Like it was real war. As long as we produced the goods, we got whatever resources and people we said we wanted.'

Looking at the lists of competencies in Table 10 above, which ones would you recommend the company management to focus on if they wish to develop these engineering project managers into general managers for UEC? How would you do it?

ACME Engineering/UEC: resolutions and outcomes

The chart below shows how the competency profile of a typical project engineer might look.

Meta-competencies	
Basic business numeracy	*Good*
Communication	*Fair*
Interpersonal competencies	*Variable*
Decision-making	*Excellent*
Organising and planning	*Excellent*
Leadership and influencing	*Excellent (at technical issues only)*
Self-awareness/reflection	*Poor*

Intermediate management competencies	
Gathering and analysing data	*Excellent*
Creating budgets for resources	*No experience*
Presentation competencies (formal, high-level)	*Good*
Formal report-writing	*Good*
Scheduling work of others	*Excellent*
Supervising work of others	*Excellent*
Handling (local) discipline	*No experience*
Handling (local) grievances	*No experience*
Interviewing	*No experience*
Identifying own training and development needs	*Limited to technical issues*
Time management	*Excellent*
Stress management	*No experience*

Complex management competencies	
Team-building	*Excellent*
Team-leading/-motivating	*Excellent*
Managing resources	*Limited*
Bargaining	*Limited*
Negotiating	*Limited*
Dispute resolution	*No experience*
Coaching	*Good on technical issues*
Developing others	*Good on technical issues*
Self-development	*Good on technical issues*

What the company did

A set of 20 project managers were selected as a pilot group. A tripartite agreement was established between the company (represented by UEC's training director), a local university business school and a college of further education.

Each of the 20 managers in the pilot group was assisted in drawing up a personal portfolio of his or her managerial skills and experience. Gaps in development were filled by a mixture of planned experience in the company, taught theoretical courses at the Business School and skills workshops provided by the FE college.

For example, most of the managers had no direct experience in recruitment and selection of staff, so managers were invited to sit in on relevant MBA classes in HRM at the Business School as non-examined participant; the FE college put on a weekend in interviewing skills and the company arranged for the managers to participate in selection interviews across the company. The project managers' progress in developing their competency profiles was factored into their performance management reviews and appraisals.

The rest of this chapter is concerned entirely with the development of one of the meta-competencies – leadership and influencing – regarded as an essential managerial competence. The section begins with a questionnaire for the reader to assess his or her own current competence level, presents essential historical and theoretical information necessary for MBA students, and returns to interpret the scoring of the questionnaire in the light both of the information given and of the relationship of the competence to the other meta-competencies.

MANAGERIAL COMPETENCIES FOR LEADERSHIP AND INFLUENCING

The *New Shorter Oxford English Dictionary* defines a leader as 'a person who guides others in action or opinion; a person who takes the lead in a business enterprise or movement', and leadership as 'the action of leading or influencing; ability to lead or influence'. Influence in turn is defined as 'an action exerted imperceptibly or by indirect means, by one person or thing on another so as to cause changes in conduct, development, conditions, etc; ascendancy, moral or political power (over or with a person or group)'.

So our initial everyday definition of leadership includes the idea of taking direct action, which conjures up the picture of issuing face-to-face instructions and performing visible personal, even physical, leadership, and the more intangible and subtle concepts of indirect power, persuasion and moral authority.

ASSESSING EXISTING COMPETENCE LEVEL IN LEADERSHIP AND INFLUENCING SKILLS

Evaluate the present level of your skill in leadership and influencing by responding to the statements below in the *Leadership and influencing competency questionnaire*.

Questionnaire

Rate your agreement or disagreement with each statement below on a scale of 1 to 10 in which **1 corresponds to 'total disagreement' and 10 to 'total agreement'**.

1 When starting a new task it is my responsibility to identify its objective and tell the others who are involved. ☐

2 A manager should always let others know what is expected of them. ☐

3 I always try to find a new and better way to undertake a project. ☐

4 I should initiate action without waiting for other people to draw my attention to it. ☐

5 I always try to give my people instructions and information in simple, clear language. ☐

6 I always look for new approaches to the job. ☐

7 I keep myself and my team informed about due dates and deadlines. ☐

8 You should discourage questions and requests for information which interfere with getting the job done. ☐

9 A manager should provide a good example for others to follow in his or her own work habits. ☐

10 I am open about my mistakes and encourage others to learn from them. ☐

11 I set goals for myself and help others to set their goals. ☐

12 I always give my team feedback on their performance. ☐

13 When assigning tasks to others I inform them of the importance and urgency of the assignment. ☐

14 When appropriate, I delegate tasks to others in accordance with their experience and capabilities. ☐

15 When assigning tasks to others I help them develop by giving them new responsibilities. ☐

16 I assign task to others in a way that encourages them to use their initiative as much as possible. ☐

17 When assigning work to others I require them to accept responsibility for finishing the job. ☐

18 I hold others and myself responsible for the quantity, quality and timeliness of completed assignments. ☐

19 I provide others with immediate feedback so that it is clearly associated with the task being evaluated. ☐

20 When giving others feedback I review their actual performance in terms of assignment and responsibility. ☐

21 I think it is my responsibility to ensure that my team have everything they need to do the job. ☐

22 If my team needs additional skills, I will organise the training. ☐

23 I personally review the performance of my team. ☐

24 I personally review the development of each of my team members. ☐

25 Each of my team members should want my job some day. ☐

We will return and consider the significance of your scores a bit later.

LEADERSHIP VERSUS MANAGEMENT

Some authorities on management and leadership clearly differentiate between the two concepts (eg Kotter, 1990) – 'management' being understood to relate to what managers do under stable organisational and business conditions, and 'leadership' describing what organisations require when undergoing transformation or when operating in dynamic conditions. On this view leaders and managers make different contributions – 'leaders have followers and managers have subordinates' (Kotter, 1990). The leader is someone who develops vision and drives new initiatives; the manager is someone who monitors progress towards objects to achieve order and reliability.

Of course, this view has never precluded the two roles from being undertaken by the same individual, but the crucial point is that they require distinct sets of skills, with the implication that one might be a competent manager without being a competent leader, or vice versa. Mintzberg (1973) suggested that in practice the distinction between effective leadership and effective management is blurred: effective managers require at least some leadership qualities.

Whetton and Cameron (2005; p.16) state that

> the recent research is clear that such distinctions between leadership and management, which may have been appropriate in previous decades, are no longer useful. Managers cannot be successful without being leaders, and leaders cannot be successful without being managers.

This is the view endorsed in this text.

LEADERSHIP AND INFLUENCE IN MANAGEMENT IN THE TWENTY-FIRST CENTURY

The 'classical' school of management theory defined a manager's work in terms of planning, organising, coordinating, commanding and controlling (Fayol, 1950; Gulick and Urwick, 1937). Mintzberg (1973) famously disputed whether managers actually behaved like that, although arguably he missed the point: a normative statement of the primary functions or obligations of management is not necessarily supposed to be a description of observable behaviour. Successful managers must somehow make and implement plans however hectic their work schedule, and whether or not it is done in a calm, reflective manner or in a busy, disjointed fashion. They have to organise activities, people and knowledge effectively, even if it is often done by informal communication such as face-to-face encounters, phone or email, rather than by formal written statements or pronouncements; by influence rather than by direct command.

This is not to say that the classical description of managerial work is adequate for the twenty-first century. Contemporary managers certainly have to plan, organise, coordinate and ultimately be accountable for, the activities and achievements of other people. But these functions are often done 'at arms' length', especially in the increasingly common cases of the self-directed team and the empowered worker. In modern organisations managers might explicitly command people relatively rarely, although they have to be able to do so when necessary, and they sometimes may have to veto some proposals from staff. They will certainly always be concerned with influencing and motivating their people, and they need to be able to be directive when required.

Control of activities, people (including teams) and knowledge ultimately rests with designated managers – but the whole thrust of work organisation and job design over the last two decades has been to move power and decision-making down the organisation to the teams and individual workers who actually perform the tasks concerned. All organisations still necessarily exercise power and control over their employees, and this is done through the management structure, but the boundaries of control and authority are typically moved further from the individual worker or team than was previously the case, giving them a higher (although ultimately still limited) degree of power and discretion.

Consequently, there have been significant differences in the emphasis given to leadership and influence. These were always both present in work, since no organisation can operate solely on the basis of direct, formal and explicit commands for all activities, but they are much more important in the era of the knowledge-worker and the self-directed and empowered team. Twenty-first-century economies require far fewer of the sort of semi-skilled and unskilled jobs that were the staple of industrialised economies until the last quarter of the twentieth century. The 'scientific management' of Taylor and others which developed to design and control such tasks was predicated on the manager always knowing more than the worker (which is one reason why skilled workers in particular so resented its application). In the twenty-first century it is understood that it is knowledge that ultimately gives an organisation sustained competitive advantage, and the twenty-first-century manager has to be able to lead and influence workers who often have more expert knowledge and skill at their own jobs than he or she does. So managers often have to play the role of 'coach' to empowered teams or workers, rather than that of supervisor, but even in those circumstances there are situations where workers and teams have to be directed – eg dealing with crises, or with major technological or cultural change.

As a general rule, the more skilled and knowledgeable the workers are, the less directive will be the style of the effective manager. But the reality is that managers have to possess a range of management styles from highly directive to a supportive, coaching approach. Also it is worth noting in this context that the empirical evidence suggests that although there have certainly been important changes in the traditional employment relationship between managers and workers, in practice there have been limits to the extent of empowerment given to workers, at least in the UK (Gallie *et al*, 1998; pp1–27): the genuinely self-managing team is comparatively rare.

Another important dimension of the manager's job that was not recognised in the classical school's description of managerial work is the role of manager as developer of others. Peter Drucker clearly stated some 50 years ago that a key characteristic of managerial work is that it simultaneously operates in the here-and-now by ensuring efficient and effective current activities, and in the future – trying to ensure that the organisation and its people *will* perform efficiently and effectively (hence the need for corporate strategy). A direct consequence of that proposition is that senior managers had the responsibility to develop junior managers who reported to them to 'grow the stock of managerial talent' for the future (Drucker, 1955). Nowadays, many organisations go further than this and expect managers to support the training and development of all who report to them, whether managers or non-managers. So effective managers have to be able to support their people, both in the short and in the long term.

Thus a range of management styles is required of the twenty-first-century manager. Goleman (2000) has used the analogy of the clubs in a golf professional's bag: all golf professionals need to be competent in the use of each club, and have the knowledge and experience to know which is the right one to use in any particular situation.

HOW DO LEADERSHIP AND INFLUENCING WORK?

In the following section we break down the leadership and influencing competency into five sub-competencies or skills: (1) *actioning* – ie initiating actions that will taken by others; (2) *managing work* – planning, assigning and delegating specific activities and responsibilities to people to enable the agreed actions to be followed, and directing and coordinating these activities where required; (3) *motivating* the people who are to carry out these actions; (4) *managing performance* – monitoring performance against targets and objectives and ensuring accountability; and (5) *supporting* – ensuring that people have the resources needed to carry out their assignments, and in the longer term helping to develop people and teams.

It is in relation to these sub-competencies that we will interpret your scores on the *Leadership and influencing competency questionnaire*. Look back at your ratings, and transfer them all to the scoring matrix below, in their appropriate positions. Add and fill in the totals in their respective slots too.

From this matrix, when completed, it should be possible to tell at once which sub-competencies are your best (your highest totals), and which you might concentrate on developing in the future (your lowest totals) towards overall competency in leadership and influencing. The Total of Totals figure might also give you some indication of how close you are currently to that overall competency.

Scoring matrix

Skill area (sub-competency)	Scores			Totals
Actioning	Question 1 ☐	Question 2 ☐	Question 3 ☐	
	Question 4 ☐	Question 5 ☐		
Managing work	Question 6 ☐	Question 7 ☐	Question 8 ☐	
	Question 9 ☐	Question 10 ☐		
Motivating	Question 11 ☐	Question 12 ☐	Question 13 ☐	
	Question 14 ☐	Question 15 ☐		
Managing performance	Question 16 ☐	Question 17 ☐	Question 18 ☐	
	Question 19 ☐	Question 20 ☐		
Supporting	Question 21 ☐	Question 22 ☐	Question 23 ☐	
	Question 24 ☐	Question 25 ☐		
			Total of Totals	

THEORIES OF LEADERSHIP AND INFLUENCING

Research into leadership can be categorised into three broad approaches: the trait approach, the behavioural approach, and the situational approach.

The trait approach

Historically, it was usually assumed that individuals who rose to prominent positions in society or its institutions did so because they possessed certain characteristics or traits which distinguished them, the leaders, from ordinary people, the led. These traits by implication were wholly or largely genetic, and thus inherited (a useful theory to support an aristocratic class system). Traits such as physical characteristics, intellectual abilities, certain personality features and interpersonal skills were all identified as being defining characteristics of leaders. The efforts of the armed forces in both the United States and the UK in selecting and training officers during World War II reflected the then dominant trait approach to leadership, and this model was very influential in management selection and training in large organisations for several decades after the war.

However, the trait approach failed to explain the generally recognised empirical fact that personality traits are poorly correlated with job success. There was also recognition that context or situation was important. Winston Churchill won fame as a young army officer and war correspondent, becoming one of the most successful politicians of his generation before he was 40 years old. By late middle age he appeared to be an isolated political failure until the outbreak of World War II and the recognition that he – and possibly he alone – had the abilities to lead Britain against the threat of Nazism. Yet the British electorate rejected Churchill in the General Election of 1945 – they respected him as a great wartime leader but feared that he would start another war with Russia. The British wanted peace and they voted for the Labour Party and its 'welfare state' policies instead. Drucker was to call Churchill 'the most successful leader of this [the twentieth] century' (Drucker, 1990; p.7), but he also said, 'to every leader there is a season' (1990; p.15).

Perhaps the British electorate sensed that Churchill did not possess the motivation or softer leadership style necessary to build a welfare state. But Churchill won the next General Election and in 1951 returned as Prime Minister. Circumstances had changed once more. His party had promised to accept the welfare state that the Labour Party had created, and the Cold War between the Soviet Union and the West was under way in earnest. Churchill was once again the people's choice for leader.

The behavioural (or 'style') approach

Following disillusionment with the traits approach, research into leadership moved from the issue of selection of leaders on the basis of personality traits to that of finding appropriate behaviour patterns or styles in which managers and other leaders could be trained. Two major research programmes, the Michigan and Ohio studies, underpinned the investigations into leadership style. These research programmes independently suggested a dichotomy in leadership styles: broadly, either (a) a considerate, participative, democratic and 'involving' leadership style, or (b) an impersonal, autocratic and directive style. Most interpretations of the results of these studies were thought to demonstrate that the former was the more effective leadership style.

The main criticism of this perspective comes from the observation that one leadership style may not be the most effective in all circumstances. Subsequent studies incorporated a context-specific or contingency aspect.

The situational approach

Tannenbaum and Schmidt presented the autocratic/democratic choice as a continuum from manager-centred leadership to subordinate-centred. An influential situational model of leadership was developed by Hersey and Blanchard (1988), in which leader behaviour is described on two dimensions: 'task behaviour' – ie the amount of direction a leader gives to subordinates, ranging from specific instructions to complete delegation – and 'supportive behaviour' – ie the amount of social back-up a leader gives to subordinates, which can range from limited communication to considerate listening.

Each of these three approaches sheds light on the complex issue of leadership, though none provides a definitive description. The approach taken in this text recognises the contribution of each of these perspectives but is influenced in particular by the situational school. Our approach is based on the assumptions that:

- certain styles of leadership are more effective in some circumstances than others

- although the ultimate effectiveness of any particular individual's leadership ability may be constrained by genetic or other more-or-less permanent factors deriving from his or her personality and psychological make-up, *all individuals can improve their effectiveness in leading and influencing others*

- no single style is intrinsically 'right' or 'wrong': different situations need different styles of leadership and influencing

- an effective leader selects the appropriate style for the particular situation.

We argue that although few of us could ever be a Steve Jobs or a Churchill or a Martin Luther King, all of us can improve our leadership and influencing skills, and learn how and when to use these to the best effect.

LEADING AND INFLUENCING OTHERS: THE BASES OF POWER AND INFLUENCE

> The processes of power are pervasive, complex, and often disguised in our society.

French and Raven (1959; p.259)

A manager has five principal 'bases of power' in exerting influence on others, each of which forms the perceptions held by the others. These bases are: (1) *reward power*, which rests on the others' perception that the manager has the ability to apply or intercede in rewards for them; (2) *coercive power*, from the perception that the manager has the ability to apply or intercede in punishments for them; (3) *legitimate power*, based on the perception by the others that the manager has a legitimate right to their authority over them; (4) *referent power*, founded on the others' admiration for and wish to identify with the manager as a person; and finally (5) *expert power*, based on the perception that the manager has some special knowledge which the others need or can benefit from.

Successful managers often exert more than one type of power at the same time. For example, a charismatic business leader like Steve Jobs possesses legitimate power as head of Apple and reward and coercive power over his subordinate colleagues and employees, but he also enjoys referent power because of his astounding business success which most people would love to emulate, and expert power as one of the men who changed the world of computing.

There can be no strict formula for successful leadership. As a manager you should examine the situation in which you are working and the people you are seeking to influence. Motivating a group of expert engineers to meet a business deadline for a design project will require a different approach from that needed to encourage a team of office cleaners to meet quality standards.

In the first case you cannot have all the expert knowledge the team of engineers collectively possess. (If you did, you might be designing the project yourself and the engineers wouldn't be needed!) Missing the deadline is likely to have a major business impact on your organisation. The engineers are likely to be successful professionals in their own right, commanding the sort of salary and market value this implies – so you probably could not easily afford to lose them.

In the second case you will probably know at least as much as the cleaners about how to do the tasks required in order to do their job, but they are likely to be poorly paid, unskilled, and not attaining much intrinsic job satisfaction. Deadlines do not come into it, but offices need to be cleaned efficiently and effectively. You can probably afford to lose any particular cleaner or team of cleaners because the low skill levels mean that replacements can be easily found from the local labour market – but you need to get the offices properly cleaned! Both scenarios will require encouragement and the use of authority, but in very different ways.

LEADERSHIP STYLE

These considerations bring us back to the question of *leadership style*. Goleman (2000) has argued for six leadership styles: coercive, authoritative, affiliative, democratic, pace-setting, and coaching. These are based on the author's previous work on 'emotional intelligence'. The styles can be thought of as occupying positions on a continuum of leadership and influencing styles from directive through to coaching.

SELECTING THE MOST APPROPRIATE LEADERSHIP STYLE

In seeking to achieve his or her objectives the manager must first decide whether leadership and influencing skills are required. Most managers have some tasks they perform themselves, such as report-writing and some planning activities, but whenever other people are involved, leading and influencing skills will be necessary.

Choice of leadership style also depends in part on the beliefs and attitudes of the manager. Some managers feel uncomfortable with highly authoritarian styles; they tend to ask employees to participate in leadership activities. Others feel that they are responsible for issuing orders to those whom they supervise. Managers who are confident in their leadership abilities will feel more confident in conferring with employees.

Further factors that influence the choice of leadership style include the manager's assessment of his or her own competencies, the needs and competencies of the employees, the nature of the situation, and the amount of time available. If the manager believes that the employees need to be told what to do in order to complete a task, that manager may use a highly authoritarian or leader-centred style. The more direction the employees need, the more appropriate is a directive leadership style. Employees who can accept responsibility need less direction, so a less directive style is appropriate.

Often, the situation itself determines which leadership style to use. In an emergency such as a fire, it would be foolish for the leader to consult with employees on whether they should leave the building: direct ordering is clearly the most appropriate leadership approach. In situations that are not emergencies, the manager should look carefully at the task. Some tasks are better accomplished by conferring with employees; others require the use of a direct style.

Time also influences a manager's choice of leadership style. If immediate action is required, the manager may choose a highly directive style; if there is time for long-range planning, a more participatory style may produce the best results.

The organisation itself is another factor. Some organisations encourage employee participation, whereas others do not. Thus the culture of the organisation can influence the manager's selection of style.

Below (as Figure 4) is an outline process model describing the managerial selection of an appropriate leadership and influencing style.

Figure 4 A leadership and influencing process model

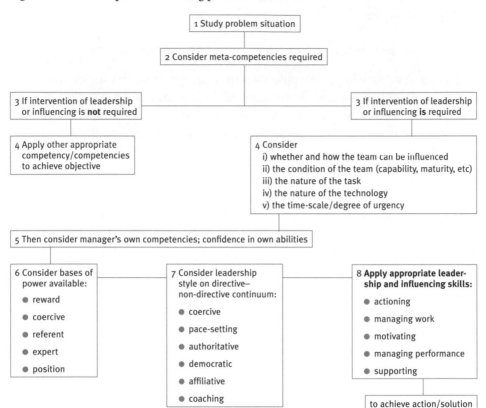

REFLECTIVE ACTIVITY

Apply the leadership and influencing process model (Figure 4) to each of the following scenarios:

1 You are the captain of a ship facing immediate shipwreck.

2 You are the newly appointed CEO of a specialist engineering firm. Your first task is to manage downsizing the firm to enable it to be competitive.

3 You are hired to manage a traditional production line for a canned fruit producer.

4 You are leading a design project employing architects and engineers to create a 'London Eye'-type showcase structure for the London Olympics.

5 You are asked to take the role of 'product champion' for a new breakfast cereal product.

6 You are team-building in a call centre environment.

7 You are creating and implementing a management development programme in a large international bank.

For each situation you are required to:

● estimate the 'influencability' of those whom you are required to lead/influence

- estimate the maturity of the team

- establish the level of complexity of the task

- establish the level of technology required for the task

- define the time-scale and level of urgency

- identify the bases of power and influence that are likely to be most important in the circumstances

- establish which leadership style is likely to be most effective.

ACTIVITY ANSWER GUIDANCE

Compare your answers with those in the boxes below.

Situation: Captain of a ship facing immediate shipwreck *Factor*	
'Influencability' of those being led	*High – used to accepting hierarchical authority*
Maturity of team	*High*
Nature of task	*Objectives clear*
Technology	*Complex, varied*
Time-scale	*Immediate*
Urgency	*Life or death*
Power source	*Position* *Reward* *Coercive* *Referent* *Expert*
Primary leadership and influencing skills required	*Actioning* *Managing work* *Motivating*
Leadership style(s)	*Coercive*

Situation: Managing the downsizing of an operation	
Factor	
'Influencability' of those being led	*Likely to be problems of poor morale*
Maturity of team	*May be mature initially, but strains of downsizing will affect team*
Nature of task	*Objectives clear*
Technology	*Generally not relevant to main situation*
Time-scale	*Short-term/immediate*
Urgency	*Usually urgent*
Power source	*Position* *Reward* *Coercive*
Primary leadership and influencing skills required	*Actioning* *Managing work* *Motivating*
Leadership style(s)	*Pace-setting*

Situation: Traditional production line management	
Factor	
'Influencability' of those being led	*Middle to high*
Maturity of team	*Probably not a team situation*
Nature of task	*Established*
Technology	*Routine*
Time-scale	*Continuous production*
Urgency	*Routine – but there will be targets on quantity and quality and frequent deadlines to meet*
Power source	*Position* *Reward* *Coercive*
Primary leadership and influencing skills required	*Actioning* *Managing work* *(Motivating)* *Managing performance*
Leadership style(s)	*Probably authoritative*

Situation: Leading a design project	
Factor	
'Influencability' of those being led	*Low – experts*
Maturity of team	*Starting from scratch*
Nature of task	*Objectives probably complex*
Technology	*Ranging from low- to high-tech from project to project*
Time-scale	*Defined time-scale*
Urgency	*Timebound – sense of urgency increases as deadline approaches*
Power source	*Referent* *Expert* *Reward* *Coercive*
Primary leadership and influencing skills required	*Actioning* *Managing work* *Motivating* *Managing performance* *Supporting*
Leadership stylc(s)	*Authoritative/affiliative/democratic as required*

Situation: Being 'product champion'	
Factor	
'Influencability' of those being led	*Say low – experts*
Maturity of team	*Starting from scratch*
Nature of task	*Complex*
Technology	*Ranging from low- to high-tech from project to project*
Time-scale	*Probably tight*
Urgency	*High degree of importance*
Power source	*Referent* *(Expert)*
Primary leadership and influencing skills required	*Actioning* *Motivating* *Supporting*
Leadership style(s)	*Democratic*

Situation: Team-building in a call centre environment	
Factor	
'Influencability' of those being led	*Variable*
Maturity of team	*Starting from scratch*
Nature of task	*Complex*
Technology	*Generally not relevant*
Time-scale	*Short-term*
Urgency	*Important to complete process within reasonable time-scale*
Power source	*Position* *Reward* *Possibly coercive* *Referent* *Expert*
Primary leadership and influencing skills required	*Motivating* *Managing work* *Managing performance* *Supporting*
Leadership style(s)	*Affiliative*

Situation: Creating/implementing a management development programme	
Factor	
'Influencability' of those being led	*High*
Maturity of team	*Not a team situation*
Nature of task	*Highly complex*
Technology	*Generally low importance*
Time-scale	*Medium to long-term*
Urgency	*No immediate urgency*
Power source	*Referent* *Expert*
Primary leadership and influencing skills required	*Supporting*
Leadership style(s)	*Coaching*

Note that from the information in the boxes above it is evident that project management is likely to be one of the most demanding and complex leadership situations for managers.

REFLECTIVE ACTIVITY

Now fill out the *Leadership and influencing competency questionnaire* again – without looking back at your answers from the first time. The questionnaire and the scoring matrix are repeated below.

AFTERWARDS compare your responses and scores with those of your first attempt. Pay particular attention to changes in responses between the two attempts. Do you understand why your answers changed?

If you keep a management log, write down the changes you think are significant and what you feel you have learned from working through the module. Note the areas of the competency where you feel you have particular strengths and weaknesses, and identify areas you wish to work on in your job.

If you use a Professional Development Plan for your continuing professional development (CPD), you should be able incorporate leadership and influencing competencies in your plan.

Questionnaire

Rate your agreement or disagreement with each statement below on a scale of 1 to 10 in which **1 corresponds to 'total disagreement' and 10 to 'total agreement'**.

1 When starting a new task it is my responsibility to identify its objective and tell the others who are involved. ☐

2 A manager should always let others know what is expected of them. ☐

3 I always try to find a new and better way to undertake a project. ☐

4 I should initiate action without waiting for other people to draw my attention to it. ☐

5 I always try to give my people instructions and information in simple, clear language. ☐

6 I always look for new approaches to the job. ☐

7 I keep myself and my team informed about due dates and deadlines. ☐

8 You should discourage questions and requests for information which interfere with getting the job done. ☐

9 A manager should provide a good example for others to follow in his or her own work habits. ☐

10 I am open about my mistakes and encourage others to learn from them. ☐

11 I set goals for myself and help others to set their goals. ☐

12 I always give my team feedback on their performance. ☐

13 When assigning tasks to others I inform them of the importance and urgency of the assignment. ☐

14 When appropriate, I delegate tasks to others in accordance with their experience and capabilities. ☐

15 When assigning tasks to others I help them develop by giving them new responsibilities. ☐

16 I assign task to others in a way that encourages them to use their initiative as much as possible. ☐

17 When assigning work to others I require them to accept responsibility for finishing the job. ☐

18 I hold others and myself responsible for the quantity, quality and timeliness of completed assignments. ☐

19 I provide others with immediate feedback so that it is clearly associated with the task being evaluated. ☐

20 When giving others feedback I review their actual performance in terms of assignment and responsibility. ☐

21 I think it is my responsibility to ensure that my team have everything they need to do the job. ☐

22 If my team needs additional skills, I will organise the training. ☐

23 I personally review the performance of my team. ☐

24 I personally review the development of each of my team members. ☐

25 Each of my team members should want my job some day. ☐

Scoring matrix

Skill area (sub-competency)	Scores	Totals
Actioning	Question 1 ☐ Question 2 ☐ Question 3 ☐ Question 4 ☐ Question 5 ☐	
Managing work	Question 6 ☐ Question 7 ☐ Question 8 ☐ Question 9 ☐ Question 10 ☐	
Motivating	Question 11 ☐ Question 12 ☐ Question 13 ☐ Question 14 ☐ Question 15 ☐	
Managing performance	Question 16 ☐ Question 17 ☐ Question 18 ☐ Question 19 ☐ Question 20 ☐	
Supporting	Question 21 ☐ Question 22 ☐ Question 23 ☐ Question 24 ☐ Question 25 ☐	
		Total of Totals

CHAPTER 9

Managing diversity: getting the best from all your people

INTRODUCTION

People are not alike. Everyone is different. Diversity therefore consists of visible and non-visible factors, which include personal characteristics such as sex, race, age, background, culture, disability, personality and work-style. Harnessing these differences will create a productive environment in which everybody feels valued, their talents are fully utilised and organisational goals are met.

CIPD, 2007f

LEARNING OUTCOMES

On completion of this chapter you should:

- understand the idea of diversity in human resource management
- be familiar with the concept of equal opportunities
- know the basis of each of the moral, legal and business cases for managing diversity
- be aware of the limitations of legislation in the field.

In many developed countries concerns about equal opportunities for women and for racial and ethnic minority groups started to find legal expression in the 1960s when governments passed laws that required employers not to discriminate on grounds of sex or race in employment matters, including pay. Other grounds such as disability or age or sexual orientation came to be included once a culture of acceptance of equal opportunities began to grow in society.

It became obvious that although a legal framework for equal opportunities was essential and achieved real progress in reducing discrimination, it had inevitable limitations in terms of producing equality of outcome

Although the business case against discrimination was always a sound one, the original impetus for equal opportunities legislation was largely moral and social: to make a fairer and better world. These concerns are still with us, of course, and as the limitations of legislation became apparent there were calls for organisations to go beyond legislative minimum standards. Because the economy has become increasingly globalised over the past 20 years – workforces, customers and other stakeholders all becoming more diverse – organisations are now urged to positively adopt diversity in their human resource management.

And it seems that no matter how big your organisation is, you really do have to take issues of diversity seriously.

In February 2007 Wal-Mart – the world's biggest retailer and owner of the Asda supermarket chain – faced the biggest sexual discrimination case in US history when an appeal court ruled that the firm had to face a class-action lawsuit involving around 1.5 million women, who claimed that the retailer discriminated against them in terms of pay and promotion.

And not just in the private sector.

Local authorities to borrow millions for equal pay claims: Government pushes for negotiations over legal action

Local authorities will be able to borrow £500 million to pay off thousands of equal pay disputes, the government has announced.

The plan will allow the 46 councils with the largest number of claims to negotiate individual agreements and reduce threats of legal action.

Public-sector union Unison welcomed the move. 'It clearly demonstrates a commitment towards the principles of equal pay,' said a spokeswoman.

'We have always maintained that collective bargaining, rather than lengthy court action, is the best way to ensure equal pay to all,' she added.

The announcement comes after comments made by Jenny Watson, chairman of the Equal Opportunities Commission, who warned that no-win no-fee lawyers were encouraging the number of women challenging employers over equal pay.

The tribunal service heard 44,103 cases from men and women last year, an increase of 155% on the previous year.

TUC general secretary Brendan Barber said: 'This is a welcome first step towards ending the stalemate in securing equal pay settlements for local government workers.'

He continued: 'However, this alone will not end the funding problems local authorities face in paying back female staff who have suffered unequal pay for many years.'

Source: *People Management*, 3 October 2007

In the UK the legal framework countering discrimination in employment has followed the approach of seeking to provide *equality of opportunity* rather than *equality of outcomes* (Kersley *et al*, 2006; p.236; Jewson and Mason, 1986). One of the aims of managing diversity is to foster a culture which assists in achieving true equality of outcome.

First, we will consider equal opportunities, and then we will proceed to discuss the somewhat wider issue of diversity.

EQUAL OPPORTUNITIES

THE DEFINITION OF DISCRIMINATION

Discrimination literally means distinguishing between people and therefore treating some differently from others. This is not always unlawful or bad management practice – for example, people are paid different wages depending on their status and skills. However, there are certain grounds on which an employer cannot lawfully discriminate against an employee. There are also other areas such as harassment and bullying of employees which might fall short of illegality but which are nonetheless both unethical and inefficient management.

If an employer treats an employee less favourably than another for an unlawful reason, the employee can take action against the employer. If an employer treats the employee unfairly for any other reason, this is not unlawful discrimination, just bad management.

TYPES OF DISCRIMINATION

Legislation protects employees from discrimination of different types.

Direct discrimination

Direct discrimination happens when an employer treats an employee less favourably because of, for example, their gender or race. (So it would be direct discrimination if an ordinary driving job was open only to male applicants.)

Indirect discrimination

Indirect discrimination is when a condition that disadvantages one group of people more than another is applied to a job. For example, saying that applicants for a job must be clean-shaven puts members of some religious groups at a disadvantage. However, the law does allow employers to discriminate indirectly if they can show a good reason for retaining the condition. For example, the condition that applicants must be clean-shaven might be justified if the job involved handling food and it could be shown that having a beard or moustache was a genuine hygiene risk.

Harassment and victimisation

Harassment means offensive or intimidating behaviour – sexist language or racial abuse, for example – which aims to humiliate, undermine or injure its target.

Victimisation means persistently treating somebody less favourably than others through spite or in a spirit of revenge – perhaps because they tried to make a discrimination complaint.

WHY BOTHER ABOUT DIVERSITY?

There are three reasons why managers should be concerned with issues of equality and diversity at work: the moral case, the legal case, and the business case.

The moral case

Managers have a moral obligation to treat all employees fairly and equally as fellow human beings. Managers are in a position of some power over their staff and they should not abuse it by showing favouritism or prejudice. Most managers (perhaps not all) would subscribe to this, and no organisation would wish to acquire a reputation for being immoral or unethical towards its own employees.

The legal case

Most countries have legal obligations not to discriminate on grounds of gender, race or religion. Other criteria are also often specified. For example, at the time of writing most employees in the UK had legal protection against discrimination on the following grounds:

- gender
- marital status
- gender reassignment
- pregnancy
- sexual orientation
- disability
- race
- colour
- ethnic background
- nationality
- religion or belief
- age.

Additionally, there were laws which forbade workers from being dismissed or treated less favourably than other workers because of:

- working part-time
- working on a fixed-term contract.

This degree of protection for employees is fairly typical of most developed economies but may be untypical of some developing ones.

The business case

Any instance of discrimination means that the optimum use of the organisation's human resources has been impaired. Another consideration, noted above in connection with the moral case, is that, quite apart from any legal sanction that might be applied, if a firm gets a reputation for discrimination, not only will this seriously affect the morale of its own employees who will fear being discriminated against personally, it will hurt its standing with customers and other stakeholders, including investors, and with potential recruits.

THE LIMITS OF LEGISLATION

Although legislation is recognised as essential in achieving equality at work, it has been found to be not sufficient and its limitations have become increasingly evident.

For example, according to the UK Government's Women and Equality Unit (website accessed 4 October 2007), in late 2006 – more than 30 years after legislation was passed outlawing pay discrimination in the UK – there was still a 'gender gap' between the pay of the sexes, with men paid on average some 13% more than women.

MANAGING DIVERSITY

In the UK the Equal Opportunities Commission, the Commission for Racial Equality and the Disability Rights Commission have all published Codes of Practice for employers which recommend practices for legal compliance. Under the Equality Act 2006, a Commission for Equality and Human Rights (effectively combining the above bodies) was established in the UK, effective from October 2007, to cover all equality issues.

It is recommended that employers follow a three-stage process to provide equality of opportunity:

- Formulate an explicit equal opportunities policy.
- Implement the policy.
- Monitor the policy to ensure its effectiveness in practice.

EMPIRICAL EVIDENCE FROM THE UK

The 2004 WERS survey found that 73% of UK workplaces (and 98% of public sector workplaces) had a written, formal equal opportunities policy or a policy on managing diversity, and 88% of UK employees in establishments were covered by such a policy – but 72% of workplaces neither negotiated, consulted nor informed employee representatives over equal opportunities.

Only 26% of workplaces reviewed selection and other procedures to identify indirect discrimination.

UK workplaces were revealed to be pretty bad at monitoring their equal opportunities practices, some 63% of workplaces doing no reviewing or monitoring at all. So it perhaps remains an open question whether the equal opportunities legislation would have a greater impact in the UK if employers exerted more effort to monitor and review their own stated policies.

JOB EVALUATION

Job evaluation schemes are used by employers to help ensure that pay and grading systems at the workplace fairly reflect the skill requirements (Chapter 7). There are a number of different types of job evaluation but there are two main classes: analytical and non-analytical. The non-analytical seeks to compare whole jobs and to use relatively simple techniques such as job ranking. Analytical schemes compare jobs on a range of common factors – eg level of skill, amount of physical effort needed, degree of responsibility, etc, each of which may be rated differently from job to job. Each factor can be weighted and then scored for each job, the total points rating for the job determining its relative position in the whole jobs hierarchy. Different jobs with the same overall points ratings are regarded as demanding an equal amount of work however different the actual tasks might be. For instance, a canteen server and a cleaner undertake different physical tasks but an analytical rating scheme might place both jobs in the same band of points and thus the jobs would attract the same basic pay.

The persistence of job evaluation schemes in the twenty-first century may seem something of a mystery in the present age of flat and flexible organisational structures and more individualised performance-related pay systems – it has a flavour of personnel management about it rather than human resource management. In fact, although the first three WERS surveys asked questions about job evaluation at the workplace, this was dropped from the 1998 survey and only reinstated for the 2004 one. The main reason it is still so important, at least for large employers, is that only an analytical job evaluation scheme can provide a legal defence against an equal pay claim at a tribunal.

The 2004 WERS survey (Kersley *et al*, 2006; pp244–7) found that 20% of all workplaces had job evaluation schemes, but the percentage rose significantly with size of the workplace as measured by number of employees: 35% of those with 100 to 199 employees had one; 36% of those with 200 to 499; and a majority – 54% – of those workplaces with 500 or more employees used job evaluation. The reason is quite clear: larger employers are more vulnerable to equal pay claims, which are often supported by trade unions. Job evaluation is also more prevalent in the public sector, 42% of all organisations in that sector operating a scheme, as opposed to 16% in the private sector. This probably reflects both size and trade union influence.

KEY ISSUES IN MANAGING DIVERSITY

Legal compliance with discrimination legislation is obviously obligatory and will be a key responsibility of your HRM function, which will take a corporate lead on the issue. But day-to-day compliance demands that line managers and supervisors are aware of company polices and procedures and must be trained accordingly. The need for compliance makes for a certain amount of unavoidable bureaucracy in monitoring. An analytical job evaluation scheme is probably a necessary evil for most larger organisations to ensure that equal pay is earned for equal work.

Compliance is necessary but is not enough. You are not going to win the war for talent if potential key employees shun you because they believe that they will be discriminated against in any way. Organisations that want to succeed must ruthlessly eliminate any discrimination in the workplace and build a genuine culture of valuing diversity.

Equal opportunities are sometimes characterised as being concerned with disadvantaged groups (women, the disabled, ethnic and racial minorities, the old). Diversity management is often described as having a more individualistic focus.

Managing diversity is a complex task and every organisation has to do it differently. The lead has to come from the top. Unless the chief executive and board members are committed, change will not occur. It requires systematic management action, with a focus on the development of an open workplace culture in which everyone feels valued and can add value. It is a continuing process, and is at least partly about managing conflict, complexity and ambiguity. Ultimately, organisations should aim to make managing diversity a mainstream issue, owned by everyone so that it influences all employment policies and working practices.

The CIPD may have the last word (CIPD Factsheet on Diversity, 2007):

'The CIPD believes that recognising and valuing diversity is central to good people management practices. HR practitioners have an important role to play in creating inclusive workplaces in which everyone can contribute to the success of the organisation. There is a compelling business case which should encourage organisations to look beyond legal compliance with anti-discrimination laws to a value-added approach enabling competitive benefits to be gained from developing good practice. Employers who sit on the sidelines regarding diversity will quickly become less attractive to existing and prospective employees.'

CHAPTER 10

People issues in mergers and acquisitions

INTRODUCTION

Companies may decide to grow in size quickly by entering into some sort of association or combination with another firm. The types of associations open to firms range from, at the simplest, the licensing of products, through alliances and partnerships, and joint ventures, lastly to mergers and acquisitions (M&A). The firms retain their identities and independence in all these possible associations except in the case of mergers or acquisitions. In a merger two firms combine to create a new company. An acquisition means that one firm absorbs the other by purchasing it, and the acquired firm ceases to exist as a legal entity.

LEARNING OUTCOMES

On completion of this chapter you should:

- understand why firms undertake mergers and acquisitions
- know why mergers and acquisitions often fail
- appreciate how mergers and acquisitions affect individuals
- be able to describe the stages of mergers and acquisitions
- be aware of the role of HRM at each stage of the merger and acquisition process.

We are concerned in this chapter with mergers and acquisitions because these types of combination have the most significant impact on the human resources of the firms involved.

There is no doubt that mergers and acquisitions represent a huge amount of economic activity. The UK Office of National Statistics reported that in 2006 UK companies were involved in a total of 777 mergers and acquisitions in the UK alone, worth some £28,000,000,000, and in nearly 400 mergers and acquisitions abroad worth a further £36,000,000,000 (Office for National Statistics, 2007).

WHY FIRMS UNDERTAKE MERGERS AND ACQUISITIONS

The most frequently cited reasons why companies undertake mergers and acquisitions include: to achieve growth, to obtain economies of scale, to control distribution channels for their products, to diversify in order to spread risk, to acquire synergies, to acquire technology, and to gain knowledge, skills and competencies. In the 'knowledge economy', increasingly, it is these last intangible resources that constitute the key motivation behind mergers and acquisitions (Gupta and Roos, 2001).

Many commentators now doubt that firms can compete in the global economy of the twenty-first century without growing and expanding through mergers and acquisitions (Schuler and Jackson, 2001).

Most commentators break the mergers and acquisitions process into three, rather obvious, distinct phases:

- Pre-combination: all the activities that take place before the firms are brought together – everything from initial research and tentative discussions with the target firm's owners and managers, through negotiations and the 'due diligence' process by which the initiating firm examines the 'books' of the target firm to verify its stated assets and liabilities (including intellectual property). As we argue in this chapter, it is increasingly held that the due diligence process should include HR issues

- Integration: the legal creation of the new entity and the actual combination of the two organisations

- Consolidation: everything that occurs after the integration phase, but specifically the process of operating and developing the new entity as a functioning and, hopefully, successful company.

WHY DO MERGERS AND ACQUISITIONS FAIL?

Despite the importance of mergers and acquisitions to the companies concerned, and to the wider economy, many are later judged to have failed in business terms. Michael Porter studied the diversification of 33 large US companies between 1950 and 1986 and concluded that 60% of the acquisitions in new businesses were later sold and that nearly two thirds of the firms eventually sold more of their acquisitions than they retained (Porter, 1987).

Mergers and acquisitions can obviously fail for many reasons. Straightforward business mistakes such as poor strategy, inept or inadequate execution of a plan, or mis-estimation of financial and economic factors will guarantee failure. But, interestingly, many mergers or acquisitions involving well-managed firms and which appear to make good strategic sense also fail. Schuler and Jackson (2001) reported that the most typical reasons given for failure in such cases concerned cultural gaps or incompatibility and loss of key talent – core HR issues, and other human factors have been identified by researchers (Napier, 1989; Cartwright and Cooper, 1990, 1996).

However, some firms seem to gain experience and acquire competence in mergers and acquisitions, learning from each successful combination (Ashkenas and Francis, 2000; Ashkenas *et al*, 2000).

FROM STRATEGIC LOGIC TO KEY PEOPLE ISSUES

Mergers and acquisitions bring about an unusual sort of major organisation change. Nothing else, other than sudden bankruptcy, can bring about change to companies on such a scale and at such speed.

In both mergers and acquisitions managers must understand and anticipate the likely effects on the people involved if they are to successfully integrate the two organisations. It will not be enough just to integrate the senior management teams. The combination will fail if middle managers and the rest of the workforce remain in conflict with the new culture, or if too many key personnel choose to leave.

Acquisitions are normally described as 'friendly' when the first bid made is accepted, and 'hostile' when the management of the target organisation recommends that shareholders refuse the offer. Of course, this distinction between 'friendly' and 'hostile' acquisitions only describes the attitudes of the shareholders and the senior management negotiators. For the typical individual employee there will be little difference in the experience of their firm's being 'merged' as opposed to being 'acquired', and either event will create considerable stress and uncertainty.

Firms which merge are more likely to be similar to each other in terms of size and other characteristics than are those involved in acquisitions. Acquiring firms are usually larger than those acquired – but not always. The flexible capital markets of the early twenty-first century have seen many occasions when smaller firms have been able to borrow sufficient funds to buy out larger ones.

THE EFFECTS OF MERGERS AND ACQUISITIONS ON PEOPLE

In this section we look at how the mergers and acquisitions process affects the individual employee. Cartwright and Cooper (1990, 1996) underlined some general propositions:

- Mergers and acquisitions are hugely stressful, and everybody in the organisation is affected emotionally.

- Management always over-estimate the speed and ease of integration after merger or acquisition.

- Organisations often lose more people than they think they will.

EVERYBODY IS AFFECTED EMOTIONALLY BY MERGERS AND ACQUISITIONS

Mergers and acquisitions might seem to be merely objective, strategic business problems to those who plan and negotiate them, but to the employees affected by the proposals they always become highly stressful, emotional events. Mirvis (1985) suggested that people in firms that have been acquired will experience the same sort of psychological response as that described in the Kübler-Ross model of grief and bereavement. This (Kübler-Ross, 1969) suggests five distinct stages:

1 Denial: 'It can't be happening.'

2 Anger: 'It's not fair!'

3 Bargaining: 'If I can just keep my job, I'll be a good employee.'

4 Depression: 'It's not worth trying to do anything anyway.'

5 Acceptance: 'Maybe it will be OK after all.'

Presumably we could also say that people in firms which merge on less than equal terms are likely to respond in this way.

Stage 1: Denial

The employees' first reaction is likely to be shock and denial. Many will seek to convince themselves that the merger or acquisition will never happen, or that when it does, little will actually change.

Stage 2: Anger

As reality is accepted, feelings of shock and disbelief will give way to anger and resentment towards the people the employee thinks are responsible – ie the old management, the new merger partner or acquiring firm, competitors, perhaps even the state of the economy and the government.

Stage 3: Bargaining

As uncertainty continues anger becomes internalised. Employees may blame themselves for not anticipating the situation and may regret their past commitment and loyalty to the firm. They worry that their existing competencies and knowledge will not be needed in the new company. The need for security of employment becomes paramount and employees would be willing to trade future prospects and perhaps even the current level of rewards in return for that.

Stage 4: Depression

Exhausted by the psychological strain of the events, people become depressed and fatalistic. It does not seem worthwhile to do anything, and people apathetically await the outcome of events.

Stage 5: Acceptance

Before they can become effective members of the new company, employees must progress beyond Stage 4 to complete the 'grieving process' and overcome the sense of loss. Those who cannot do so will eventually wish to leave the organisation, or may be compelled to because they will be unlikely to be able to function productively. A positive acceptance of the change cannot start to develop until the individual employee realises that continual denial and resistance is pointless and that the new situation must be accepted. Once this stage of acceptance has been reached, it is possible for the employee to rebuild his or her psychological contract with new organisational entity, work productively and pursue future career opportunities in the new firm.

At the same time that employees may be dealing with feelings of loss, they have to cope with the uncertainty associated with major organisational change, which is also likely to be stressful. So it is a 'double whammy' for the average employee in terms of stress (Cartwright and Cooper, 1996; Panchal and Cartwright, 2001).

Cartwright and Cooper (1996) interviewed in depth some 200 managers and their employees who were affected by mergers and acquisitions, and surveyed more than 600 other managers and employees of merged and acquired companies. The emotional detachment and accompanying uncertainty experienced by employees showed itself in five immediate areas: a sense of loss of identity; a perception of lack of information and increased feelings of anxiety; an obsession with survival in terms of continued employment; a loss of talent as people left – both involuntarily and voluntarily – coupled with resentment on the part of some of those left; and finally, negative effects on family life as stress, and the perceived need to demonstrate loyalty to the company by working longer hours, spilled over into people's home lives.

IT'S NEVER AS EASY (OR AS QUICK) AS YOU THINK

Management always seem to over-estimate how easy it will be to complete the integration of the organisations after merger or acquisition and how quickly it will happen.

Cartwright and Cooper (1996) found that most acquiring firms were realistic in expecting difficulties, but that they generally seriously underestimated the scale of the 'people problems' they were to face and the length of time it would take to integrate cultures and systems. Firms usually failed to anticipate the loss of key customers and personnel or the amount of managerial time and effort that the integration and consolidation of the two companies would require.

Many organisations are prepared to complete mergers and acquisitions without making any management plan for human resources, or even making any appraisal of the talent and competencies they are about to acquire. When an acquisition is made, it is often thought to be unnecessary to understand the culture of the acquired organisation. The acquiring firm may simply assume that their organisational culture is superior to that of the acquired firm and expect that it will be adopted unproblematically. However, the acquired workforce may not share this sense of the superiority of the acquirer's culture, and culture change can then become a longer and more difficult process.

YOU MIGHT LOSE MORE PEOPLE THAN YOU THINK

Mergers and acquisitions usually involve job losses and redeployment of personnel because cost-cutting resulting from rationalisation of functions and the elimination of duplication of roles is typically part of the business rationale for the merger or acquisition in the first place.

In addition to these planned rationalisations of resources, organisations often deliberately choose to replace some people to accelerate the process of culture-change. The senior managers of the acquired organisation are vulnerable to this and sometimes are disposed of as a whole, despite any individual abilities and competencies that might be useful to the new firm.

However, these planned reductions in staffing are very often followed by unplanned and unexpected additional losses, often of key employees. Fear of redundancy is of course one of the most common concerns of people as they anticipate a merger or acquisition. The ruthlessness of the initial rationalisations may indeed often be necessary, but an unavoidable consequence is that the 'survivors' of the first purges feel even less secure, and those with external options are more likely to take them.

WHY ARE PEOPLE ISSUES IGNORED IN MERGERS AND ACQUISITIONS?

Schuler and Jackson (2001) suggested that there are several reasons why people issues are often ignored in mergers and acquisitions, despite being crucial to their success, including:

- a lack of understanding, or consensus, within the acquiring firm that they really are important
- the belief that they are too complex to manage
- the lack of a spokesperson or 'HR champion' to articulate their importance
- the lack of a systematic framework or model to manage HR issues in mergers and acquisitions
- a focus on mainstream business activities such as finance, accounting and operations leading to neglect of HR issues.

MANAGING HUMAN RESOURCES AT EACH STAGE OF THE MERGER OR ACQUISITION

THE PRE-COMBINATION STAGE

The primary HRM tasks in this phase are as follows:

- getting HR input into identifying the rationale for a merger or acquisition – eg identifying key competencies and knowledge or specific personnel which the firm should acquire
- getting HR input into the task of selecting a specific target organisation for merger or acquisition
- creating a merger/acquisitions team and selecting or recruiting a leader for the team – 'a capable leader who can focus entirely on the mergers and acquisition process' (Schuler and Jackson, 2001; p.244)
- getting HR input into the decision on the most appropriate style of negotiations
- undertaking 'soft' due diligence which includes:

- obtaining from the target company as much relevant data as possible on the existing human resources: HR strategies, plans and procedures, staffing levels, competency frameworks, training and development policies, reward and performance management data, turnover and absence rates, and suchlike

- undertaking cultural assessments of both firms – identifying, for example, their values and leadership styles, organisational structures, reward strategies, acceptance of risk, relative power of stakeholders, and their people management philosophies and approach. The cultural assessment should conclude with an evaluation of how compatible the two company cultures are and the challenges of merging them into one integrated culture for the new organisation

- being fully familiar with existing communication structures and channels because communication is a major influence on combination success

- formulating HRM strategy, policies and procedures for the new organisation

- planning to ensure that the organisation learns from the merger or acquisition process.

THE INTEGRATION STAGE

The announcement of the acquisition or merger is the legal endorsement of the new organisational combination. It also marks the ending of the existing psychological contract between the employees and their original organisation, and the starting point for developing a new one with the new organisation.

The ultimate success of a merger or acquisition crucially depends on how the integration is managed in the early months. This is when employees will assess the culture of the new organisation and evaluate its attractiveness for them.

The key HR issues at the integration stage are:

- selecting a leader for the new organisation

- selecting an 'integration manager'

- communicating with stakeholders

- introducing the new culture

- formulating and implementing HRM strategy, policies and procedures for the new organisation

- resourcing the new organisation.

1 Selecting a leader for the new organisation.

Effective leadership at this stage is perhaps the single most important factor in achieving success in mergers and acquisitions (Schuler and Jackson, 2001; p.246).

2 Selecting an 'integration manager'

Dealing with people issues and problems as a result of mergers or acquisitions is time-and energy-consuming and there is the danger that they will be neglected because initially priority will be given to systems and procedures. It is therefore advantageous at the outset to nominate a specific individual to take the responsibility of monitoring and facilitating human resource integration. This person will not be one of the executives charged with running the new combination as a business. He or she will focus exclusively on managing the HR aspects of the integration of the two organisations and might be an experienced outsider hired for their expertise in just this task. The person appointed must possess good negotiating skills and have a 'diplomatic' manner. He or she will act as an 'ombudsman' to whom people can present their complaints for any people issues related to the merger or acquisition. This 'integration manager' will be part of the executive committee charged with managing the whole integration process, and will be assisted by a set of integration teams. These integration teams should be composed of members of both organisations, irrespective of the terms of the merger or acquisition.

3 Communicating with stakeholders

Primarily this means with the employees of the target firm, although the needs of the acquirer's workforce should not be neglected. The merger/acquisition announcement will be the first and most important source of information that the acquired or merged workforce will have about their future and about the culture of the organisation they will be expected to integrate with. Once formed, attitudes and behaviour are often resistant to change. Yet in practice acquisition announcements often display inadequate information, insensitive handling and poor timing. In one of Cartwright and Cooper's (1996) case studies, 11% of middle managers first heard the news through a telephone call from a manager of the other merger partner. Information that is potentially worrisome is always best communicated in person, so face-to-face communication of the merger/acquisition announcement by means of group announcements or presentations is preferable to using the written word or email. It is better to make such announcements on-site rather than at an outside location because employees are likely to feel less insecure on familiar territory. Wherever possible, the aim should be to inform everybody simultaneously, and before any press release or other media announcement.

The golden rule is: 'If in doubt, over-communicate.' Another reason for recommending face-to-face announcements of the merger or acquisition is that it allows time to be left for employees' questions. This will improve the communication process and help to dispel unhelpful rumours that are certain to have arisen. Both the integration and consolidation phases must include clear, open communication channels which operate both ways – from the company to employees, and vice versa.

4 Introducing the new culture

One aspect of mergers and acquisitions that is often overlooked is that the uncertainty and stress involved in the process often results in people's 'closing ranks' in both of the organisations, not just the target one, to meet the expected changes (Cartwright and Cooper, 1996). This increases the difficulty in both organisations of introducing a new culture or new management priorities and practices.

The acquiring company has to present its own culture positively and effectively. The period from the merger/acquisition announcement to the time when the consolidation process begins to work is the time when the new organisation is most vulnerable to losing key employees – the people you want to become core employees in the new company. Attractiveness of the new culture will be a crucial factor in encouraging potential core employees, who will have market value in their knowledge and competencies, to stay with new organisation. Although a new culture will develop over time, it will be deeply affected by the culture of the dominant company in the merger/acquisition. It is important, therefore, that key employees are given a clear, consistent and realistic understanding of that culture as early as possible, and that they find it attractive. Employees' attention should be focused on areas of similarity and common ground between the two cultures. The culture of the acquired firm should never be dismissed or despised. On the contrary, the positive achievements of the firm should be praised. The surest way to lose the best employees is to give the impression that you think they have been wasting their time for years by working for a company that has now been seen to fail.

5 Formulating and implementing HRM strategy, policies and procedures for the new organisation

The most important will be: recruitment, rewards, performance management, people development, and employee relations. Of course, all of these should have been well planned in advance, during the pre-combination stage, although it is unlikely that even with the most extensive 'due diligence' process specific HR policies and procedures could be finalised in detail before the new company is formed.

6 Resourcing the new organisation

This means dealing directly and immediately with redundancies and other employee exits, new recruitment and other resourcing issues.

In both the integration and the consolidation phases we must remember the Kübler-Ross model. If we want to retain key people, we must create an environment which helps them to get through to Stage 5 of the model – acceptance of the change. Only then can a new psychological contract be developed that will help to retain and motivate these core employees.

THE CONSOLIDATION STAGE

As we saw in Chapter 3, according to Kurt Lewin (1951) organisational change can be viewed as a three-stage process involving (i) 'unfreezing' the status quo, (ii) changing to the new situation, and (iii) 'refreezing' or establishing the new situation. So we can think of the consolidation stage of a merger or acquisition as constituting the third stage of Lewin's change management process. A merger or acquisition can only be considered to have been consolidated when a clear, coherent and unified culture has developed throughout the organisation, and when employees generally share and accept the new organisational values and goals. It is impossible to predict with any precision the length of time the consolidation process will take in any particular case, but we may say that consolidation will have been completed when problems cease to be described as 'merger/acquisition-related' and once again become simply 'organisational' or 'management' problems.

In addition to the continued implementation and management of the HRM strategies policies and procedures required for the new organisation ('HRM business as usual', we might say), the HRM function has a number important specific roles in the consolidation stage:

- building the new culture
- coordinating review and learning from the merger/acquisition project
- monitoring the progress of consolidation.

Building the new culture

As we saw in Chapter 5, people development is a vital HR activity in any successful twenty-first-century organisation. All HRM activities are significant in creating the new culture in the post-merger/acquisition situation, but in the longer term people development is perhaps the single most important activity in building and reinforcing a new organisational culture. Management development is particularly useful.

Coordinating review and learning from the merger/acquisition project

We noted at the start of the chapter that some firms do seem to acquire an organisational competency in managing mergers and acquisitions successfully

(Ashkenas and Francis, 2000; Ashkenas *et al*, 2000), and this may be essential if a company wishes to compete in the twenty-first-century global economy. Every merger and acquisition, whether successful or not, should be reviewed and treated as an opportunity to learn more about the process.

Monitoring the progress of consolidation

The importance of monitoring the integration cannot be over-emphasised. The acquiring or merging management have to stay in touch with the rest of the workforce, particularly its middle managers. The importance of communication was underlined in our examination of the integration stage. Once consolidation is under way, the primary function of communication should be to supplement the initial information and to help translate cultural values and norms into practice. Consolidation can be monitored by the use of staff attitude surveys and regular liaison meetings throughout the organisation. Feedback mechanisms introduced in the early stages should remain in place and operate for some time post-merger/acquisition.

KEY ISSUES IN MERGERS/ACQUISITIONS

Undertaking mergers and acquisitions is an increasingly popular way for firms to grow, and it has even been argued that it will be essential for firms who wish to compete globally in the twenty-first century to acquire competence in this area. Many mergers and acquisitions seem to fail, often for HR-related issues – especially the failure to build a viable new culture or the inability to retain key personnel. Mergers and acquisitions are highly stressful events which affect everyone in the organisation. Managers usually underestimate both how hard the integration of two companies will be to achieve and how long it will take. They also almost always lose more people than they anticipate – often including key employees.

HRM has a crucial role to play at each stage of any merger or acquisition: at the pre-combination, the integration and the consolidation stages.

REFLECTIVE ACTIVITY

Read the Corus case study – A merger in practice – below.

Using the framework for mergers and acquisitions given in this chapter, consider what lessons can be drawn from the case.

CASE STUDY

A merger in practice

Corus of disapproval

Britain's steel industry suffered another body blow last month when Anglo-Dutch firm Corus announced huge losses. How big a part have cultural misunderstandings played? Zoë Roberts reports.

Bad news has been unrelenting for Corus since the company was created in 1999 from the merger of British Steel and Dutch firm Koninklijke Hoogovens. But last month was particularly bad.

Corus's British management suffered a bitter defeat when Dutch courts blocked attempts to sell off the Netherlands-based aluminium division. The case was brought when Corus's Dutch supervisory board voted against the sale (see panel below).

Corus is now a company in crisis. After the merger it became the fourth-biggest steel company in the world, with a market value of £4.1 billion. Today its market value is just 3% of that. The inside story reveals deep divisions between what are still two separate companies.

In 2000 Allan Johnston, executive director responsible for HR, and his Dutch counterpart Kees Blokland spoke to *PM* about HR's involvement in the merger. Johnston said their aim was to acknowledge the differences between the two companies by creating a very decentralised management structure. This, he said, showed willingness to accept differences in the way business was conducted in the Netherlands and the UK.

Metal fatigue

Corus is not yet four years old, but already it has had a particularly turbulent life.

The non-sale of the Corus aluminium arm has scuppered hopes of raising £534 million to help finance further UK restructuring. It will probably mean the loss of yet more British jobs.

1999: Merger between Hoogovens and British Steel.

2000: Joint chief executives John Bryant and Fokko van Duyne resign after disagreements over the company's direction.

2001: 6,050 job losses and under fire from Downing Street over failure to inform and consult government over redundancies.

2002/2003: Row with Dutch supervisory board over sale of aluminium arm. Corus UK management board says the supervisory board acted 'irresponsibly and unreasonably'. It takes the case to the Enterprise Chamber of the Amsterdam Court of Appeal, but loses.

2003: Losses of £458 million announced, along with the resignation of chief executive Tony Pedder.

Bargaining, policy-making, works councils and union relationships were all left devolved. It now appears that this policy has backfired.

'We might have put in place a different governance structure had we known then what we know now,' Johnston admitted to *PM* just two weeks ago.

Duncan Angwin, mergers and acquisitions expert at Warwick Business School, is more explicit. 'The companies wanted to stay distinct, but this flaw in the merger design is now holding them hostage,' he says.

But Johnston believes the main problem lies primarily with the Dutch supervisory board and its independent structure.

In the Netherlands, independent supervisory boards oversee the activities of management boards. They are made up of executives who are forbidden to be employees or hold significant stock in the company. At Corus, this board of four independent directors, chaired by former shipping executive Leo Berndsen, blocked the sale of the aluminium division.

The board wanted a guarantee that money from the sale would go to the Netherlands and that the effectiveness of the restructuring in the UK would be reviewed.

According to Johnston, the supervisory board did not act in the best interests of the company. He maintains that the Dutch and UK management boards were in agreement over the sale.

However, Peter Prud'homme of the Dutch-based consultancy Cross-Cultural Organisations says the problem is not the supervisory board. He says the blocking of the aluminium sale is just one move in a power struggle that encompasses the whole of the organisation.

'This goes way beyond the present disagreement. It is about the two parts using their different powers to fight it out,' he says. 'The supervisory board was using its powers in the name of the whole Dutch workforce.

'People feel that they were promised a merger and were told that that the Dutch side would have just as much importance and play an equal role in the company,' he says. This view is supported by Peter Joosten, a mergers and acquisitions consultant at Dutch firm Fuhri Snethlage Joosten & Flohil.

'There always has been the feeling that the Dutch side is supporting the loss-making UK,' he says.

'Many people were very unhappy with the merger in the first place, as the British steel industry was seen as very traditional and not very modern in its management style.'

Joosten claims the Dutch side believes that UK management wants to restructure old British Steel debt by 'selling off Dutch diamonds'.

Frits van Wieringen, chairman of the Corus Central Works Council in the Netherlands,

agrees. The works council also voted against the sale on the grounds that it did not believe it was a strategic move. Following the court case, van Wieringen said he believed UK managers had only been thinking of securing their own future.

So why did Corus not tackle these differences during the merger and ensure that the Dutch workforce felt fully consulted and involved in decision-making processes?

Johnston says it is a question of corporate governance. 'This issue was not on my radar screen at all. In terms of corporate structure the design was driven by financial and taxation issues,' he says. 'If we went into another merger tomorrow I would not have responsibility for corporate governance.'

This is a widespread problem. The CIPD is undertaking a major research project looking at the role of HR in cross-cultural mergers. Fran Wilson, the CIPD's international specialist, says the results show that HR involvement is critical, but it still isn't happening at the very early stages of a merger. And last year Mercer Human Resource Consulting found that although people management issues came far down the list of priorities in mergers, they were often the most difficult to address. Over 40% of large companies surveyed said they found harmonising different company cultures very difficult.

Duncan Angwin believes that the HR team at Corus should have been highlighting the kind of people issues that the taxation and financial departments would not spot. However, he adds: 'It is probably harsh to say that HR has failed here, although people will be looking for scapegoats. It is likely they tried very hard within the scope that they were allocated, maybe with one hand tied behind their back.'

Angwin believes that without creating a workable model for decision-making during the merger, Corus was 'papering over the cracks'.

'The Corus management was much too narrow in its mandate of what constitutes cultural differences. I am not convinced that they fully thought through the implications of allowing the different cultural norms to exist.'

He says that British Steel management may have been lulled by the success of other Anglo-Dutch mergers such as Shell and Unilever. 'The problem is that the Dutch are seen as a very good nation to merge with because of their focus on consensus. Maybe it was felt that cultural issues would not be too much of a problem,' he says.

But there are major differences in UK and Dutch decision-making structures. Under Dutch law, large companies are required to have works councils and supervisory boards. The unelected structure of the supervisory board may seem strange to UK companies, but tackling these differences is key to any cross-cultural merger.

'Very often the national culture is linked to the organisational culture,' says Linda Holbeche, director of research at Roffey Park. 'UK management is relatively ignorant about the strength of work councils, supervisory boards and the latent strength of an organised workforce. These are largely more cohesive than unions and they can make or break mergers and deals,' she warns.

The Netherlands, both in political and business life, operates on a consensus-based model, involving continuous consultation and co-operation between social partners (the government, employers' associations and trade unions).

Holbeche says it was naïve to believe that this could sit easily with a hierarchical Anglo-Saxon style of decision-making.

However, Johnston told PM that the decentralised management style at Corus meant that these two cultures should not have clashed. 'We are very much a decentralised organisation in Corus,' he says. 'We don't beam down too much from the head office to out there.'

This isn't how the unions see it. 'British Steel's management thought that they could manage in Holland with the same arrogance that they manage in the UK,' says Michael Leahy, general secretary of UK steel union ISTC.

'They did not go to the supervisory board and put the decision forward – instead, they just announced it. They thought that they could run Corus in the way they ran British Steel – without consultation.'

The union is holding a series of protests aimed at removing Sir Brian Moffat, chairman of Corus. 'It was his lack of consultation and contempt for Dutch consultation procedures that led directly to this failure in agreement,' Leahy says.

In the light of all these factors, could the merger have ever worked? Johnston insists that external rather than internal circumstances played a major part in the firm's difficulties. 'If the company had not hit such choppy waters, then all of this difficulty would not have occurred and we would not have a "them and us" situation,' he says.

There can be little doubt that Corus has been unlucky. The exchange rate against the euro seriously damaged Corus's UK business; UK manufacturing has shrunk and many of the company's big customers, such as Black & Decker, have moved abroad.

'If the environment had been more hospitable, then after a few years there might have been a gentle coalescence between the two sides – but the context moved faster than the integration,' agrees Angwin.

It also seems that context moved faster than the restructuring of Corus's UK business could. 'Corus in the UK has some serious efficiency problems,' says one City analyst. 'Although there have been major attempts to improve this, they have not worked.' Analysts say that the basic structure of the company, which is based on four sites around the UK, is a serious impediment to efficiency. They also believe that the company is overmanned, a hangover from its days as British Steel.

'This is very difficult to change,' says another analyst. 'No UK politician or union will countenance large-scale redundancies or the closure of one of the sites.'

However, internal divisions are the major problem now. Analysts claim that any attempt at a de-merger would be a disaster and would just provide rich pickings for the lawyers. Johnston stresses that there is no question of the company either de-merging or 'going bust'.

Angwin believes Corus management must decide what it wants. 'They need to decide if they are going to run the business the UK way, the Dutch way, or the best of the two; they cannot just leave it,' he says.

If ever there were a case study to alert CEOs to the importance of HR in mergers, then Corus is it.

People Management, 3 April 2003

CHAPTER 11

HRM in international companies

INTRODUCTION

This chapter is concerned with HRM issues in the context of the multinational organisation, and specifically with the interface between national and company cultures. Approaches to HRM in multinational organisations is first considered, from the ethnocentric through to the geocentric. Hofstede's concept of dimensions of culture is explored. Issues of selection, training and support for managers on expatriate assignments are discussed.

LEARNING OUTCOMES

On completion of this chapter you should:

- be able to appreciate the different approaches to HRM that may be possible in multinational companies (MNCs)

- know about Hofstede's concept of dimensions of culture and what these can tell us about managing people in the interface between national and organisational culture

- understand something of the complexity inherent in selecting, preparing and supporting personnel for expatriate assignments.

The cultural background to HRM as an approach to managing people is, as we have seen in this text, predominantly North American. It has been largely through the agency of multinational companies that HRM practices have spread internationally. However, not all the world shares all features of North American work culture. It is more individualistic and more achievement-oriented than most other countries (Hofstede, 1980), and this is reflected in employment practices and employee relations legislation in that country.

But it can also be said that, for instance, the European Union is unique in having its members committed to an international level of legislation which affects the employer–employee relationship, and in the context of HRM, Europe can be distinguished from the USA in a number of other important ways. Western Europe is still a relatively heavily unionised continent. Although unions have lost members in most European countries, recognition by employers remains high, as does trade union influence, although there are some significant differences in this among the various European nations.

The high Western European levels of educational and vocational training and government support for the labour market are quite different from those in America. Patterns of ownership are also different.

The newly developing markets in Eastern Europe, even those within the EU, are still significantly different from those in Western Europe in many respects.

Then there is Japan and the 'Tiger economies' of the Pacific Rim, and of course the emerging new economic superpowers of India and China. All of these countries have unique features of culture, employment law and regulation of the labour market. The global economy is enormously diverse.

Clearly, the idea of 'international HRM' is a huge subject. We will deal with just one important aspect of it: how operating in different countries affects the HRM of companies that operate in different countries – multinational corporations or companies (MNCs).

One definition (Armstrong, 2003; p.88) of international human resource management (IHRM) is:

> the process of employing and developing people in international organisations which operate ... globally.

APPROACHES TO IHRM

A widely used typology of the approaches which an MNC can take to its subsidiaries in other countries is that devised by Perlmutter (1969). This identified four different approaches:

- *the ethnocentric approach*, in which the MNC simply transfers the HR practices and policies used in the home country to foreign subsidiaries. Expatriates from the home country manage the foreign subsidiaries and the MNC

- *the polycentric approach*, where each subsidiary can develop its own HR policies appropriate to its circumstances: local managers are hired to manage HRM activities

- *the regiocentric approach*, in which for a given regional grouping of subsidiaries (eg Europe, Asia, or the Americas) HR policies are co-ordinated within the region, but may vary from region to region. Subsidiaries may be staffed by managers from any of the countries within in the region

- *the geocentric approach*, in which the firm views itself as a single international business rather than one with a home base and a number of foreign subsidiaries. HR policies are developed to meet the global goals of the enterprise. HRM and other activities are managed by the individuals judged to be most appropriate without regard for their own nationality – so a Dutch manager might handle HRM in a British plant, and vice versa.

Many factors may influence the IHRM approach taken by a particular MNC. These include national politics and legislation, managerial culture, educational and technological development in the host and subsidiary countries, production technology and the nature of the product, the organisational life cycle, and national cultural differences.

When asked by researchers to identify the most important global pressures on IHRM (Roberts *et al*, 1998), senior HR managers in MNCs nominated

- getting the right knowledge, skills and competencies to where they were needed globally

- disseminating knowledge and innovation effectively throughout the organisation

- identifying and developing talent globally.

NATIONAL CULTURES: THE WORK OF HOFSTEDE

Geert Hofstede researched the interface between company and national culture. In the 1970s with colleagues at the University of Limburg in the Netherlands, he surveyed IBM employees' attitudes in over 70 countries. This work took into account responses of over 110,000 questionnaires and has been described as by far the largest organisationally based study ever to have been undertaken (Pugh and Hickson, 1995). A total of 20 different-language versions of the questionnaire had to be made.

It was assumed that national cultural differences found within the company would reflect those existing within the countries at large. The survey was repeated after four years and found reliable results, supporting the conclusion that valid cultural differences had been found.

Hofstede initially identified four basic dimensions of the differences between national cultures, and thereafter positioned each of the cultures on a scale from high to low on each of the four dimensions, giving each culture a distinctive profile.

The initial four dimensions were:

- Power-distance
- Uncertainty avoidance
- Individualism/collectivism
- Masculinity/femininity.

The **power-distance** dimension measures how close or how distant subordinates feel from their superiors, and is a index of power inequality in a culture. In high-inequality cultures (eg India or France) where people are respectful of traditional authority, it is unlikely that employees will be expected, or will wish, to challenge their superiors in the workplace. The management style is more likely to be autocratic or paternal. Organisations will usually be hierarchical and decision-making will be centralised.

In low-inequality cultures (eg Israel, Australia) employees will feel able to voice disagreement with their managers and will not see this as disrespectful. Employees will expect to be consulted by their managers when major decisions affecting their jobs and careers are to be made. The management style is therefore likely more likely to be participative or consultative, and the organisational structure will tend to be flat and flexible. Networks and self-managed teams are more likely to flourish in low-inequality/high-equality cultures.

The **uncertainty avoidance** dimension shows how easily the culture copes with innovation and change and can tolerate ambiguity. In strong uncertainty-avoidance cultures, such as Japan and Greece, people feel the need for clarity and order, and risk-taking is not pursued or encouraged. Employees are attracted to long-term careers with the same company. In a weak uncertainty-avoidance culture – eg Denmark and Hong Kong – uncertainty is more easily accepted. A pragmatic view is taken of the need to change, or occasionally break, company rules. Employees do not seek or expect the long and stable employment patterns typical in the high uncertainty-avoidance countries and are more likely to be entrepreneurial in their behaviour. Organisations are more likely to be decentralised and a higher degree of empowerment granted to employees.

The **individualism/collectivism** dimension shows the degree to which the culture encourages individual as opposed to collective concerns. In an individualist culture such as the USA or the UK, the emphasis is on personal initiative and achievement. It is also accepted that everyone has a right to a private life and opinion. In a more collectivist culture such as Iran or Peru, there are tighter social frameworks and people are seen more as members of extended families or clans, which protect them in exchange for loyalty. Careers are pursued to increase standing in the family by being able to help other members of it. In collectivist cultures the aim is to be a good member, whereas in individualist ones it is to be a good leader (Pugh and Hickson, 1995).

In individualist cultures the relationship is contractual – that is, employees offer their labour for commensurate pay during their working hours. Most employees, especially non-managerial and non-professional ones, will not expect to work beyond the normal hours of work without being paid overtime, and they will not expect their relationship with their employing organisations to overlap with social or private lives. In collectivist cultures, by contrast, the employee–workplace relationship is emotional as well as contractual and the boundary between private and professional spheres of life in many instances is blurred. The superior is not just a manager but could also be a father or mother figure to seek advice from on private issues, such as the need for a loan to buy a house or get married. Most employees are prepared to work well beyond the official working hours if required, without expecting additional pay. In addition to the pay in exchange for labour as stated in the formal employment contract it is understood that the workplace looks after the employees' total well-being in return for loyalty and commitment (Tayeb, 2008).

The **masculinity/femininity** dimension is not about discrimination or liberation in gender terms. It refers to the value placed on traditionally male or female values as traditionally understood in most Western cultures. 'Masculine' cultures such as Japan, Italy and Australia value competitiveness, assertiveness, ambition, and the accumulation of wealth and material possessions whether pursued by males or females. 'Feminine' cultures such as the Netherlands and Sweden place more value on relationships and quality of life, and service rather than ambition is valued. 'Anglo' cultures such as the USA and the UK are moderately 'masculine'. The terminology is somewhat offensive or embarrassing to many readers of Hofstede's work and this dimension is often renamed 'quantity of life versus quality of life'.

Hofstede later developed a fifth dimension of culture – that of long-term versus short-term orientation. This describes the 'time horizon' of a society. China, Japan and the Asian 'Tiger' countries scored very highly on this dimension; most Western countries scored rather low, and many less developed countries scored very low.

Hofstede's work has been criticised for identifying culture with individual nation states. It may seem plausible for small countries – but can we really talk about one single culture for the USA or China or India? Many people are sceptical on this point. Nonetheless, Hofstede's work has been very influential and if we accept that, at best, his conclusions are very broad generalisations to which there will be many exceptions in all countries, it can prove helpful in providing a starting point in thinking about the cultural differences between countries.

Culture not only influences an MNC's overall approach to IHRM, it has a potential impact on every HR function.

Example

Pugh and Hickson (1995) used Hosfstede's framework to analyse the use of *management by objectives* (MbO) in an MNC with subsidiaries in Germany and France.

American companies pioneered the use of MbO for the performance appraisal of managers, and it has been claimed that this technique has had more success there than in many other countries. Hofstede's analysis of culture may give an answer.

MbO requires that:

- the subordinate is sufficiently independent to negotiate meaningfully with the boss (ie low power-distance)
- both are willing to take some risks – the boss in delegating power, the subordinate in accepting some responsibility (low uncertainty avoidance)
- the subordinate is personally willing to 'have a go' and try to make his/her mark (high individualism)
- both regard high performance and results as important (high masculinity).

Germany's work-culture has low power-distance, which is appropriate for MbO, but is high on uncertainty avoidance, which suggests a lack of willingness to take the risks and tolerate the ambiguity needed to accept 'stretch' goals. France has high power-distance and high uncertainty avoidance, suggesting that MbO may be highly inappropriate there as a means of managerial performance appraisal. In fact, research indicates that in Germany MbO can be successful but takes a more participative approach than in the USA, reducing the uncertainty. In France MbO has never really been popular.

TRUST AND LEADERSHIP

One of the major factors that will influence the extent to which managers are willing to delegate power and authority to their subordinates is whether they can trust them (Tayeb, 1988, 2008). Firstly, are they technically capable of making decisions on their own, and do they possess the requisite knowledge and competence? Secondly, will they put the company's interests before theirs?

The level of trust in other people's good intentions varies widely between cultures, dependent on such factors as the extent of corruption prevalent in public bureaucracies and in private companies as well.

If a culture is such that the people are in general honest, with a traditionally good work ethic, and the society possesses an educated workforce, managers will be able to trust them to make decisions on their own. In cultures characterised by corruption or by low levels of skills and competence and a poor work ethic, to protect their own interests and those of their company managers are likely to delegate decision-making authority only to a few trusted employees and by preference to members of their own clan, their relatives or friends.

PREFERENCE FOR CERTAIN LEADERSHIP BEHAVIOURS

People in cultures which have low tolerance for ambiguity and risk-taking tend to prefer major decisions affecting the community to be taken by their leaders as 'benevolent autocrats', whereas in cultures with a higher tolerance for ambiguity people usually prefer to participate in decision-making or at least have their leaders to take their views into account when making decisions on their behalf.

The preference for leadership models is reflected within organisations. For instance, in cultures with a preference for benevolent autocratic leaders, managers may well be looked up to as 'father figures' who usually know best. In cultures with a preference for a participative consultative model, the manager is seen as another team member who contributes to the discussions the same as anyone else.

A comparison between Japanese and British leadership styles (Tayeb, 1994b) also showed that there are some behaviours that are associated with a high employee-oriented behaviour by respondents in one country but which are perceived quite differently by people in another country.

The Japanese see it as high employee-oriented behaviour when a supervisor or manager

- spends more time at work than official work hours
- expects to discuss an employee's personal difficulties with other team members in the employee's absence

- talks with the subordinates frequently about progress in relation to a work schedule
- spends some time with the subordinates socially
- spends time with subordinates discussing their career plans
- evaluates performance on the work of the group as a whole
- meets the group frequently for social or recreational purposes, and
- consults the subordinates when substantially new work procedures are being discussed.

British employees see a supervisor as showing high employee-oriented behaviour when he or she

- frequently uses or demonstrates how to use any of the equipment used by the group
- makes it possible for subordinates to put forward suggestions for work improvement
- discusses with the group if he or she believes that there is a substantial problem in the group's work procedures, and
- may be addressed by first name.

For a supervisor to discuss a subordinate's personal difficulties behind their back with other group members was very definitely regarded by the British (unlike the Japanese) as anything but high employee-oriented behaviour. The British considered such an act an invasion of personal privacy and unacceptable.

These findings reflect the cultural characteristics of the countries. Strong features of British culture are the willingness to take account of other people's opinions, consultation and participation, a love of privacy and 'minding their own business', and individualism. The Japanese, in contrast, do not seem to mind their superiors' discussing their personal affairs with others in their absence, which is consistent with a more collectivist culture.

IHRM AND THE SELECTION PROCESS: SELECTING EXPATRIATES

The management of expatriate employees is a particularly challenging task in IHRM, and the failure rate of expatriate assignments is high. Scullion (1995) found that UK MNCs experience lower failure rates than do US ones because UK managers tended to have a more international outlook than did US ones. UK firms valued international experience more highly, and they tended to have more effective HR polices on expatriation, especially with respect to selection of personnel for expatriate projects.

Research has shown there are identifiable attributes which contribute to the success or failure of expatriates employees:

- personality traits – the ability to tolerate ambiguity; behavioural flexibility; the ability to be non-judgemental; the level of cultural empathy and ethnocentrism; interpersonal skills (Mendenhall and Oddou, 1985; Tung, 1986)

- motivational state – belief in the mission; congruence of assignment with career path; interest in overseas experience; interest in the host-country culture; a willingness to learn new behaviour patterns and attitudes

- family situation – the willingness of a partner to live overseas; the adaptability and supportiveness of the partner; the stability of the relationship with the partner

- language skills – an ability to quickly learn the host-country language; a facility also in non-verbal communication.

EXPATRIATE RE-ENTRY

The task of effectively repatriating employees after foreign assignments is often initially overlooked by organisations and, indeed, by expatriates themselves and their families.

Adler (1991) found that 20% of US expatriates leave their firms within a year of returning home. Many seemed to find returning home a greater culture-shock than moving abroad. They and their families exhibited a typical pattern of emotion on returning: joy and elation for less than a month, followed by relative dissatisfaction and disappointment for two to three months, then an acceptance stage.

The problems associated with re-entry adjustment can be divided into those related to general cultural readjustment and those dealing specifically with readjustment to the job.

General cultural readjustment

Re-entry often brings a feeling of cultural and social loss. The international assignment may have presented an exciting and fulfilling experience for the employee and his/her partner together with a considerably higher standard of living – possibly including the provision of servants and a desirable social life. Children may experience difficulties in readjusting to school. There may be unexpected financial difficulties in reverting to domestic salary levels. All these can result in marital strain.

Job readjustment

Returning expatriates often find that their 'home office' has not planned for their return and they typically feel isolated from changes that have occurred during their foreign assignment. They may feel that they have fallen behind with new technology, and they may feel that they have missed promotion opportunities. Very often the expatriate enjoyed a higher level of authority and responsibility while on the foreign assignment and may find it difficult to accept their former, less responsible, role. (It is a particularly difficult transition to make.) All these difficulties mean that many returning expatriates are vulnerable to feelings of demotivation and may be more likely to accept employment offers from other organisations.

REFLECTIVE ACTIVITY

Defend or refute this statement:

It is not a good idea to send female managers to countries that have a very masculine work culture.

ACTIVITY ANSWER GUIDANCE

It is acknowledged that there are special issues regarding female expatriates (Fisher *et al*, 1993; pp804–7) but clichés must be examined rather than taken at face value.

In a survey of over 600 North American MNCs only 3% of 13,338 expatriates were identified as women. In another survey of 60 US firms, 54% indicated a reluctance to place women in expatriate positions, giving as their reasons (i) the belief that many foreigners were prejudiced against women managers, and (ii) the belief that international assignments for women often caused problems for dual-career marriages (Adler, 1984a; Adler, 1984b).

Yet a survey of over 1,100 graduating MBA students from seven management schools in North America and Europe found that 84% (with no difference between male and female students) wanted an international assignment at some point in their careers. So it would seem that potential female international managers represent a significantly under-used source of managerial ability and expertise (Adler, 1984c; Adler, 1986).

In a different study 52 female expatriates were interviewed about recently completed Asian assignments (Jelinek and Adler, 1988; Adler, 1987): 92% described their assignments as successful; many suggested that the most difficult part had been getting their firms to agree to send them abroad. Some suggested that they were more discriminated against by Western expatriates than by local

Asian businessmen. Throughout the interviews one common theme emerged: female expatriates were regarded first and foremost as foreigners: normal local rules about female behaviour were not applied. So, just because a society discriminates against its own women does not mean that it will not accept female expatriates.

'In selecting individuals for foreign positions, it seems most rational to look for the kinds of attributes associated with success in foreign assignments, regardless of the sex of the candidate' (Fisher *et al*, 1993; pp806–7).

REFLECTIVE ACTIVITY

By what criteria would you judge the success of an expatriate re-entry?

ACTIVITY ANSWER GUIDANCE

Feldman (1991) has outlined outlined six criteria that should be met before a re-entry can be judged successful. The returning expatriates should:

1 perform at a level and quality expected by their managers

2 exhibit a reasonable level of job satisfaction with the new position

3 be able to use the skills developed during the foreign assignment

4 be able to maintain a career progression comparable to cohorts who did not go abroad

5 remain (or at least intend to remain) with the employer for a reasonable period of time after returning

6 avoid dysfunctional levels of stress during re-entry.

The main factors that affect successful re-entry are:

- the similarity of the international and domestic assignments
- the amount of change in the home organisation
- the nature and personality of the expatriate
- the support available to the returning expatriate
- the career planning system of the organisation.

HRM in action

No place like home

The way some relocation specialists talk, you'd think taking a job overseas was simply a question of booking a man with a van.

But the real issues behind moving abroad these days are psychological, spiritual and cultural. More people are thinking twice about uprooting themselves for an overseas job, even though it may be an astute career step.

Take Carrie, who works for an insurance company in Cheltenham and lives with her IT consultant husband Chris and six-year-old son Jed. If her employer asked her to go to Cairo for two years, Chris's business would suffer and Jed would be wrenched away from his school. The expatriate life wouldn't appeal since they belong to a community of friends in Cheltenham. International schools? The local ones are among the best in the country. Carrie's worried about uprooting her family, terrorism and the unpopularity of the British in the Middle East since the Iraqi invasion. What if she stays at home and visits Cairo regularly? Saying no wouldn't be the end of her career, simply a personal statement about work–life balance. This isn't just psychological, spiritual and cultural – it's personal too.

People Management, 27 July 2006

HRM in action

Send the right people to the right places

A failure to take into account different business cultures, and ways of working, when arranging overseas assignments is costing international organisations dear.

Sending senior business executives abroad is an expensive undertaking. Yet research suggests that around 40% of those who take on an expatriate assignment fail, at a cost to their employer of two to four times their annual salary. So what causes this surprisingly high failure rate?

The Global Personality Inventory (GPI) contains data gathered by Personnel Decisions International (PDI) from more than 12,000 managers and executives who have gone through its leadership screening process across the globe. It suggests that the chief cause of the high failure rate for expatriate assignments is the inability of managers to appreciate differences between their own business cultures and foreign work environments. In other words, troubles often arise because of personality-based perceptions rather than substantive business issues.

According to the GPI data, 'agreeableness' and emotional balance accounted for 85% of differences between managers and executives working across countries. That is, the tendency to seek group harmony versus fostering individuality, or to have quick and deep emotional reactions to events rather than muted emotional responses. Problems arise when an individual's own attributes in these areas don't match those of the culture where he or she is sent. A leader who favours individuality will rub up the wrong way co-workers in a country where group needs traditionally take precedence. Likewise, an even-keeled leader in a culture where emotional expression is the norm risks being seen as cold and unfeeling.

By matching individuals' personality traits in these two key areas to the cultural norms of the countries to which they are being assigned, businesses can achieve greater success than by relying on 'gut instinct'. For example, tackling business problems as a team is common practice in the UK, while working solo is the norm in China. The French most closely match their colleagues in Mexico in business leadership style, placing strong emphasis on individuality. By contrast, Japanese executives are more in tune with their colleagues in Saudi Arabia, both nationalities placing strong emphasis on maintaining group harmony.

PDI then grouped together similar cultures and drew up a shortlist of the most valuable managerial skills for potential expatriates. The top six on this list were the ability to act with integrity, to champion change, to build relationships, to demonstrate adaptability, to use sound judgement, and to coach and develop others. The two with most significant between-country differences were the ability to act with integrity and to champion change.

The lesson for HR, as well as leaders working across borders, is obvious. Smart businesses will take cultural similarities and differences into account when working across the globe.

People Management, 13 July 2006

CHAPTER 12

Review

In Chapter 1 we defined 'people management' as

> all the management decisions and actions that directly affect or influence people *as members of the organisation rather than as job-holders.*

We concluded that sustainable competitive advantage can only come from the skills, experience, creativity, imagination and brainpower of people. So all managers must know about managing people and need to understand the basic concepts and practices of HRM, both to deal with day-to-day HR issues that have been devolved to the line and to be able to work with HR specialists.

THE EMERGENCE OF HRM

We have seen that over the last few decades a consensus evolved that post-Taylorist organisations required a new approach to managing people. Sustainable competitive advantage in a technologically advancing global economy could ultimately only come from the talents and efforts of an organisation's core employees. This approach to people management has become known as human resource management (HRM). It differs from the earlier personnel management (PM) paradigm in taking a strategic view of the use of human resources and in aiming to achieve the willing commitment of employees rather than their coercion. It also favours an individualist rather than collective employment relationship.

Few if any organisations practise pure HRM or pure PM and the people management of most will be a combination of the two paradigms. But HRM is in the ascendant: there is good empirical evidence that many HRM initiatives have become well-established and that line and general managers are more directly involved in people management issues than previously.

We have seen how Ulrich's (1998) recommendations on the relevance of the HRM function has set the agenda for HRM in the twenty-first century:

- HRM should become a 'partner' with senior and line managers in strategy execution.

- It should become an 'expert' in the way work is organised and executed, delivering administrative efficiency to ensure that costs are reduced while quality is maintained.

- It should become a 'champion for employees', vigorously representing their concerns to senior managers and at the same time working to increase employees' contribution.

- It should become an 'agent of continuous transformation', shaping processes and a culture that together improve an organisation's capacity for change.

HRM has developed few, if any, new techniques of people management and it is mainly in the manner and intent of their use in which HRM differs from PM.

We noted the Harvard model (Beer *et al*, 1984) as one of the first and most important models of HRM. The central issue here is performance – managing human resources to achieve positive HR outcomes in terms of a committed workforce, working in harmony with the objectives of the organisation and achieving competence and cost-effectiveness. These outcomes in turn lead to positive long-term consequences: firstly, organisational effectiveness, but also individual and society's well-being.

There have been significant developments in management theory and practice since the Harvard model was conceived, its biggest single deficiency probably being its neglect of learning and development. However, we concluded that the model had proved to have remarkable utility and durability, and that it still provided a good initial map of the 'HRM territory' for general managers.

A characteristic of this model was its emphasis on policy choice, which implied that although situational factors and stakeholder interests might have some impact on managerial decisions on HRM, none of these would determine which HRM policies were followed. Managers had at least some degree of discretion in their HR policies. This was the viewpoint adopted throughout the present text.

THE UNIVERSALIST VERSUS CONTINGENCY DEBATE

We saw how this question which runs through all management thinking and practice finds expression in the 'best fit' versus 'best practice' debate in HRM. Our view, that of strategic choice, avoids the extremes of the argument. There may well be some generic HR practices at some level which all organisations should adopt, but these have yet to be unambiguously identified. And if someday they are, it seems certain that their scope will be limited and that there will always be contingent factors that have to be taken into account.

Empirical evidence suggests that 'bundles' of HR practices have significant impact on organisational performance but that the precise composition of the effective bundles will vary from industry to industry.

The framework presented by the Harvard model is a contingency model, but it can accommodate a variety of 'best fit' practices in various specific environments (eg industries, technology groups or cultures) as determined by the situational factors and stakeholder interests.

KEY THEMES IN HRM FOR THE TWENTY-FIRST CENTURY

We identified a number of key themes in HRM for the twenty-first century.

The adoption of *'high-performance' work practices* – also known as 'high-commitment' or 'high-involvement' work practices – which are intended to achieve better individual, team and organisational performance by increasing employee commitment and involvement. These are typically thought of as comprising 'bundles' of sophisticated HR practices in the areas of employee involvement, resourcing (eg in recruitment) and rewards and commitment.

A *'flexible organisation'* with a *'core'* of key employees (including non-managerial employees) with greater investment in these human resources; and a *'peripheral'* workforce of other workers who typically enjoy less secure and less attractive terms and conditions of employment and less HR development. But in efficient organisations the barriers to the core will be permeable to hard-working and capable employees on the periphery.

The organisation of work at a micro-level – teamworking, cross-training, multi-skilling and problem-solving groups to increase functional flexibility, participation in the design of work processes, and the sharing of task-specific knowledge.

Sophisticated HR practices in recruitment and selection – eg the use of psychometric testing and personality profiling and competency and performance tests for a wide range of key or core employees including non-managerial ones.

Employee relations in a unitarist environment – trade unions are in a historically precipitous decline in most advanced economies and especially in new industries, but all but the smallest employers need to find means of communicating with their employees and achieving perceptions of fairness and legitimacy in pay rates and conditions of employment agreement.

Change management – 'the only constant is change' has become a cliché but reflects the acknowledgement now that the competitive global economy and continuous increasing technological advances are realities. Physical resources are relatively easy to change; human ones are much more challenging. HRM is often tasked with taking a lead and coordinating change across the organisation.

The 'learning organisation' – defined as an organisation which encourages learning at all levels and thereby brings about continuous (and by definition often unpredictable) change to itself. This is a consequence of the realisation that employees are expected and encouraged to learn all the time, and should employ their learning by being innovative and enhancing performance; that 'to pay someone to work is to pay them to learn'.

Knowledge management – 'using the ideas and experience of employees, customers and suppliers to improve the organisation's performance' (Skapiner, 2002).

Leadership – to initiate and effect change and to achieve high-performance working.

In all of these areas it will usually be the line or general manager who initiates action and carries responsibility to make it happen, but he or she will increasingly rely on HRM specialists, who may have a lead role within the organisation in coordinating activities across the organisation.

We can do no better to conclude our study of HRM than by quoting again the words of Linda Holbeche (Holbeche, 2007; pp10–11) that

building organisational capability is HR's heartland,

and that HR managers

can help make capitalism human,

and suggesting that her last phrase should be applicable to all managers.

References

Adler, N. J. (1984a) 'Women in management: where are they?', *California Management Review*, Vol.26, No.4, 78–89

Adler, N. J. (1984b) 'Expecting international success: female managers overseas', *Columbia Journal of World Business*, Vol.19, No.3, 79–85

Adler, N. J. (1984c) 'Women do not want international careers, and other myths about international management', *Organizational Dynamics*, Vol.13 No.2, 66–79

Adler, N. J. (1986) 'Do MBAs want international careers?', *International Journal of Intercultural Relations*, Vol.10, No.3, 277–300

Adler, N. J. (1987) 'Pacific-Basin managers: a *gaijin*, not a woman', *Human Resource Management*, Vol.26, No.2, 169–92

Adler, N. J. (1991) *International Dimensions of Organizational Behaviour*. Boston, MA: PWS-Kent

Adler, P. S., Goldoftas, B. and Levine, D. I. (1997) 'Ergonomics, employee involvement and the Toyota production system: a case study of NUMMI's 1993 model introduction', *Industrial and Labor Relations Review*, Vol.50, No.3, 416–37

Aitken, H. G. J. (1960) *Taylorism at Watertown Arsenal*. Cambridge: MA: Harvard University Press

Appelbaum, E., Bailey, T., Berg, P. and Kalleberg, A. L. (2000) *Manufacturing Advantage: Why high performance work systems pay off*. London: Cornell University Press

Argyris, C. and Schön, D. A. (1974) *Theory in Practice: Increasing professional effectiveness*. London: Jossey-Bass

Argyris, C. and Schön, D. A. (1978) *Organizational Learning*. Reading, MA: Addison-Wesley

Armstrong, M. (1993) *Managing Reward Systems*. Buckingham: Open University Press

Armstrong, M. (2001) *A Handbook of Human Resource Management Practice*, 8th edition. London: Kogan Page

Armstrong, M. and Murlis, H. (1998) *Reward Management*, 4th edition. London: IPM/Kogan Page

Ashby, W. R. (1940) 'Adaptiveness and equilibrium', *Journal of Mental Science*, Vol.86, 478–83

Ashkenas, R. N. and Francis, S. C. (2000) 'Integration managers: special leaders for special times', *Harvard Business Review*, Nov–Dec, 108–14

Ashkenas, R. N., Demonaco, L. J. and Francis, S.C. (2000) 'Making the deal real: how GE capital integrates acquisitions', *Harvard Business Review*, Jan–Feb, 165–78

Atkinson, J. (1984) 'Manpower strategies for flexible organizations', *Personnel Management*, August, 28–31

Bailey, K. D. (1994) *Typologies and Taxonomies: An introduction to classification techniques.* Quantitative Applications in the Social Sciences Series, No. 02. London: Sage

Bandura, A. (1969) *Principles of Behaviour Modification.* New York: Holt, Rinehart & Winston

Bandura, A. (1977) *A Social Learning Theory.* Upper Saddle River, NJ: Prentice Hall

Barney, B. (1991) 'Firm resources and sustained competitive advantage', *Journal of Management*, Vol.17, No.1, 99–120

Bass, B.M. and Barratt, G.V. (1981) *People Work and Organisations: An introduction to industrial and organisational psychology.* Boston, MA: Allyn & Bacon

Beaumont, P. B. and Hunter, L. C. (1992) 'Competitive strategy, flexibility and selection: the case of Caledonian Paper', in B. Towers (ed.) *The Handbook of Human Resource Management.* Oxford: Blackwell

Beaumont, P. (1993) *Human Resource Management: Key concepts and skills.* London: Sage

Becker, B. and Gerhart, B. (1996) 'The impact of human resource management on organizational performance: progress and practice', *Academy of Management Journal*, Vol.39, No.4, 779–801

Beer, M., Eisenstat, R. and Spector, B. (1990) 'Why change programs don't produce change', *Harvard Business Review*, Nov–Dec, 158–66

Beer, M., Spector, B., Lawrence, P. R., Mills, D. and Walton, R. E. (1984) *Managing Human Assets*. New York: Free Press

Belbin, M. (1981) *Management Teams: Why they succeed or fail*. London: Heinemann

Blyton, P. and Turnbull, P. (1992) *Reassessing Human Resource Management*. London: Sage

Boxall, P. and Purcell, J. (2006) *Strategy and Human Resource Management*. Basingstoke: Palgrave Macmillan

Boyatzis, R. E. (1982) *The Competent Manager: A model for effective performance*. London: Wiley

Braverman, H. (1974) *Labour and Monopoly Capitalism: The degradation of work in the twentieth century*. New York: Monthly Review Press

Brown, W. (1989) 'Managing Renumeration' in K. Sissons (ed) *Personnel Management in Britain*. Oxford: Basil Blackwell

Brown, W. and Walsh, J. (1994) 'Managing Pay in Britain' in K. Sissons (ed) *Personnel Management: A comprehensive guide to theory and practice in Britain*. Oxford : Basil Blackwell

Buchanan, D. (1994) 'Principles and practice in work design', in D. Sissons (ed.) *Personnel Management: A comprehensive guide to theory and practice in Britain*. Oxford: Blackwell

Cannon Working Party Report (1994) *Progress and Change 1987–1994*. Corby: Institute of Management

Cartwright, S. and Cooper, C. L. (1990) 'The impact of mergers and acquisitions on people at work: existing research and issues', *British Journal of Management*, 1, 65–76

Cartwright, S. and Cooper, C. L. (1996) *Managing Mergers Acquisitions and Strategic Alliances: Integrating people and cultures*. Oxford: Butterworth-Heinemann

Cartwright, S. and Cooper, C. L. (2000) *HR Know-how in Mergers and Acquisitions*. London: IPD

Chandler, A. D. (1991) *Strategy and Structure: Chapters in the history of the American industrial enterprise*. Cambridge, MA: MIT Press [first published 1962]

Cheetham, G. and Chivers, G. (1996) 'Towards a holistic model of professional competence', *Journal of European Industrial Training*, Vol.20, No.5

Cheetham, G. and Chivers, G. (1998) 'The reflective and competent practitioner: A model of professional competence which seeks to harmonise the reflective practitioner and competence-based approaches', *Journal of European Industrial Training*, Vol.22, No.7, pp.267-76

Child, J. (1972) 'Organisational structure, environment and performance – the role of strategic choice', *Sociology*, Vol.6, 1–22

Child, J. (1984) *Organisation: A guide to problems and practice*, 2nd edition. London, Paul Chapman

Child, J. (1997) 'Strategic choice in the analysis of action, structure, organisations and environment: retrospect and prospect', *Organization Studies*, Vol.18, No.1, 43–76

CIPD (1994) *People Make the Difference*. London: CIPD

CIPD (2005) *What Is Employee Relations?* London: CIPD; also available online at: http://www.cipd.co.uk/subjects/empreltns/comconslt/empvoice

CIPD (2006a) *Managing Change*, Factsheet. London: CIPD; also available online at: http://www.cipd.co.uk/onlineinfodocuments

CIPD (2006b) *Recruitment, Retention and Turnover, Annual Survey*. London: CIPD; also available online at: http://www.cipd.co.uk/onlineinfodocuments

CIPD (2006c) *Psychological Testing*, Factsheet. London: CIPD; also available online at: http://www.cipd.co.uk/onlineinfodocuments

CIPD (2006d) *Learning and Development Survey*. London: CIPD; also available online at: http://www.cipd.co.uk/onlineinfodocuments

CIPD (2007a) *Employee Engagement*, Factsheet. London: CIPD. Also available online at http:www.cipd.co.uk/onlineinfodocuments

CIPD (2007b) *Employee Voice*, Factsheet. London: CIPD; also available online at: http://www.cipd.co.uk/onlineinfodocuments

CIPD (2007c) *Management Development*, Factsheet. London: CIPD; also available online at: http://www.cipd.co.uk/onlineinfodocuments

CIPD (2007d) *Competence and Competency Frameworks*, Factsheet. London: CIPD; also available online at: http://www.cipd.co.uk/onlineinfodocuments

CIPD (2007e) *Learning and Development: Annual survey report 2007*. London: CIPD; also available online at: http://www.cipd.co.uk/surveys

Coffield, F., Moseley, D., Hall, E. and Ecclestone, K. (2004) *Should We Be Using Learning Styles? What research has to say to practice*. London: Learning and Skills Research Centre

Cully, M., Woodland, S., O'Reilly, A. and Dix, G. (1999) *Britain At Work: As depicted by the 1998 Workplace Employee Relations Survey*. London: Routledge

Davis, T.W., and Luthans, F. (1980) 'A social learning approach to organisational behaviour', *Academy of Management Review*, Vol.5, pp.281-90

Department of Trade and Industry and Department for Education and Employment (1997) *Partnerships at Work*. London: HMSO

Dodgson, M. (1993) 'Organizational learning: a review of some literatures', *Organizational Studies*, Vol.14, 375–94

Drucker, P. F. (1955) *The Practice of Management*. London: Heinemann

Drucker, P. (1974) 'New templates for today's organizations', *Harvard Business Review*, Jan–Feb, 221–34

Drucker, P. (1990) 'The emerging theory of manufacturing', *Harvard Business Review*, May–June, 94–102

Drucker, P. (1993) *Post-Capitalist Society*. Oxford: Butterworth-Heinemann

DTI/CIPD (2005) *High-Performance Work Practices: Linking strategy and skills to performance outcomes*. London: HMSO; also available online at: www.dti.gov.uk

Du Gay, P. and Salaman, G. (1992) 'The cult(ure) of the customer', *Journal of Management Studies*, Vol.29, No.5, 615–33

Duncan, C. (1989) 'Pay and payment systems', in B. Towers (ed.) *A Handbook of Industrial Relations Practice*. London: Kogan Page

Dunlop, J. T. (1984) *Dispute Resolution: Negotiation and consensus building*. Dover, MA: Auburn House

Dyer, L. and Reeves, T. (1995) 'Human resource strategies and firm performance: what do we know and where do we need to go?', *International Journal of Human Resource Management*, Vol.6, No.3, 656–70

Earnshaw, J. and Cooper, C. (1998) *Stress and Employer Liability*. London: IPD

Eggert, M. (1991) *Outplacement: A guide to management and delivery*. London: IPM

Emery, F. E. (1963) *Some Hypotheses About the Ways in Which Tasks May Be More Effectively Put Together to Make Jobs*. London: Tavistock Institute of Human Relations

Fandt, P. M. (1994) *Management Skills: Practice and experience*. St Paul, MN: Weat

Farnham, D. (2000) *Employee Relations in Context*, 2nd edition. London: IPD

Farnham D. and Pimlott J. (1995) *Understanding Industrial Relations*, 4th edition. London: Cassell

Fayol, H. (1916/1950) *Administration industrielle et generale*. Paris: Dunod

Feldman, D. C. (1991) 'Repatriate moves as career transitions', *Human Resource Management Review*, Vol.1, No.3, 163–78

Fernie, S., Metcalf, D. and Woodland, S. (1994) *Does HRM boost employee-management relations?* Working Paper 548. London School of Economics: Centre for Economic Performance

Fisher, C. D., Schoenfeldt, L. F. and Shaw, J. B. (1993) *Human Resource Management*, 2nd edition. Boston, MA: Houghton Mifflin

Fombrun, C. J., Tichy, N. M. and Devanna, M. A. (1984) *Strategic Human Resource Management*. New York: Wiley

Foulkes, F. K. (1980) *Personnel Policies in Large Non-Union Companies*. Englewood Cliffs, NJ: Prentice-Hall

Fox, A. (1966) *Royal Commission on Trade Unions and Employers' Associations Research Papers 3: Industrial Sociology and Industrial Relations*. London: HMSO

French, J. and Raven, B. (1959) 'The bases of social power' in D. Cartwright (ed) *Studies in Social Power*. Ann Arbor, MI: Institute of Social Research, University of Michigan

Gallie, D., White, M., Cheng, Y. and Tomlinson, M. (1998) *Restructuring the Employment Relationship*. Oxford: Clarendon Press

Goleman, D. (2000) 'Leadership that gets results', *Harvard Business Review*, March-April, pp78-90

Guest, D. (1987) 'Human resource management and industrial relations', *Journal of Management Studies*, Vol.24, No.5, 503–21

Guest, D. (1989) 'Human resource management: its implications for industrial relations and trade unions', in J. Storey (ed.) *New Perspectives on Human Resource Management*. London: Routledge

Guest, D. (1990) 'HRM and the American Dream', *Journal of Management Studies*, Vol. 27, No.4, 377–97

Guest, D. (1991) 'Personnel management: the end of orthodoxy?', *British Journal of Industrial Relations*, Vol.29, No.2, 149–75

Guest, D. (1995) 'Human resource management, trade unions and industrial relations', in J. Storey (ed.) *Human Resource Management: A critical text*. London: Routledge

Guest, D. (1996) *The State of the Psychological Contract in Employment*. London: IPD

Guest, D. E. (1997) 'Human resource management and performance: a review and research agenda', *International Journal of Human Resource Management*, Vol.8, No.3, 263–90

Guest, D. (2000) 'HR and the bottom line – has the penny dropped?', *People Management*, Vol.20, July, 26–31

Guest, D. and Hoque, K. (1993) *Are Greenfield Sites Better at Human Resource Management?*, CEP Working Paper No.435. London School of Economics: Centre for Economic Performance

Guest, D., Michie, J., Conway, N. and Sheehan, M. (2003) 'Human resource management and corporate performance in the UK', *British Journal of Industrial Relations*, Vol.41, No.2, 291–314

Gulick, L. and Urwick, L. (eds) (1937) *Papers on the Science of Administration*. New York: Columbia Press University Press.

Gupta, O. and Roos, G. (2001) 'Mergers and acquisitions through an intellectual capital perspective', *Journal of Intellectual Capital*, Vol.2, No.3, 297–309

Gyllenhammar, P. G. (1977) *People at Work*. Reading, MA: Addison-Wesley

Hakel, M. D. (1982) 'Employment interviewing', in K. M. Rowland and G. R. Ferris (eds) *Personnel Management*. Boston, MA: Allyn & Bacon

Hamel, G. and Prahalad, C. K. (1994) *Competing for the Future*. Boston, MA: Harvard Business School Press

Hammarström, O. and Lansbury, R. D. (1991) 'The art of building a car: the Swedish experience re-examined', *New Technology, Work and Employment*, Vol.6, No.2, 85–90

Handy, C. (1985) *Understanding Organizations*. New York: Penguin

Handy, C., Gordon, C., Gow, I. and Randlesome, C. (1988) *Making Managers*. London: Pitman

Harrison, R. (1997) *Employee Development*. London: IPD

Henderson, I. S. and Dowling, M. (2008) *Managing Personal Competencies*. Edinburgh: Edinburgh Business School

Herzberg, F. (1966) *Work and the Nature of Man*. Cleveland, OH: World Publishing

Herzberg, F., Mausner, B. and Snyderman, B. B. (1959) *The Motivation to Work*. London/New York: Wiley

Hofstede, G. (1980) *Culture's Consequences*. London: Sage

Holbeche, L. (2007) 'Building high performance – the key role for HR', *Impact: Quarterly Update on CIPD Policy and Research*, No.20, 10–11

Hollinshead, G. and Leat, M. (1995) *Human Resource Management: An international and comparative perspective*. London: Pitman

Honey, P. and Mumford, A. (1989) *A Manual of Learning Opportunities*. Maidenhead: Peter Honey.

Howard, A. (1990) 'An assessment of assessment centres', in G. R. Ferris, K. M. Rowland and M. R. Buckley (eds.) *Human Resource Management : Perspectives and issues*, 2nd edition. Boston, MA: Allyn & Bacon

Huselid, M. (1995) 'The impact of human resource management practices on turnover, productivity and corporate financial performance', *Academy of Management Journal*, Vol.38, No.3, 635–72

ILO/IFTDO (2000) *Supporting Workplace Learning for High-Performance Working*. London/Geneva: International Labour Organisation; www.ilo.org/

Incomes Data Services (1991) *Guide to Incentive Payment Schemes*. London: IDS

Income Data Services (1992) *IDS Study No.500*

Incomes Data Services (2001) *Competency Frameworks*, IDS Study 706. London: IDS

Institute of Management (1994) *Management Development to the Millennium*: the Cannon and Taylor Working Party Reports. London: IM

Institute of Personnel and Development (1997) *The IPD Code of Professional Conduct and Disciplinary Procedures*. London: IPD

International Labour Organisation (1984) *Payment by Results*. London/Geneva: ILO

IRS (1993) *Multi-employer Bargaining*, *IRS Employment Trends* No.544, 6–8

Jelinek, M. and Adler, N. J. (1988) 'Women: world class managers for global competition', *Academy of Management Executive*, Vol.2, No.1, 11–19

Jewson, N. and Mason, D. (1986) 'The theory and practice of equal opportunities policies: liberal and radical approaches', *Sociological Review*, Vol.34, No.2, 307–34

Johnson, G. and Scholes, K. (1997) *Exploring Corporate Strategy*. London: Prentice Hall

Kanter, R. (1989) *When Elephants Learn to Dance*. New York: Touchstone

Keenan, T. (2005) *Human Resource Management*. Edinburgh: Edinburgh Business School

Kennedy, G., Benson, J. and McMillan, J. (1984) *Managing Negotiations*, 2nd edition. London: Business Books

Kenney, M. and Florida, R. (1993) *Beyond Mass Production: The Japanese system and its transfer to the U.S.* Oxford: Oxford University Press

Kennoy, T. (1999) 'HRM as hologram: a polemic', *Journal of Management Studies*, Vol.36, No.1, 1–23

Kersley, B., Alpin, C., Forth, J., Bryson, A., Bewley, H., Dix, G. and Oxenbridge, S. (2005) *Inside the Workplace: First Findings from the 2004 Workplace Employment Relations Survey*. Abingdon: Routledge

Kersley, B., Alpin, C., Forth, J., Bryson, A., Bewley, H., Dix, G. and Oxenbridge, S. (2006) *Inside the Workplace: Findings from the 2004 Workplace Employment Relations Survey*. Abingdon: Routledge

Kessler, S. and Bayliss, F. (1992) *Contemporary British Industrial Relations*. London: Macmillan

Kirkpatrick, D. L. (1967) 'Evaluation of training', in R. L. Craig and L. R. Bittel (eds) *Training and Development Handbook*. New York: McGraw-Hill

Klemp, G. O. (1980) *The Assessment of Occupational Competence*. Report to the National Institute for Education. Washington DC

Kochan, T. A., Katz, H. A. and McKersie, R. B. (1994) *The Transformation of American Industrial Relations*. New York: Basic Books

Kolb, D. A., Rubin, I. and McIntyre, J. M. (1971) *Organizational Psychology: An experiential approach*. Englewood Cliffs, NJ: Prentice Hall

Kotter, J. (1999) *John Kotter on What Leaders Really Do*. Cambridge, MA: Harvard Business School Press

Kübler-Ross, E. (1969) *On Death and Dying*. New York: Macmillan

Kuhn, T. (1970) *The Structure of Scientific Revolutions*, 2nd (enlarged) edition. Chicago: University of Chicago Press

Landy, F. J. and Conte, J. M. (2007) *Work in the Twenty-First Century: An introduction to industrial and organizational psychology*, 2nd edition. Oxford: Blackwell

Legge, K. (1989) 'Human resource management: a critical analysis', in J. Storey (ed.) *New Perspectives on Human Resource Management*. London: Routledge

Legge, K. (1995) *Human Resource Management: Rhetorics and realities.* Basingstoke: Macmillan Business

Legge, K. (1997) 'The morality of HRM', in C. Mabey (ed.) *Experiencing Human Resource Management.* London: Sage

Legge, K. (2001) 'Silver bullet or spent round? Assessing the meaning of the high-commitment management/performance relationship', in J. Storey (ed.) *Human Resource Management: A critical text* 2nd edition. London: Thomson Learning

Lewin, K. (1951) *Field Theory in Social Science.* New York: Harper & Row

Lorsch, J. W. (1970) 'Introduction to the structural design of organisations', in G. Dalton, P. Lawrence and J. Lorsch (eds) *Organizational Structure and Design.* Homewood, IL: Richard Irwin

Mabey, C. and Salaman, G. (1995) *Strategic Human Resource Management.* Oxford: Blackwell

Mabey, C. and Thomson, A. (2000a) *Achieving Managerial Excellence.* London: Institute of Management

Mabey, C. and Thomson, A. (2000b) 'The determinants of management development', *British Journal of Management*, Vol.11, Special issue, S3–S16

Mabey, C., Salaman, G. and Storey, J. (1998) *Human Resource Management: A strategic introduction*, 2nd edition. Oxford: Blackwell

MacDuffie, J. P. (1995) 'Human resource bundles and manufacturing performance: organizational logic and flexible production systems in the world auto industry', *Industrial and Labor Relations Review*, Vol.48, 197–221

Mangham, I. and Silver, M. (1986) *Management Training: Context and practice.* London: Economic and Social Research Council

Maslow, A. (1943) *A Theory of Human Motivation.* New York: Harper

mcKersie, R. B. (1987) 'The transformation of American industrial relations: the abridged story', *Journal of Management Studies*, Vol.24, No.5, 434–40

McKinlay, A. and Starkey, K. (1998) *Foucault, Management and Organization Theory.* London: Sage

Meister, J. (1998) 'Ten steps to creating a corporate university', *Training and Development*, Vol.52, 38–43

Mendenhall, M. and Oddou, G. (1985) 'The dimensions of expatriate acculturation: a review', *Academy of Management Review*, Vol.10, No.1, 39–47

Miles, R. E. and Snow, C. C. (1978) *Organizational Strategy, Structure and Process.* New York: McGraw-Hill

Miles, R. E. and Snow, C. C. (1984) 'Designing strategic human resource systems', *Organizational Dynamics*, Summer, 36–52

Millward, N. (1993) 'Industrial relations in transition: the findings of the third Workplace Industrial Relations Survey'. Paper presented to BUIRA, York, July

Millward, N. (1994) *The New Industrial Relations.* Poole: Policy Studies Institute

Millward, N., Stevens, M., Smart, D. and Hawes, W. R. (1992) *Workplace Industrial Relations in Transition.* Aldershot: Dartmouth

Mintzberg, H. (1973) *The Nature of Managerial Work.* New York, Harper & Row

Mintzberg, H. (1975) 'The manager's job: folklore and fact', *Harvard Business Review*, Vol.53, No.4, 49–61

Mintzberg, H. (1978) 'Patterns in strategy formation', *Management Science*, Vol.24, No.9, 934–48

Mintzberg, H. (1987) 'Crafting strategy', *Harvard Business Review*, July–August, 66–74

Mirvis, P. H. (1985) 'Negotiations after the sale: the roots and ramifications of conflict in an acquisition', *Journal of Occupational Behaviour*, 6, 65–84

Morris, J. F. (1978) 'Management development and development management', in J. Burgoyne and R. Stuart (eds) *Management Development: Context and strategies.* Aldershot: Gower

Muchinsky, P. M. (1986) 'Personnel selection methods', in C. L. Cooper and I. T. Robertson (eds) *International Review of Industrial and Organisational Psychology.* London: Wiley

Napier, N. K. (1989) 'Mergers and acquisitions, human resource issues and outcomes: a review and suggested typology', *Journal of Management Studies*, Vol.26, No.3, 271–89

Nisbet, R. A. (1969) *Social Change and History: Aspects of the Western theory of development.* London: Oxford University Press

Nonaka, I. and Takeuchi, H. (1995) *The Knowledge-Creating Company.* Oxford: Oxford University Press

Office for National Statistics, Quarterly, First/News/Press Release; also available online at: http://www.statistics.gov.uk/

Osterman, P. (1994) 'How common is workplace transformation, and who adopts it?', *Industrial and Labor Relations Review*, Vol.47, No.2, 173–88

Panchal, S. and Cartwright, S. (2001) 'Group differences in post-merger stress', *Journal of Managerial Psychology*, Vol.16, No.6, 424–33

Pearn, M. A., Kandola, R. S., Mottram, R. D. and Pearn Kandola Associates (1987) '*Selection Tests and Sex Bias*', Equal Opportunities Commission Research series. London: HMSO

Pedler, M., Burgoyne, J. and Boydell, T. (1991) *The Learning Organisation*. Maidenhead: McGraw-Hill

Perlmutter, H. V. (1969) 'The tortuous evolution of the multinational corporation', *Columbia Journal of World Business*, Vol.4, 9–18

Peters, T. (1987) *Thriving on Chaos: Handbook for a management revolution*. London: Macmillan

Pfeffer, J. (1994) *Competitive Advantage Through People*. Boston, MA: Harvard Business School Press

Pfeffer, J. (1998) *The Human Equation: Building profits by putting people first*. Boston MA: Harvard Business School Press

Polanyi, M. (1966) *The Tacit Dimension*. London: Routledge & Kegan Paul

Porter, M. E. (1980) *Competitive Strategy: Techniques for analysing industries and competitors*. New York: Free Press

Porter, M. E. (1985) *Competitive Advantage: Creating and sustaining superior performance*. New York: Free Press

Porter, M. (1987) 'From competitive advantage to corporate strategy', *Harvard Business Review*, May–June, 43–57

Prahalad, C. K. and Hamel, G. (1990) 'The core competence of the corporation', *Harvard Business Review*, Vol.68, May–June, 79–91

Pugh, D. S. (ed.) (1990) *Organizational Theory – Selected Readings*, 3rd edition. London: Penguin

Pugh, D. and Hickson, D. J. (1995) *Writers on Organisations*, 5th edition. London: Penguin

Purcell, J. and Ahlstrand, B. (1994) *Human Resource Management in the Multi-Divisional Company*. Oxford: Oxford University Press

Purcell, J. (1989) 'The impact of corporate strategy on human resource management', in J. Storey (ed.) *New Perspectives On Human Resource Management*. London: Routledge

Purcell, J. (1999) 'Best practice and best fit: chimera or cul de sac?', *Human Resource Management Journal*, Vol.9, No.3, 26–41

Quinn, R. E., Faerman, S., Thompson, M. P. and McGrath, M. (2003) *Becoming a Master Manager: A competency framework*, 3rd edition. New York: Wiley

Rankin, N. (2004) *The New Prescription for Performance: The eleventh Competency Benchmarking Survey*. Competency and Emotional Intelligence Benchmarking supplement 2004/5. London: IRS

Roberts, J. (1990) *Harmonization: Whys and wherefores*. London: IPD

Roberts, K., Kossek, E. and Ozeki, C. (1998) 'Managing the global workforce: challenges and strategies', *Academy of Management Executive*, Vol.12, No.4, 93–106

Robinson, D., Perryman, S., and Hayday, S. (2004) *The Drivers of Employee Engagement*. Brighton: Institute for Employment Studies

Roethlisberger, F. J. and Dickson, W. J. (1939) *Management and the Worker*. Cambridge, MA: Harvard University Press

Roscow, J. and Casner-Lotto, J. (1997) *People, Partnership and Profits: The new labor–management agenda*. New York: Work in America Institute

Schein, E. (1985) *Organizational Culture and Leadership*. San Francisco, CA: Jossey-Bass

Schmitt, N., Gooding, R. Z., Noe, R. A. and Kirsch, M. (1984) 'Meta-analysis of validity studies published between 1964 and 1982, and the investigation of study characteristics', *Personnel Psychology*, Vol. 37, 407–22

Schon, D.A. (1983) *The Reflective Practitioner: How professionals think in action*. New York: Basic Books

Schuler, R. and Jackson, S. (1987) 'Linking competitive strategies and human resource management practices', *Academy of Management Executive*, Vol.1, No.3, 207–19

Schuler, R. and Jackson, S. (2001) 'HR issues and activities in mergers and acquisitions', *European Management Journal*, Vol.19, No.3, 239–53

Scullion, H. (1995) 'International human resource management' in *Human Resource Management*, ed. J. Storey. London: Routledge, pp.352-82

Senge, P. (1990) *The Fifth Discipline: The age and practice of the learning organization*. New York: Doubleday

Sisson, K. (ed.) (1989) *Personnel Management in Britain*. Oxford: Blackwell

Skapiner, M. (2002) *The Change Agenda*. London: CIPD

Sloan, A. P. (1967) *My Years with General Motors*. London: Pan Books

Smith A. (1976) *An Inquiry into the Nature and Causes of the Wealth of Nations*. Chigaco: University of Chicago Press [first published 1776]

Storey, J. (ed.) (1989) *New Perspectives in Human Resource Management*. London: Routledge

Storey, J. (1992) 'HRM in action: the truth is out at last', *Personnel Management*, April, 28–31

Storey, J. (1995) HRM: *A critical text*. London: Routledge

Storey, J. (ed.) (2001) *Human Resource Management: A critical text*, 2nd edition. London: Thomson Learning

Storey, J., Edwards, P. and Sisson, K. (1997) *Managers in the Making: Careers, development and control in corporate Britain and Japan*. London: Sage

Tannenbaum, R. and Schmidt, W.H., (1973) 'How to choose a leadership pattern', *Harvard Business Review*, May-June, pp.162-80

Tayeb, M. H. (1987) 'Contingency theory and culture: a study of matched English and Indian manufacturing firms', *Organization Studies*, Vol.8, 241–62

Tayeb, M. H. (1988) *Organizations and National Culture: A comparative analysis*. London: Sage

Tayeb, M. H. (1994a) 'National culture and organizations: methodology considered', *Organization Studies*, Vol.15, No.2, 429–46

Tayeb, M. H. (1994b) 'Japanese managers and British culture: a comparative case study', *International Journal of Human Resource Management*, Vol.5, No.1, 145–66

Tayeb, M. H. (1998) 'Transfer of HRM practices across cultures: an American company in Scotland', *International Journal of Human Resource Management*, Vol.9, No.2, 332–58

Tayeb, M. H. (2000) *The Management of International Enterprises: A socio-political view*. Basingstoke: Macmillan

Tayeb, M. H. (2008) *Managing People in the Global Markets*. Edinburgh: Edinburgh Business School

Taylor, F. J. W. (1994) *Working Party Report: The way ahead 1994–2001: Management development to the millennium research*. Corby: Institute of Management

Taylor, F.W. (1911) *Principles of Scientific Management*. New York: Harper

Thompson, J. (1967) *Organisations in Action*. New York: McGraw-Hill

Thompson, P. and McHugh, D. (2002) *Work Organisations: A critical introduction*, 3rd edition. Basingstoke: Palgrave Macmillan

Thomson, A., Mabey, C., Storey, J., Gray, C. and Iles, P. (2001) *Changing Patterns of Management Development*. Oxford: Blackwell

Thornton, G. C. and Byham, W. C. (1982) *Assessment Centres and Managerial Performance*. New York/London: Academic Press

Toplis, J., Dulewicz, V. and Fletcher, C. (1987) *Psychological Testing: A practical guide for employers*. London: IPM

Torrington, D., Hall, L. and Taylor, S. (2002) *Human Resource Management*, 5th edition. London/New Jersey: FT/Prentice-Hall

Trist, E. A. and Bamforth, K. W. (1951) 'Some social and psychological consequences of the longwall method of coal-getting', *Human Relations*, Vol.4, 3–38

Tuckman, B. W. (1965) 'Development sequence in small groups', *Psychological Bulletin*, Vol.93, No.3, 384–99

Tuckman, B. W. and Jensen, N. (1977) 'Stages of group development revisited', *Group and Organisation Studies*, Vol.2, No.3, 419–27

Tung, R. L. (1986) 'Selection and training of personnel for overseas assignments', *Columbia Journal of World Business*, Vol.16, No.1, 68–78

Ulrich, D. (1998) 'A new mandate for human resources', *Harvard Business Review*, January–February, 124–34

US Dept of Labor (1993) *High-Performance Work Practices and Work Performance*. Washington DC: US Government Printing Office

Valery, N. (1974) 'Importing the lessons of Swedish workers', *New Scientist*, Vol. 62. No. 4 April, 27–8

Vitiello, J. (2001) 'New roles for corporate universities', *Computerworld*, Vol.35, No.15, 42

Walton, R. E. (1985) 'From control to commitment in the workplace', *Harvard Business Review*, Vol.85, No.2, 77–84

Webb, J. and Liff, S. (1988) 'Play the white man – the social construction of fairness and competition in equal opportunities policies', *Sociological Review*, Vol.36, No.3, 532–51

Weber, M. (1949) *The Methodology of the Social Sciences*, translated by E. A. Shils and H. A. Finch. Glencoe: Free Press

Whetton, D.A. and Cameron, K.S. (1983) 'Management skill training: A needed addition to the management curriculum', *Organizational Behavior Teaching Journal*, Vol.8, pp.10-15

Whetton, D. R. and Cameron, K. S. (2005) *Developing Management Skills*, 6th edition. Harlow/New Jersey: Pearson/Prentice-Hall

Whetton, D. R., Cameron, K. S. and Woods, M. (2000) *Developing Management Skills for Europe*, 2nd edition. Harlow: Pearson Education

White, M., Hill, S., Mills, C. and Smeaton, D. (2004) *Managing to Change? British Workplaces and the future of work*. Basingstoke: Palgrave Macmillan

Whyte, W. F. (1955) *Money and Motivation*. New York: Harper & Row

Wood, S. and Albanese, M. T. (1995) 'Can we speak of high-commitment management on the shop floor?', *Journal of Management Studies*, Vol.32, No.2, 215–47

Wooton, B. (1955) *The Social Foundations of Wages Policy*. London: Allen & Unwin

Work Foundation (2004) Report: *Achieving Strategic Alignment of Business and Human Resources*; also available online at http://www. theworkfoundation.com/products/publications/azpublications/ achievingstrategicalignmentofbusinessandhumanresources.aspx

Youndt, M., Snell, S., Dean. J. and Lepack, D. (1996) 'Human resource management, manufacturing strategy and firm performance', *Academy of Management Journal*, Vol.39, No.4, 836–66

Index

Diagrams and tables are given in italics

U
UK Training Agency 157
Ulrich, David 4, 68, 228
uncertainty avoidance 216
unitarist perspective 10, 230
Universal Electric Company (UEC) 167
'universalist/contingency' debate 13–14,
    34–5, 229
upward problem-solving 134
US Dept of Labor 39

V
vertical loading 55

W
Wal-Mart 190
'war of talent' 86
Washington Mutual (WaMu) 108–9
Watson, Jenny 191

Wealth of Nations, The (Smith) 50
Weber, Max 16–17
websites
    www.acas.org.uk 89, 123
    www.ebsglobal.net 113
    www.tiger.gov.uk 89
welfare 20
West Sussex County Council 118
Westminster City Council 78
Whetton, D. R. 163–4, 172
Wieringen, Frits van 210
Wilson, Adrian 109
Wilson, Fran 210
Work Study 143
work-in-progress (WIP) 56
work-life balance, explanation 66
work-related model (competencies) 157
working patterns 65–6